T0114792

WHY YOU'RE WRONG ABOUT THE RIGHT

Behind the Myths:
The Surprising Truth
About Conservatives

S. E. CUPP AND BRETT JOSHPE

THRESHOLD
EDITIONS

New York London Toronto Sydney

Threshold Editions
A Division of Simon & Schuster, Inc.
1230 Avenue of the Americas
New York, NY 10020

First Threshold Editions hardcover edition May 2008

THRESHOLD EDITIONS and colophon are trademarks of Simon & Schuster, Inc.

For information about special discounts for bulk purchases, please contact Simon & Schuster Special Sales at 1-800-456-6798 or business@simonandschuster.com.

Designed by Jan Pisciotta

Manufactured in the United States of America

10   9   8   7   6   5   4   3   2   1

Library of Congress Cataloging-in-Publication Data

Cupp, S. E.
        Why you're wrong about the Right : behind the myths : the surprising truth about conservatives / S. E. Cupp and Brett Joshpe.
    p. cm.
1. Republican Party (U.S. : 1854-)   2. Republican Party (U.S. : 1854-) —Public opinion.   3. Conservatives—Public opinion.   4. Conservatives—Attitudes.   5. Public opinion—United States.   I. Joshpe, Brett.   II. Title.
JK2356.C87 2008
324.2734—dc22
            2007050499
ISBN-13: 978-1-4165-6284-9
ISBN-10:   1-4165-6284-2

To all the brave American men and women
—of every political view—
who have ever worn a uniform. Thank you.

CONTENTS

FOREWORD

by Tucker Carlson

I remember the day I decided I wasn't a liberal. It was a Saturday morning in 1976 and I was having breakfast with my brother and my father in our kitchen in Southern California. The three of us were sitting around the table eating cereal in our undershorts when the doorbell rang. It was Mrs. Raymond, my first-grade teacher. Mrs. Raymond was about twenty-eight and, I now realize, a living period piece. Visualize every fashion cliché of the 1970s— eight-inch earrings, high-heel sandals, earth tone blouse opened one button too low—and you've got Mrs. Raymond. She had politics to match.

Even at seven I sensed where Mrs. Raymond was coming from ideologically. We spent entire school days making solar ovens, or weaving Native American god's eyes out of popsicle sticks and yarn. She lectured us on the evils of the class system, and of white bread. One day, she combined the two, explaining with obvious pleasure that medieval lords died younger than their serfs, since the latter couldn't afford to have their grain finely milled and therefore ate darker bread. (It was years before I realized this was ludicrous, but it was too late; to this day I've never tasted Wonder Bread.) She made frequent and nasty references to President Ford.

One day Mrs. Raymond's politics got the best of her. We came back from recess and found our classroom dark. Mrs. Raymond was sitting alone in the gloom. In a quavering voice, she told us to put our heads on our desks and close our eyes. This was a couple of years before Jonestown, but it was still creepy as hell. Even the unruly kids obeyed. Then she started sobbing, loudly. "The world is such a bad place," she wailed. "So unfair. So mean. You don't even understand."

We definitely didn't understand. I didn't think my father would understand either, so I didn't tell him about the sobbing incident. Which is probably why he'd hired Mrs. Raymond to come to our house on Saturday morning and tutor my brother and me in subjects she had neglected to teach during the week, like penmanship and reading. My father didn't know she was crazy.

Once inside the house, Mrs. Raymond made a beeline for the kitchen table, apparently to find out what we'd been eating. What she saw stopped her cold. "Cap'n Crunch!" she shouted. "Mr. Carlson, you're letting your boys eat Cap'n Crunch! How could you do that?" She had a look of shock and horror on her face, the look of a priest who has stumbled into a black Mass.

I can't remember precisely what happened next (I've repressed it deeply), but I know my father didn't react well. I'm pretty sure there was profanity involved. In any case, Mrs. Raymond left and never came back.

It was a traumatic experience, but instructive. I decided right then that there are two kinds of people in this world: people who want to control what sort of breakfast cereal you eat, and those who don't. This is the basic division, and it matters. A busybody is merely an ineffective totalitarian. If Mrs. Raymond ever gained absolute power, a lot of people would die. I sensed that then. I know it now.

I spent sixteen more years of school in the grip of various Mrs. Raymonds, mediocrities whose basic desire wasn't to teach but to control, and if possible, to indoctrinate. By the time I got to college,

I'd become pretty cynical about formal education. Senior year, I signed up for Introduction to Women's Studies. I wasn't especially interested in the subject (I haven't taken feminism seriously since the first time someone tried to explain to me, with a straight face, that women have less power than men in society) but I was short on credits, and by that point I understood the rules: denounce the penis, pass the course. For a lazy man, it was found money. I wrote paper after schlocky paper about the horrors of the patriarchy and the dignity of the oppressed. Guaranteed Bs, every one.

It got boring after a while, so for my final project I wrote a long, supposedly biographical essay about my mother, whom I described as "my feminist hero." The idea was to see how far I could push it. The answer: pretty far. The paper opened with my mom, a spunky pioneering female journalist, walking through a phalanx of hateful, jeering male reporters on her first day in the newsroom. "They spit on her because she was a woman, but they could not break her spirit. She persevered. . . . "

To this day, it may be the most florid thing ever to leave my keyboard, and I'm including my subsequent stint as a newspaper editorial writer. Not a word was true, and not only that, it was pretty obviously fiction. Or it should have been obvious. I got a B, about the highest possible grade a non-woman could receive.

The experience got me wondering: Does anybody in the academic world ever get the joke? To find out, one of my roommates and I decided to create a fake environmental terrorist group (this was pre-9/11, when the idea seemed a lot funnier) to see what would happen. We posted handbills announcing that our "radical eco-action coalition" had "spiked all trees larger than six inches in diameter on campus. No longer will our green siblings fall defenselessly to the saws and scythes of the capitalist stooges known as 'buildings and grounds.'" We went on to call for the forced removal of all aerosol deodorant products from campus, and demanded that the bookstore stop selling Fruit Stripe gum, on the grounds that key ingredients in the cherry flavor were "produced in Brazil by underpaid and oppressed workers." We threatened violence if our demands were ignored.

Nobody paid the slightest attention. We sent our manifesto to the school newspaper. Still no response. At the time I wondered if the campus was too apathetic to care. Now I realize that in the context of college our positions didn't seem that unusual. It's hard to see something as bonkers if you agree with it.

That was almost twenty years ago, but I suspect the school hasn't changed much. There's nothing more hidebound or reactionary than an ostensibly liberal college. Conservatism, on the other hand, has changed. After two terms of George W. Bush, it's harder than ever to know what it means to be a conservative, though for a working definition, this book is an excellent place to start. Cupp and Joshpe have thought it through, and write with the sort of easy wit we could use more of on the right.

As for my own definition, I'm not much for litmus tests, but if I had to design one I'd say a conservative instinctively sides with the individual over the group. He understands that not every choice is a moral issue, that sometimes people just prefer plastic to paper, a Suburban to a Prius, and that's okay. He's for diversity, in the true sense. You can eat any kind of breakfast cereal you want in front of a conservative. He won't judge you.

INTRODUCTION

By S. E. Cupp

Popularity's a funny thing. Growing up, when popularity is of course most important, my level of "in-ness" ran the gamut, from eating lunch at the "head table" to eating lunch in the bathroom. One year I had six different boyfriends, and another it was as if I'd been crop-dusted by anthrax. And of course it mattered—it mattered desperately—but to cope with the capricious unpredictability of the popularity see-saw, I became very friendly with that old childhood adage, "I know you are, but what am I?"

But as you get older, popularity comes to mean other things. There are no more school cafeterias, awkward dances, or year-book superlatives to tell you who's in and who's out. Now we go to our newspapers, magazines, the internet, and television for that—whether it's the society pages, business, sports, or celebrities, popularity is judged now by an editor and circulation numbers. Or box office returns, television ratings, the *Billboard* charts, and web hits. And even though the celebrities, athletes, business tycoons, musicians, and movie stars may wonder if they're more popular than their competitors, you're not Beyoncé, so what the hell do you care? Indeed, in your day-to-day life, when are you ever touched by the callous and catty whim of popularity's chilly hand?

Well, if you're a young Republican in New York City—all the time. Sure, I might be the toast of Topeka, but here in New York, and undoubtedly in the rest of the blue states and even bluer big cities, I'm a pariah, the worst of the worst. I'm like the ex-con who just moved across the street from the elementary school, or the punk rocker who rented the place above yours, or the weird old lady who throws rocks off her porch and has long conversations with a broom handle. I'm a nuisance, a bad seed, a danger to the community, even.

So when my college friend Brett approached me to write a book about conservatism, I was once again confronted by that childhood dilemma that sends so many of us to therapy. *We're going to be so unpopular.*

Our friends are already repulsed by us. Sure, they love us on the surface, where it counts, but deep down they wish us long, slow deaths that leave us identifiable only by dental records. Our neighbors, the ones who know our dark secret thanks to copious amounts of mail from the RNC, look at us askance in the elevator and secretly hope our apartments will be ransacked by thieves, left as empty as our souls. And our coworkers think that every paycheck we cash might as well go straight into Satan's bank account.

But because I've held "unpopular beliefs" for so long, I've developed thick (yet remarkably soft to the touch) skin. So I decided to throw caution, and some may say common sense, to the wind, and I did it with alacrity and unbridled enthusiasm. I relished the chance to stick to my guns, regardless of who liked it and who didn't. No more tiptoeing around my political beliefs, couching them in less offensive and more popular sentiment, or biting my tongue altogether. I was going to put it out there. So in the summer of 2005, we began.

The original premise of the book was simple: We'd try to convince readers that Republicans are not necessarily what you'd expect them to be. Brett and I were perfect examples—we grew up in the liberal Northeast, went to very liberal colleges and graduate schools, lived in liberal New York City, and worked primarily with liberals, I at the *New York Times,* and he at a large law firm, a job that he'd later leave to more rigorously tend to this book. (Note: Regardless of my politics, I'd like it to be known that I love my job, and hope to keep it a very, very long time. The *New York Times* is a great place to work!) Furthermore, we fancied ourselves hip and smart, two adjectives liberals generally like to think they own. We lived among liberals, worked with liberals, socialized with liberals. We couldn't avoid them. They were our deliverymen, our dry cleaners, our waitresses and video store clerks. They taught our classes, poured our drinks, sat next to us at New York Mets games. And yet, Brett and I disagreed fundamentally with everyone around us, from the ubiquitous antiwar protesters to my friend who thinks taxes are a nice way to say an annual thanks to the government. What were we doing here?

There had to be more people like us. Surely we'd met other Republicans in New York, and there were probably a few in Los Angeles and even in Boston and Miami. (And I'm sure I saw one or two in Chicago.) And they might have some pretty interesting stories. So the plan was to find these "surprising conservatives" and tell their stories, with the idea that if we could find enough of them, we could prove conservatism isn't all that unpopular, even in places considered liberal. But therein lay the problem: finding them. We knew only a handful, and a few posts on websites like Craigslist netted some very unsavory results. One gentleman out of Portland, Oregon, for example, was indeed an unlikely conservative—a skateboard designer who headlined a heavy-metal band. But he was also, we discovered, a skinhead.

It became clear that, unless we wanted to invest in some high-tech surveillance equipment, we'd never know just whom we were endorsing, and a gaffe like that could jeopardize the whole operation. So after a few months of searching, we decided to shift our goals—to what, we didn't know, but shifting of some kind would definitely take place.

Meanwhile, we learned that through a circuitous connection, we could get to conservative writer and culture critic David Horowitz. We decided we'd interview him, if he'd agree, and see what we had when it was over, hoping to gain some kind of new direction out of our conversation. Horowitz was game, and we sat in Brett's bedroom, my ancient, practically Amish tape recorder rolling, cell phones on speaker, and talked with him for two hours. We felt very official. I wore a suit. It was a great interview, punctuated alternately by incredibly insightful analysis and the kind of hilarious outbursts that spice up any good interview (like his insistence that "Tom Cruise is a nut, a phony"). And when it was done, we thought: Why not parlay this interview with a well-known conservative pundit into another? So on a whim, I emailed my favorite pundit, Tucker Carlson, through his literary agent. To my surprise, she returned my request with a phone number, and said he was expecting my call. He agreed without hesitation to speak with me and—I have to gush for a moment—was one of the nicest, friendliest, funniest, smartest people I've ever interviewed. (Granted, that not-so-extensive list was then headlined by actor Jerry O'Connell, whom I'd profiled for my college paper, but nonetheless, I was smitten.)

So from there our goal was clear—interview as many well-known conservatives, Republicans, neoconservatives, far-Righters, libertarians, and moderates as we could find and write a book about the stereotypes surrounding the Right, in their voices and ours. And, as we soon learned, the stereotypes were many. Republicans, according to popular culture, are racist, misogynistic, homophobic, closed-minded, fanatical, stupid, redneck, elitist, uncaring, uncharitable, prudish, and most offensively, unfunny. In fact, we stumbled on one definition of "Republican" that made particularly adroit use of more than one of these stereotypes:

Republican: An individual who believes that the white male Christian God should be the only object of worship on the planet, that power and wealth should remain in the hands of 1% of the world's population while the remaining 99% starve, that health care should be privatized so the poor can't afford basic medication, that a rape victim living on welfare should be forced to care for a baby she didn't even ask for, and that America is the only real country on Earth while all those other countries they read about are just fakes invented by communists . . . oh wait, it's terrorists now, isn't it?"[1]

Eventually, as the project evolved, the goal became not only to erase those stereotypes and prove them false, but to prove that not all conservatives behave, talk, and think alike. And when all was said and done, we'd asked more than forty "experts" to comment. (Actually, we asked more than two hundred, but only forty agreed to help. We now call them "God's children.") Some were, like Tucker, easy to reach and more than happy to help us out. For others it took months upon months of negotiating with handlers, agents, lawyers, and producers who wanted to vet every aspect of our project before agreeing to contribute. Some, like Lisa "Kennedy" Montgomery and Jonah Goldberg, were hilarious—so funny we couldn't keep from laughing. And others gave us the kind of straight-up answers you'd never expect to hear from someone in the public eye.

And not all were total strangers to us. Jon Zimmerman and Jeremy Rabkin, both published experts in their fields, were once my professors. We met former White House advisor K. T. McFarland at a city council fund-raiser, and Deroy Murdock, a syndicated columnist, at another. And I met NASCAR driver Tony Stewart at his 2005 championship luncheon at the 21 Club in New York. Others became friends through the process. After months of emailing with former New York Mets pitcher Al Leiter, we finally arranged a get-together. After about four hours of great interview, and several beers later, we ended up going out to dinner, and then out for drinks. When the Mets blew their playoff chances in 2007, it was somewhat comforting to know we could vent our frustrations with a former player—and we did.

As the months rolled on, we grew confident—cocky, even—in our project. When people like Newt Gingrich and Ted Nugent take your phone calls, it can go to your head. We imagined ourselves the next Woodward and Bernstein, forty pounds overweight from our many medals and trophies, living large in our mansions with regular visits from sitting and past presidents. I would get a dachshund and wear only gold lamé. We were going to be beloved (like so many Republicans). When we had enough interviews in the can, we decided it was time to take the next step. And that's where everything fell apart.

Getting a literary agent is the first job of any writer looking to publish a book. Nonfiction or fiction, most publishing houses won't even consider your proposal or manuscript if you're unrepresented. You'd think people would line up for the contractual right to take 15 percent from you, but it's very much the other way around. So we began what we knew would be a difficult search for an agent who wanted to represent not only a conservative project, but also two conservative writers. Since most agents were headquartered in New York City, we knew this was an almost impossible endeavor. We queried dozens, conducting exhaustive research to find agents who considered themselves either apolitical or sympathetic to conservative politics. You'd also think that, as businesspeople, agents would make finding the next great idea and making a boatload of money priority one. But this was decidedly not the case. Even Ann Coulter, who one could certainly argue has no trouble getting her opinions out there, wrote:

> While the radio and Internet can bring conservatives to people's homes with the flick of a dial or modem, conservative books have to clear three sets of liberal censors before making their way to readers. First the books have to be published. Then the public has to know the book exists. Finally, potential readers have to

find a bookstore where they can buy it. All this is complicated by the fact that publishers don't like conservative books, the major media ignore them, and bookstores refuse to stock them.[2]

And that first liberal censor was proving to be an incredibly powerful one. Upon querying one of New York's top agents, for example, we received the following response, via email to *Why You're Wrong About the Right*:

> I don't think I am wrong. And this lot in power are venal, corrupt, think the law is only for them when it benefits them, determined that their view of the world is the only one that counts and that anyone who disagrees should be punished in some form (including making the rest of the world sicker because of their "moral" stances on issues), secretive and conspiratorial to the point of undermining the constitution of the republic, up to their ears in the blood of our children, and have made us more vulnerable to attack not less, while making the top 3% immorally richer at the expense of the rest of us. I have no interest in a book that intends to exonerate these people from their responsibilities. God knows, they refuse to do it themselves. Sorry.

Not only were we being rejected, we were also being scolded. Another top agent wrote to us, dismissively:

> This is the kind of query that makes me wonder if writers read our profiles at all. If you'd bothered to go to our website, or really read my profile on writers.net or agentquery.com, you'd find that we have a reputation for progressive politics. Something like this would never be appropriate for our agency.

Something "like this"? What's more progressive than a book by a new generation of urban conservatives at a time when the cult of liberalism is so de rigueur, it's almost boring?

And then there were the responses of pity and sympathy. The "I wish I could, but…" replies. One agent wrote us, "I'm sympathetic, since I sometimes think I'm the only political conservative in the New York publishing industry, and have certainly experienced the same frustrations you describe." Another agent wrote, "As luck would have it, you've found one of probably a half dozen people in New York publishing who aren't crazy radical Leftists." Both felt our pain. Both passed.

Of course we also received dozens of standard "no" replies, and still another agent called me just to say he hoped my teeth fell out. I'd sent out my first query on April 5, 2006, and ten months later, our manuscript was collecting dust. We started to consider taking the book to a less-established agent outside the city, or even publishing it ourselves. I dreaded the phone calls I'd have to make to our contributors. "Thanks for everything, but we just can't sell the thing." But then, as it goes in the movies, on February 15, 2007, our query found itself on the right person's desk. John Talbot would take us on—and he was shocked it had taken us so long to find an agent. He thought it was perfect for Threshold, a conservative imprint at Simon & Schuster, and predicted he'd sell the book within two weeks—and he did. If one day I name my firstborn John, you'll all know why.

Back to popularity. The point of this book is not to echo popular sentiment, or to feed a demographic what it wants or expects to hear for the sake of book sales. The Left already does that very well. If you're looking for that scathing profile of President Bush, or the book on stupid Americans, look no further than Al Franken or Michael Moore. This book intends to surprise, shock, even alarm, and we hope it does so in a provocative and even humorous way. Furthermore, whether this is naiveté or booze talking, we honestly believe that this book is for everyone. It's for the conservative, looking for ammunition to better argue with his liberal friends. It's for the undecided, sick of getting her political "news" from the blow-hards on television. And, yes, it's for the liberal, who, as a smart and cultured person of the world, wants to be better informed and speak the language of authority, instead of the language of hyperbole and hypocrisy. (And it's also for my mother, who can't wait to see my name in print, but that's neither here nor there.)

As for Brett and me, we're no experts, and don't claim to be. We're simply Republicans with an axe to grind. But if you got to know us, we think you'd really like us! We love sports and movies and music. We enjoy a fine glass of whiskey and cheap, American beer. We love a forty-dollar steak as much as a two-dollar Nathan's hot dog. We live in cramped New York City apartments that we can barely afford and love it (though if you're giving out rent-stabilized apartments in the West Village, we won't say no). We're close to our families and have wonderful friends, despite their weird political views. We're often funny, and our parents say we're not half bad-looking. We also have a healthy helping of crazy, which makes us colorful and fun to be around. Brett, for example, can imitate the batting stances of nearly every famous Mets player, past and present. And I once put a balloon in my shirt, went to a swanky hotel bar, ordered a cocktail, and pretended to be drunk and pregnant—out of sheer boredom! Sometimes when we go out we'll change our names and pretend to be CIA agents, just to mess with people. And we're full of fascinating contradictions. For example, I'm a longtime atheist pursuing a master's degree in religious studies. I find Hollywood repulsive, but I'm totally ad-dicted to perezhilton.com. I love to fish, but am afraid of the water. Brett is bored by art and rarely gets to a museum, but is himself an amateur artist and photographer. He hates Washington, D.C., but hopes to one day go into politics. In other words, we're just every-day twenty-somethings who happen to be conservatives.

Though we may be fun, we know that alone does not sell books. We're nobodies, which speaks volumes about the character of our many contributors—all of whom had little to gain by investing in a project that could easily have gone nowhere. And that's why we went to them—to say the things we have no business saying. I, a white, twenty-something woman, can't speak with authority on race relations or the civil rights movement. But Shelby Steele can. We can't speak expertly on global warming, the history of education, the popularity of NASCAR, or being a devout Christian in Major League Baseball, but Naomi Orsekes, Jon Zimmerman, Andrew Giangola, and Curt Schilling can. And when mixed together, their opinions and knowledge, along with our research, combine—like a really meaty, Republican bouillabaisse—to create a better, more comprehensive and nuanced picture of the conservative viewpoint, one that reflects its incredible diversity and intellectual integrity.

So we say to you, go forth and buy many copies. I have a feeling our battle with popularity is only just beginning. Which reminds me—it might be time to dust off that comeback for the liberals who continue to insist that Republicans are racist, homophobic, uncaring, uncool, uptight, stupid, and the rest. To them I say, "I know you are, but what am I?"

WHY YOU'RE WRONG ABOUT THE RIGHT

CHAPTER 1

Republicans Are Racist

The Myth of the White Supremacist

They say a leopard can't change its spots and Republicans can't change their "negro-lynching," white robe wearing, and card-carrying membership ways of the KKK. . . . To Limbaugh and Republicans we say, "If you can't stand the heat, don't stand so close to the burning cross."[1]

—A. Alexander

Comedian Dave Chappelle's *Chappelle's Show* featured a sketch in which he plays a blind "white supremacist" who doesn't know he's actually black. While utterly hilarious, the sketch is also an ingenious and provocative depiction of the folly and blind ignorance of racism, and a reminder to all of us to take a quick glance in the mirror once in a while. Nearly twenty-five years after Steve Martin, the whitest guy in America, famously opened *The Jerk* with the line, "I was born a poor, black child . . ." Chappelle gave us a clever reverse-take for the new millennium. While no point was made about the character's politics, one could draw a convincing parallel between the blind, black, white supremacist and the hackneyed image of the "Republican Racist," the backward hillbilly who knows not what he does, or worse, knows *exactly* what he does . . . and likes it. Why is it that comedians seem to have the keenest take on race today? Kanye West saying "George Bush doesn't care about black people" in the middle of a benefit for victims of Hurricane Katrina wasn't profound, or funny—it was awkward. But Chris Rock, mocking West shortly thereafter at another Katrina victims' benefit by saying "George Bush hates midgets" was hilarious, and pointed out the absurdity of West's claim. It seemed for Rock (and the rest of intelligent America) that George Bush's alleged contempt for black people was just as responsible for the Katrina disaster as was his contempt for the vertically challenged, which is to say, not at all. Maybe we should appoint Chris Rock, Dave Chappelle, and Steve Martin (circa *The Jerk*, not *Cheaper By the Dozen 2*) overseers of U.S. race relations?

Racism, more than a century and a half after the Civil War and more than forty years after the civil rights movement began, is still an issue in the United States, and pinning the "racist" label on a powerful group of people is a highly effective means of deflating their influence, regardless of the veracity of the claim. So the carefully crafted and desperately clung to image of the Republican Racist remains at the top of the liberal tool box, and it doesn't take much (of any real substance) to get them to whip it out.

But is it true? The answer is complicated. Racism is both a historical and a current fact, and a great many have contributed to its continuation over the centuries, including, in some cases, blacks and minorities themselves. But one thing is certain: History has been hijacked and rewritten to implicate Republicans as the most racist folk in the history of the world, despite a stellar and often-forgotten record of civil rights success.

Historical Republican achievement in racial equality extends back to the party's roots, of course, with the first Republican president, Abraham Lincoln, who led the Union to victory over the slave-owning Confederacy in the Civil War. As Republican Party historian Michael Zak points out, this wasn't really a war between the North and South, it was a war between Republicans and Democrats. "The Democrats chose to become the slavery party. No Republican ever owned a slave. That's not semantics, that's a fact."[2] Indeed, Republicans passed the first Civil Rights Act following the Civil War. They then passed the Fourteenth Amendment, which protected all persons from deprivation of due process or equal protection by the states. Every Democrat in Congress voted against its passage. Similarly, 98 percent of Republicans voted for the Fifteenth Amendment, which gave blacks the right to vote, and 97 percent of Democrats voted against it.

The Democratic Party is also the party whose national slogan in 1868 was, "This is a White Man's Government," a reflection of the racist paranoia of the era.[3] It is the same party whose members have included George Wallace, the former Democratic governor of Alabama, who raised the Confederate flag above the state capitol in 1963; Hugo Black, Supreme Court justice and former Ku Klux Klansman; Robert Byrd, former Ku Klux Klansman and West Virginia senior senator; and former South Carolina senator Ernest Hollings, who said during the 1984 presidential primary that "you had wetbacks from California that came in here for Cranston," to explain why his opponent finished second in a straw poll.[4] Even former attorney general Robert F. Kennedy directed the FBI to wiretap the home telephone of Martin Luther King, Jr.

Recent Republican presidents have only improved on the party's legacy of progressive race relations. The elder George Bush appointed Clarence Thomas to the Supreme Court, only the second black ever appointed to the high court. George W. Bush appointed two consecutive black secretaries of state, the first and second in history, and Condoleezza Rice has remained one of his most trusted advisors. Yet, as *National Review* managing editor Jay Nordlinger asserts, "No one cares. Because [Bush] doesn't care. If Clinton did this, he'd be talking about it constantly. Maryland governor Bob Ehrlich said to me in an interview that if Condi Rice were a Democrat, they'd have parades for her. She'd be on the cover of *Time* magazine every week."[5]

And in desperate efforts to preserve the image of the racist Republican, Democrats minimize the accomplishments of Republicans in racial equality by effectively demeaning members of the very constituency they claim to represent. Popular talk-radio host and author of the best-seller *Shut Up and Sing!* Laura Ingraham observes that the elevation of conservative blacks to high posts is somehow perceived by the Left as less legitimate or important. "Condoleezza Rice, Colin Powell, Clarence Thomas, and the list goes on of black Americans elevated to the highest positions in government by a Republican president—yet they somehow don't count."[6]

Furthermore, there is a pervasive notion among many on the Left that "black Republican" is somehow an oxymoron, and that blacks who vote Republican are doing a disservice to their race. As if that weren't insulting enough, some even go so far as to insist that blacks who align with conservative ideology are—knowingly or not—just trying to suck up to the so-called white establishment. In 1999, Bill Maxwell, a black columnist for the *St. Petersburg Times,* wrote a scathing critique of black Republicans that should make anyone, regardless of skin color, bristle:

> By all standards, some creatures are just plain strange, making us do double takes because their compositions or habits or appearances defy our sense of logic and our way of viewing reality. Take the wildebeest, the warthog, the hyena, the brown pelican, the Shar-Pei. These animals, seemingly wrought by committee, make us laugh or shake our heads. Another such creature, of the human kind—and perhaps the strangest of all—is the black Republican. Do not laugh. This is a serious

matter, given yet another Alan Keyes run—absurd as it may be—for the White House. He is the talk show host who exhibits an obnoxious Messianic complex that emerges each time he appears on TV to debate his white counterparts. My grandfather, a smart Pentecostal pastor who died five years ago, would have said that Keyes, along with others like him, is "out there cuttin' up 'round them white folks." This was my gramps' portrayal of black sycophants, whose raison d'etre was pleasing their white "superiors."[7]

Deroy Murdock, a nationally syndicated columnist and contributing editor with *National Review Online*, discussed this hostility toward black conservatives, the skewed version of history, and why he votes for Republicans even though he is black. "The Republican Party and conservatives generally have spent the last 147 years trying to liberate black Americans and make them self-reliant, while Democrats and liberals have spent most of that time either trying to hold blacks behind or making them dependent on big-government solutions. While the Right generally has tried to create a society built on equal opportunity where race matters less, the Left usually has tried to amplify the importance of race while apportioning power and privilege on the basis of skin color."[8]

But there was a shift. Despite a history of unfettered commitment to racial equality by Republicans, the Left somehow got black Americans to side with them. Ted Hayes is a homeless advocate in Los Angeles. Hayes administered one of the most successful homeless shelters in the country, Dome Village, and then voluntarily decided to live there himself. (Incidentally, he was unable to renew the lease to Dome Village once his landlord demanded much higher rent—after learning that Hayes was a black Republican.) He discussed the surprising transition from Republicans as the party of racial equality to Democrats.

"I began to realize that we abandoned our base. We were deceived by welfare and food stamps, clothing, housing and

Medicaid and foster care. We got ripped off and went right back into slavery."[9]

And the shift was very successful. Democrats embraced the racial equality cause vocally, if not always in practice, then in promise, and blacks embraced Democrats, thanks in no small part to the mistakes of a few high-profile Republicans. Trent Lott, for example, celebrated segregation-era politics when he said in 1984 that the "spirit of Jefferson Davis" still exists in the party. Hayes blames the shift not on overt hostility or racism, but on a slow and gradual history of neglect and indifference. "[Republicans] don't deal with social prejudices, and that's their fault because they have strayed from the foundations of the Republican Party, particularly of 1854. The party of 1854 was based primarily on the eradication of slavery and social, political, and economic injustice in America and throughout the world. And unfortunately, even though they never attacked black people or minorities or poor people, they never really retook the battlefield of social issues. Basically, modern Democrats took us the route of socialism and welfare, which has destroyed poor, black people in America."[10]

That route began with the "political realignment of 1964," when Lyndon Johnson's civil rights accomplishments, combined with Republican nominee Barry Goldwater's opposition to the Civil Rights Act, further contributed to this profound shift in voting patterns of blacks. But that historical moment has also been rewritten. Contrary to the popular myth, Goldwater was known as an integrationist who supported equal rights but opposed the Civil Rights Act not out of hostility toward blacks, but for denying private businesses certain rights of association and demanding that they serve all people, which he saw as a stripping away of the rights of private business owners. Additionally, twenty-seven out of thirty-one Republican senators supported the bill, whereas twenty-one Democrats voted against it, including Sam Ervin, Robert Byrd, and Al Gore, Sr. It was Republican minority leader Everett Dirksen who wrote and introduced the 1964 Civil Rights

Act and who delivered a speech in favor of the act with the words, "Nothing is so powerful as an idea whose time has come."[11]

But the legacy of the shift is still very visible today in the collective suspicion of the Republican agenda as it applies to blacks and minorities. The cult of the Republican Racist is both a product of revisionist history and a political weapon of necessity. That political necessity helps to keep the myth of the Republican Racist alive. Byron York, the White House correspondent for *National Review*, explains that "for years Democrats have portrayed themselves as the sole guardians of civil rights, not only because they support the cause but also to obscure the fact that for so many years the Democratic Party was an obstacle to civil rights. Now, of course, Democrats depend on receiving 90-plus percent of the African-American vote in presidential election years. Even with that vote, they lose, and if they received even slightly less than that, they would never, ever win. So their survival depends on the need to portray Republicans as racists, or at least as insensitive to civil rights. I think that message is often megaphoned in the media, and so Republicans find themselves constantly on the defensive."[12]

Regardless of who started what, the legacy of racism in the United States is, of course, all of ours now. And as both sides work eagerly to figure out ways to solve existing problems (and appeal to valuable voting constituencies), the question of who is doing a better job is often raised—by the media, by popular culture, by the parties themselves. The answer has much to do with differing views on agency, opportunity, and oppression.

Indeed, those who argue that blacks and other minorities suffer from a lack of opportunity that is ubiquitously afforded to whites often embrace programs and initiatives like welfare and affirmative action meant to counter that imbalance. But while the imbalance may be real, the programs are not the answer, and are in fact a huge part of the problem.

Shelby Steele, the renowned race relations expert, academic, and author, asserted that progress in this country is hindered by a double standard that is part of what he calls "white guilt." "Affirmative action is a perfect example," says Steele. "It gives something to somebody without asking anything. It ought to be contingent on performance; at least you ought to have to meet a certain elevated grade point average. It's up to black people to pull themselves together and become competitive in American life, in our economic life. No one can make you equal. You have to do that yourself."[13]

Agency, something rarely addressed by today's most vocal black leadership, is a hugely important part of dissecting race relations, and Steele makes no small point of it.

"If you want to help [blacks], the first thing you have to do is ask something from them. And you have to make all reform contingent on their performance. If they don't perform, they don't get any rewards. The Great Society asks nothing. 'We white people will put our shoulders to the wheel but we're not going to ask black people. In fact we're going to take responsibility off your shoulders.' It's the sickest, most absurd social reform ever created. It never worked, it never will. It made black America worse. Black kids today, on the SAT exam, score lower than they did in 1990."[14]

Several years ago Bill Cosby made remarks that few would dare to utter when he said, "Ladies and gentlemen, the lower economic people are not holding up their end in this deal. These people are not parenting. They're buying things for the kid—$500 sneakers—for what? They won't spend $250 on *Hooked on Phonics*."[15]

These were comments that some undoubtedly found offensive, but that others, including some blacks, believed to be the kind of honest statements that could lead to true progress. Again, it seems to be the comedians who have the best perspective (or maybe just the most freedom of expression).

Ted Hayes said about Cosby, "I'm 100 percent in his corner.

Bill Cosby is the voice of the next generation. He and people like him are the foundation-layers for the next forty years, but the last forty years have been nothing but devastation for our people."[16]

In his seminal piece *The Case for Democracy,* Natan Sharansky lays out his platform for achieving peace, stability, and democracy throughout the world. The historical model that he uses to describe his proposal is the United States' response to the Soviet Union during the Cold War. He notes that when several members of Congress, including conservative Democrat Henry "Scoop" Jackson, brought Soviet persecution of their *own* political dissidents to light and started tying U.S. benefits to Soviet internal reform, the political tide in the Kremlin changed, paving the way for the erosion of a totalitarian communist regime.

Sharansky uses the Soviet experience as the framework for achieving reform in other areas of the world. He argues that all democratic societies have something in common: They treat their own people with respect. Conversely, the most oppressive leaders and societies can be defined not by how poorly they treat outsiders, but by how little dignity they afford insiders. Nobel Prize–winning economist Amartya Sen likewise concluded that a nation that practiced true democracy would never experience famine, since democracies put the livelihood of their people in their own hands. Sen used India as an example, pointing out that, despite the Third World conditions in some regions, India has not experienced famine since gaining its independence in 1948. It is in the nondemocratic societies that leaders have the greatest capacity to shift attention from their own failures to artificially created scapegoats, such as the United States. This only functions to perpetuate the leader's power as he points to the scapegoat, whose continued existence provides the leader with continued relevance.

Sharansky does not address race in America, although his discussion of democracy aptly applies to racial politics in this country.

Much of the black leadership in America has arguably done a great disservice to its own people, as a number of race relations experts have dared to point out. Unfortunately for the black community, their progress has been shunted, not expedited, by their own leadership, as public figures like Jesse Jackson and Al Sharpton claim any setback as the work of men like George W. Bush. People, like countries, do not progress by pointing to others. Success comes only with self-agency.

Today's left-wing racial equality advocates are, by any standards, horrendous spokespeople for an incredibly important cause. Much was made of President Bush's refusal to attend the NAACP convention for several consecutive years. Although many used the absence to once again disparage the president for his lack of racial consciousness, the Bush administration pointed to the lack of respect given Bush and Republicans by Julian Bond, chairman of the NAACP. Bond said Republicans' idea of equal rights "is the American flag and the Confederate swastika flying side-by-side."[17] Jesse Jackson's anti-Semitism is well known and well documented, thanks to shocking statements like, "I'm sick and tired of hearing about the Holocaust," and referring to New York City as "Hymietown" in 1984.[18] Democratic congressman Charles Rangel said that "George Bush is our Bull Connor,"[19] a reference to the former Birmingham, Alabama, police commissioner who used dogs and hoses to disrupt civil rights marches. Connor was a Democrat. Rangel. Bond. Sharpton. Jackson. These "leaders" have severely deprived their constituencies by pursuing political scapegoats at the expense of dignity and fairness. And even worse, when someone on the left makes blatantly racist comments stemming from utter ignorance, they are rarely checked. Equal opportunity offender Joe Biden, Democratic senator from Delaware, offered this explanation for why Iowa's schools performed better than those in Washington, D.C.: "There's less than one percent of the population of Iowa that is African American. There is probably less than four or five percent that are minorities. What is it in Washington?

So look, it goes back to what you start off with, what you're dealing with." The left-leaning *Washington Post* called this offense a mere "stumble."[20]

Characters such as Chappelle's blind, black, white supremacist help to shed some light on racism, but Republicans will find this particular myth very hard to escape, thanks to the Left's desperate reliance on its persistence. A 2002 *Time* magazine article by Jack White, "Lott, Reagan and Republican Racism," offered a suggestion to Republicans looking for more black votes: "Here's some advice for Republicans eager to attract more African-American supporters: don't stop with Trent Lott. Blacks won't take their commitment to expanding the party seriously until they admit that the GOP's wrongheadedness about race goes way beyond Lott and infects their entire party. The sad truth is that many Republican leaders remain in a massive state of denial about the party's four-decade-long addiction to race-baiting."[21]

Whose race-baiting? So the myth persists.

CHAPTER 2

Republicans Are Elitist WASPs

The Myth of the Yachtsman Conservative

> Bless this ship, and all who sail on her. I christen thee *The Flying WASP.*
>
> —*Caddyshack*

In a particularly hilarious episode of *Curb Your Enthusiasm,* Larry David and Jeff Green find themselves kicked out of their country club for removing a five-wood from the casket at a club member's funeral, and are faced with the prospect of joining the so-called gentile club. Susie, Jeff's wife, was not in favor. "There's like three fucking Jews in the whole club, okay? It's not for us. It's WASP, WASP, Republican city." When Larry and his wife attended the club's interview, they made sure to affect a WASPy, "Republican" lifestyle. Larry went to great lengths to explain during the interview that he went to school in New Haven, drove a Hummer, belonged to the National Right to Life Committee, and that he and his wife had met while campaigning for Ronald Reagan. Of course, in the world of Larry David, a WASPy country club must be a Republican country club.

There are two confounding and contradictory myths about the typical Republican: He is both the gun-toting hick, driving barefoot and shirtless in his pickup truck, *and* the loafer-wearing WASP, sipping scotch on a yacht or lounging in the polo club. The latter stereotype may include the benefits of sophistication and wealth, but by no means extends to likeability. CNN Headline News pundit and radio personality Glenn Beck said of this contradictory imagining of the Republican elite by the Left, "When you think of red states, do you think of homes on Central Park and in the Hollywood Hills, or do you think of stupid, redneck hicks in Oklahoma? The media can't have it both ways. There is only one elite, and it's the Left, and that's why the Democrats have solidly lost their connection to the Democrats that were like my grandparents."[1]

Examples of the Republican-as-Elitist-WASP stereotype abound in popular culture. Certain common characterizations of the WASP in particular have emerged over the years, some of which are more puzzling than astute. One is that WASPs are notorious alcoholics.

Of course, the generalization does not just refer to Republicans. How could it? There have been numerous and well-documented misadventures of some notorious alcoholic Democrats, including Ted Kennedy, his son Patrick Kennedy, Ann Richards, and Gavin Newsome.

Additionally, there is the categorization of WASPs as socially awkward—out-of-touch geezers who are more at home on the trading floor than the dance floor. Gawker.com, a website that reports on New York media and gossip, recalled this version of the WASP in a behind-the-scenes blog from inside the 2004 Republican National Convention parties, held in New York City:

> The best part was when they started playing the Electric
> Slide and everyone ran out to the dance floor. Two hundred

Republicans of varying degrees line-dancing—it was like a tacky bat mitzvah gone wrong. Maybe if the WASPs and Southern Baptists had had a little more exposure to that scene, they wouldn't have been so quick to kick off their shoes?[2]

And then there's the version that paints the WASP as a snobby, aloof, and downright cruel misanthrope, eager to step on his friends, family members, or the crippled and elderly to get ahead. A famous line in the Oliver Stone movie *Wall Street* has the clearly Republican Gordon Gekko say, "I just got on the board of the Zoological Society. Cost me a million. That's the thing with WASPs—they like animals but they can't stand people."

With all of these varying versions of the WASP floating around in the pop culture ether, it's easy to forget that it's actually a fairly derogatory term, and one that doesn't inherently apply to Republicans. Since white, Anglo-Saxon Protestants represented some of the earliest American settlers, saying that Republicans tend to be WASPy is a bit like saying they tend to be religious: it is often the case for *Americans*, regardless of their political affiliations. The first known use of the term was by Andrew Hacker in a 1957 article entitled "Liberal Democracy and Social Control," in the *American Political Science Review*. He wrote, rather brazenly:

> These "old" Americans possess, for the most part, some common characteristics. First of all, they are "WASPs"—in the cocktail party jargon of the sociologists. That is, they are white, they are Anglo-Saxon in origin, and they are Protestant (and disproportionately Episcopalian). To their Waspishness should be added the tendency to be located on the Eastern seaboard or around San Francisco, to be prep school and Ivy League educated, and to be possessed of inherited wealth.[3]

Though that may, to many liberals, sound like today's typical Republican, this too is a misconception. While Republicans do benefit from some WASP support, they by no means have a monopoly on it. In the 2006 elections, Protestants voted for Republicans more than Democrats by a relatively narrow margin of 54 percent to 44 percent.[4] While WASPs in the South have remained largely Republican, the blue New England states might as well be called the "WASP Block" for Democrats, as five out of the six states have voted consistently Democratic, with the exception of swing state New Hampshire.[5] And some of the Democrats' most outspoken liberals are WASPs, including Howard Dean and Ned Lamont.

Conversely, many northeastern Republicans today, like George Pataki and Tom Ridge, are Catholic. Mitt Romney is Mormon. The list goes on and on, and although the term is often associated with "non-Catholic Christian," a survey of the U.S. Senate illustrates how inaccurate it is to classify Republicans as the WASP party. There are nine Republican Roman Catholic senators. There are also six Baptists, four Mormons, one Church of Christ member, one Greek Orthodox, one International Church of the Foursquare Gospel member, one McLean Bible Church member, and two Jews.[6]

Recently, Jewish Americans have become increasingly right-leaning. Historically, Jews have tended to vote overwhelmingly Democratic, which most likely stems from the communist, labor origins of many Eastern European Jews, as well as general sympathy toward midcentury social programs in the United States. Given the perception by many that the Roosevelt administration did not do enough to help displaced Jews during World War II, it is somewhat surprising that Jews have clung to their New Deal roots. However, there is little debate now that Republicans have become the party that most consistently defends Israeli policies and the Zionist cause, and George W. Bush and Ronald Reagan were two of the most pro-Israel presidents in history. In the 2004 election, President Bush received an estimated 25 percent of the Jewish vote, a number representing significantly higher Jewish support than in the past.[7] And, although all Americans tend to be more supportive of

Israel than are our allies, Republicans have proved to be its biggest supporters. A 2002 Gallup Poll showed that 67 percent of Republicans side with Israel in the Israeli-Palestinian conflict, compared to 45 percent of Democrats. Support for the Palestinians is at 8 percent among Republicans, versus 21 percent among Democrats.[8]

In addition to conservative support for Israel, left-wing anti-Americanism has also been increasingly associated with anti-Israel views. Jimmy Carter, along with other notable Democrats, such as Jesse Jackson and Al Sharpton, has faced the accusation of anti-Semitism, and recently, in Carter's case after publication of his book *Palestine Peace Not Apartheid.* Carter is quoted on the Republican Jewish Coalition website as saying the United States' decision not to support Hamas is "criminal."[9] Monroe Freedman, former executive director of the Holocaust Memorial Council, said about Carter, "Anti-Semite is a range of things. You go from, say, Nazi is a ten. Country club discreet anti-Semite's at one. I'd put Carter at three."[10] Abraham Foxman, chairman and director of the Anti-Defamation League, said, "One should never judge a book by its cover, but in the case of former President Jimmy Carter's latest work, *Palestine Peace Not Apartheid,* we should make an exception. All one really needs to know about this biased account is found in the title."[11]

In fact, often the staunchest supporters of Israel come from the Christian Coalition wing of conservatives. Journalist, historian, and Middle East analyst Daniel Pipes wrote that Christians "are increasingly the bedrock of Israel's support in the United States, more solidly pro-Israel and more robustly Zionist than many in the Jewish community."[12] He went on to say, "To those who wonder why Washington follows policies so different from the European states, a large part of the answer these days has to do with the clout of Christian Zionists, who are especially powerful when a conservative Republican like George W. Bush is president. (In contrast, Christian Zionism has nearly died out in Great Britain.)" However, this has not always translated into Jewish votes for the Republican Party, as Jews tend to be mistrustful of the motives of the Christian Coalition.

* * *

Although Jewish voters still overwhelmingly support Democratic candidates, Jewish Republicans are undoubtedly becoming more mainstream within the party. The Republican Jewish Coalition has become an increasingly powerful group that identifies with Republican policies. The RJC's website articulates its platform and why it supports Republican policies, including President Bush's aggressive war on terror, a buildup in military strength, strong support for Israel, school vouchers, individual achievement rather than affirmative action, economic freedom, social security reform, and a criminal justice system that punishes criminals.[13] The neoconservative movement, which has become very influential in the modern Republican Party, is also heavily grounded in Judaism and is thought of as an outgrowth of leftist Jews who came to support more conservative policies over time. Notable supporters include Frank Meyer, cofounder of the *National Review,* and Irving Kristol, who described himself as a "liberal mugged by reality."[14]

There is also substantial Roman Catholic support for Republicans, including the South Florida Cuban voting block. Cubans represent one of the most reliable groups of Republican voters and are significantly more conservative than Hispanics at large, as they identify with the tough stance that Republicans have taken with communist regimes like Fidel Castro's.

Vietnamese Americans also overwhelmingly vote Republican, which can likewise be attributed to their past communist regimes and the firm stance that Republicans have historically taken against those regimes. In 2004, 72 percent of Vietnamese Americans polled in eight eastern states said they voted for George Bush. Historically, Vietnamese Americans disdained the Democratic Party because it was perceived as the party that was less supportive of the Vietnam War.[15] This may shed some light on the sort of voting patterns we can expect from future Iraqi Americans.

President Bush has also increased Republican support among

Hispanics. In 2004, Bush collected 44 percent of the Hispanic vote. He also collected 44 percent of the Asian vote, although both numbers declined for Republicans running for Congress in 2006. Arab Americans tend to support Republicans at about the same rate as they do Democrats, and well-known Arab-American Republicans include California congressman Dan Issa, who led the recall election to remove California governor Gray Davis in favor of Arnold Schwarzenegger. Before the 2000 election, the American Muslim Political Coordinating Council Political Action Committee endorsed President Bush, citing his outreach to the Muslim community. Obviously, none of these voters are the country club WASPs we've been trained to expect.

But somewhat surprisingly, considering the recent influx of non-Protestants and non-Caucasians to the Republican Party, the president has been a frequent target of the Republican WASP stereotype. Sure, Bush comes from an elite, privileged background, attending Andover, Yale, and Harvard, and vacationing in Kennebunkport, Maine. But then, so do a great many American leaders, who have benefited from the best education and opportunities, from John F. Kennedy to John F. Kerry. Kerry in particular epitomizes the Brahmin image of the cultural elite, growing up in France and Massachusetts, attending Fessenden, Yale, and Boston College, and vacationing in Martha's Vineyard. But unlike Kerry, Bush has always possessed the ability to come across as a regular guy—a family man who hangs out on the ranch and wears cowboy boots

Even Alexandra Pelosi, daughter of House Democratic Leader Nancy Pelosi, in her documentary *Journeys with George,* had to admit that there was something relatable about him. While chronicling Bush's 2000 campaign for president, Pelosi eventually befriended Bush, earning romance advice from him, sharing his Cheetos, and gossiping about the other journalists. In fact, there were rumors that some in Bush's camp were worried that he was *too* relatable, and that the film would make him look less presidential.[16] The folksy, fun-loving, easygoing Everyman Bush onscreen was far from the moody, contemptuous, condescending characterization that would be expected from someone of his considerable background and position—less like a WASP and more like the Waltons. A 2006 *Wall Street Journal* column by Daniel Henninger, entitled "Bush is Back. Will it Matter?"[17] commended President Bush for a speech he delivered in Wheeling, West Virginia, in defense of the war. Henninger was so blown away, in fact, that he resorted to a comparison that would shock and disturb any liberal into seizure: "I'll pay him the highest possible compliment: It was Clintonesque."

Henninger went on to anoint Bush with even more name-dropping. "Ronald Reagan, Franklin Roosevelt and Winston Churchill reside in the Valhalla of great communicators, but Bill Clinton and Harry Truman thrived as mere mortals, not only connecting with the mythic 'common man' but somehow bonding to them. George Bush joined that class in Wheeling on Wednesday."

Bush's relatability, likeability, and general ease make him, to many, a guy you'd like to share a beer with, see a ballgame with, watch *South Park* with. As Henninger said, "OK, it wasn't Demosthenes, but it was George W. Bush at his Everyman best. . . . This is the man, liberal mockery and amazement notwithstanding, who won two hard-fought presidential elections, not as spin has it, only by Rovian genius but by connecting with audiences."

So is the Republican Party beholden to Nantucket or Kentucky? Is today's conservative named Buffy or Biff? Are they white, Anglo-Saxon Protestants from the colonies or uncultured, fanatical evangelicals from the Bible Belt? Well, it's whichever the Left finds more useful and convenient at the time. So fire up the yacht and pour me a scotch, Bitsy—we're sailing to Little Rock.

CHAPTER 3

Republicans Are Humorless

The Myth of the Unfunny Conservative

The Nixon I remembered was absolutely humorless; I couldn't imagine him laughing at anything except maybe a paraplegic who wanted to vote Democratic but couldn't quite reach the lever on the voting machine.[1]

—Hunter S. Thompson

A left-of-center friend who writes for a left-leaning online magazine once half-joked, "Television is liberal because liberals are the funny ones. Conservatives aren't funny. And they kind of smell."

We'll get to body odor in a minute. But first, the broad and boldly stated hypothesis that conservatives aren't funny is a difficult one to prove or disprove. And the use of humor in the political sphere is no small point. Politics and comedy have enjoyed a long and mutually beneficial relationship. From political cartoons to satire, mockumentaries to late-night television, court jesters to

Jon Stewart, comedy brings levity to politics, and politics provides comedy with endless fodder.

But what of the notion that liberals are funnier than conservatives? Republicans have long been painted as humorless, uptight, stiff, and sober, thanks in large part, one must assume, to well-meaning men like Dick "My Cardiovascular Health Is No Laughing Matter" Cheney, Dan "Don't Make Fun of My Spelling!" Quayle, and Rudy "Feces Isn't Art" Giuliani. CNN Headline News pundit Glenn Beck, an unabashedly funny conservative, said of the caricature, "I don't know at what age conservatives were taught that they have to lodge a stick deep inside of them. I've missed that step."[2] Dry-witted conservative columnist George Will (who routinely gives us gloriously glum quips like "Childhood is frequently a solemn business for those inside it"[3]) also weighed in on the stereotype. "It seems to me there is no ideological monopoly on humor. But I do think the essence of humor is to see incongruities and I think that conservatives are particularly good at seeing the incongruities in the world that limit the possibility of perfection. So liberals tend to have sometimes a painful earnestness."[4]

Indeed, the indelible image of the dour-faced, dark-suited, tie-strangled Republican has convinced most of America that all conservatives must own stock in Brooks Brothers. Sharon Stone once told the *Washington Post*, "It's traumatizing for me to come to Washington during a Republican administration because I don't have any Republican clothes."[5]

Stammering conservatives who eagerly rattle off a very short list of names of popular right-leaning funny men (Ben Stein, Larry Miller, Drew Carey, Dennis Miller, P. J. O'Rourke) just provide more fodder for the chock-full-of-funny Left, and those who make unqualified declarations like "Bush's friends say he's a funny guy!" seem even more humorless.

Lisa "Kennedy" Montgomery, a former MTV VJ, political satirist, and television personality, was a longtime Republican who now considers herself a libertarian. Fed up, in part, with the self-important sobriety of some of the Right's leading personalities, she discusses the uneasy marriage between entertainment and politics and acknowledges the humor problem:

> So many TV Republicans pander, and they're just humorless. Ann Coulter used to be really, really funny, and then she started taking herself so seriously. She started to really buy into her own punch lines. And they were funny when they were just sort of the outrageous exclamations on the end of her sentences, but now she really takes them so seriously. She's defining herself with these more extreme views. I find her to be humorless as time goes on, which is a shame, because she started out as a beacon for conservative humor that had been missing from literature and TV for a long time. P. J. O'Rourke is probably the greatest conservative writer of this generation, and he will be remembered for defining his brand of conservatism with logic and humor, which are seldom bedfellows, sadly. I thought Ann was going to, if not take his place, at least pacify people until P.J. started writing more books. But she really buys into this unattractive side of the conservative coin.[6]

Conservatives who take earnest whiffs at funny don't usually fare any better, if public opinion is any barometer. When the Republican governor of California, Arnold Schwarzenegger, makes a joke during a speech, funny or not, the public pounces, eager to make fun of his quirky accent or corny, overacted delivery. Michael Moore's documentary *Fahrenheit 9/11* features a scene in which President Bush speaks to a room full of wealthy Republicans ("The haves . . . and the have mores") and captures an inarguably funny Bushism: "Some would call you 'the elite.' I call you 'my base.'" But instead of laughing, liberals immediately rebuke him for his politically incorrect and classist brand of humor. They forget that, for a United States president, that's a pretty funny joke.

But it's impossible (and should, in fact, be illegal) to call conservatives humorless after reading anything by vaunted American satirist P. J. O'Rourke. For example: "Imagine a weight-loss program at the end of which, instead of better health, good looks, and hot romantic prospects, you die. Somalia had become just this kind of spa."

Former *Crossfire* cohost Tucker Carlson wrote a hilarious book, "Politicians, Partisans, and Parasites: My Adventures in Cable News." When *The Daily Show* host Jon Stewart appeared on *Crossfire,* however, Carlson was lambasted for everything from his bow tie to his journalism skills. Stewart, a funny guy, had the *Crossfire* audience roaring with laughter, and the show was talked about for weeks, with much of the media lauding Stewart for his comedic prowess, sharp wit, and even, inexplicably, his "bravery." Some suggested that the performance even affected Carlson's career, as shortly thereafter *Crossfire* was canceled and Carlson was shipped from CNN to MSNBC.

While most liberals were patting themselves on the back for what became a collective effort to flex the comedic muscles of an entire political demographic, others (liberals *and* conservatives) saw the segment as a cheap and immature playground stunt in which Stewart was actually the humorless one, bullying Carlson over his wardrobe, name-calling ("You're still a dick"), and petulantly refusing to play along with Tucker's request to "be funny." It was reported that after the show Stewart had to be forcibly removed from the *Crossfire* studio, where he spent hours airing his political grievances to producers backstage. Regardless of who won the throwdown, many saw it as the final nail in the coffin, proof that conservatives, alas, *definitely* aren't funny.

But too little is made of the humorlessness of the Left, and it's a lack of levity that stretches beyond the bounds of comedy and has begun to envelop the liberal ideology and further the myth of the unfunny conservative. To that end, Carlson says:

> Liberals take politics far more seriously because they take government more seriously. Most of the conservatives I know

have a "fuck you" sensibility that's much cooler than sucking up to the establishment. I spent a lot of time covering campaigns, and the staff on the Republican side would go out for dinner and drinks and say, "Our guy's a good guy. We don't know if he's the best guy, but he's a good guy, and he's probably better than the other guy. And if he doesn't win we'll move on and do other things." But on the Democratic side they're much more emotionally invested. They see their candidate as the final barrier between civilization and the Visigoths. A lot is at stake; it's a totally different level of intensity. For Democrats, politics is so much more personal. Conservatives have an easier time being friends with liberals than liberals do with conservatives.

In fact, a fascinating book by University of Virginia psychologist Jonathan Haidt called *The Happiness Hypothesis* attempts to examine inherent psychological and philosophical differences between conservatives and liberals (among other things) as a way of locating biological and environmental influences on morality—and seems to prove Tucker's point. In the book Haidt asks questions about the origins of disgust. Haidt found that liberals, especially extreme liberals, were less likely to attach meaning to moral systems that protected the group, and were far more likely to invest in morals that support the individual. Conservatives, on the other hand, saw more value in protecting the group, but were also able to see value in protecting the individual. "Because conservatives do give some weight to individual protections, they often have a better understanding of liberal views than liberals do of conservative attitudes, in his view," wrote Nicholas Wade in his *New York Times* story on Haidt.[7]

Because of these differences, to which Carlson and others throughout *this* book attribute liberal misperceptions about the Right, it would seem conservatives have been *forced* to adopt a healthy sense of humor about their odd station in American civilization. (That station is called "Feared and Avoided.") But, as Haidt, a liberal himself, points out, conservatives also seem to maintain more moral pragmatism, for which the nation should, in fact, be supremely grateful. "A liberal morality will encourage much greater creativity but will weaken social structure and deplete social capital. I am really glad we have New York and San Francisco—most of our creativity comes out of cities like these. But a nation that was just New York and San Francisco could not survive very long. Conservatives give more to charity and tend to be more supportive of essential institutions like the military and law enforcement."[8] But what's all that worth if you can't make fun of it on *The Daily Show* and in the *New York Times*?

The conservative who hasn't faced the Disbelieving Liberal hasn't gotten out much. The DL is, after all, everywhere. He is on planes and trains, in restaurants and bars, in classrooms and office lunchrooms, and he just . . . can't . . . believe . . . ("Are you serious?!") that you—his drinking buddy, his ballgame buddy, the guy he discusses sexual misadventures with—are a conservative. And after grilling you on your stand on assorted political issues (and then running to the bathroom to wash his hands) he will leave you, betrayed and shocked, as if he just found out he was adopted. Carlson related one particular brush with the DL (presumably one of many). "I'll be on a plane out of LAX and by the time we're flying over Arizona with a couple cocktails in our systems someone will invariably say to me, 'So you don't actually believe that stuff you say, do you?' And you know, I want to tell them that I'm a lot more extreme than you think. I'd like to move to Idaho, have a couple guns and live in peace. But that's inexplicable to a liberal, because liberals don't have a category for someone they like personally but dislike politically."[9]

This very storyline plays out daily in every corner of the country. In May 2006, PETA-loving *Clueless* actress Alicia Silverstone made an appearance on *The View* just days after a very public spat between hosts Rosie O'Donnell and token conservative Elisabeth

Hasselbeck about the war in Iraq. In what read like a high-school lunchroom move, Silverstone refused to hug or acknowledge Hasselbeck, but embraced Rosie and the other hosts, making her allegiance abundantly clear—and allaying the concerns of all who feared that the B-lister might get through the segment without weighing in on the war at all. Later, one of O'Donnell's staffers was removed from the studio when she was caught defacing posters of Hasselbeck. Even more recently, in September 2007, Barry Manilow canceled an appearance on *The View,* and told online gossip source TMZ.com, of Hasselbeck, "I strongly disagree with her views. I think she's dangerous and offensive. I will not be on the same stage as her."[10] To be clear, these are adults.

The painful earnestness of the liberal elite is exaggerated most by their inability to recognize and acknowledge the smart and funny conservative in their midst. According to many, popular culture either evades or lampoons conservatives, whereas liberals (wink, wink) are somehow innately "in on it." They seem to miss the joke that is actually on them. A number of pundits, academics, and culture critics are addressing this issue in more nuanced ways. Brian C. Anderson, author of the wildly popular *South Park Conservatives,* made the argument in his book that the animated television show *South Park,* the brainchild of Trey Parker and Matt Stone, espouses more conservative views than Hollywood would like to admit—and it's hilarious.

> The smartest funny show in the history of television is *South Park,* and it is not liberal. The success of Parker and Stone shows just how much material there is for humorists to exploit—I'd like to see more of it. A show like *South Park* regularly skewers the Left (the Right, too, of course); much of the comedy on Comedy Central has an anti-PC flair, which can sometimes seem right-wing since the left has been largely responsible for PC conformities.[11]

Jonah Goldberg, writer for *National Review,* acknowledges that *South Park* takes funny and clever potshots at the Left, but draws the line at calling the show conservative.

My friend Brian Anderson wrote a book called *South Park Conservatives,* and even though my blurb is on the front cover, I'm actually quite critical of some of it. I hate generational politics, I hate youth politics, I hate identity politics of all kinds. And if conservatism is about ideas, then you can take it too far and think that somehow these "South Park Conservatives" represent something truly new, and the whole point of conservatism is that there's nothing new under the sun. It can be taken too far. There's a real difference between attacking political correctness and attacking the Left for its silliness, and being a conservative. *South Park* is very good, and *The Simpsons* was very good, at attacking the false pieties of the Left. That's where their humor really came from.

A lot of people are recognizing now that liberals are the ones who are sort of becoming the sticks in the mud, dogmatic, humorless people. They're sort of taking the place of conservatives because they're the ones who have all these pieties and dogmas about political correctness. Mocking some of that stuff, that is a very healthy positive sign in the popular culture, because it shows that the hold of liberalism on this next generation is less than the stereotypes that liberals have about young people would have you think. Liberals think that young people have to be liberal. They're synonymous, when what it really is is a projection of baby-boomer nostalgia about the 1960s upon young people. Young people don't have to be liberal. They don't all have to act alike.

And Goldberg offers some advice to those who may be interested in erasing that stick-in-the-mud stereotype. "If you can at least show that in the popular vernacular you've got other things going on in your life than translating Thomas Aquinas into English, you can appeal to people and you can get someone to listen to your point of view for two seconds longer than some of the old style conservatives who were all about Latin puns. I think that's been very successful."[12]

Politics, the media, and the entertainment industry will always use one another, attack one another and subjugate one another, for mutual gain. As for my friend's original point, he's clearly wrong that conservatives aren't funny. And if Richard Nixon, Steve Forbes, and Don King are any proof, we're also pretty funny-looking. As for his other quip that Republicans "kind of smell"? Recent evidence to the contrary just surfaced in Berlin. In preparation for the G8 summit, where German authorities were expecting hundreds of violent left-wing protesters, they reportedly used scent-tracking to keep tabs on particularly dangerous offenders.[13] Identifying left-wing protesters by scent may sound funny, but if you've ever been to a Moby concert—or stood next to Michael Moore for more than thirty seconds—you know this kind of makes sense.

Unlike offensive body odor, humor is, of course, subjective. But not unimportant. Consider the April 2006 issue of *GQ*, which listed the overwhelming advantages of sleeping with Republicans. Reason No. 4: "A Sense of humor. Republicans are happy to watch Jon Stewart with you. They think he's a riot. They don't parse every word he says in an effort to figure out if 'The Huffington Post' will approve. They just laugh, pour another cocktail, and decide upon which couch they will fuck your brains out after the show."[14] So there. Not only are Republicans funny, but they're great in the sack. But that's another chapter.

CHAPTER 4

Republicans Don't Care About Education

The Myth of the Leave-All-Children-Behind Conservative

The Bush regime doesn't believe in funding education because if you fund education you will have a more educated populace. If you have a more educated populace, you will have critical thinking. If you have critical thinking, you cannot push this agenda that they have and you won't have as many people that are so willing to serve in the armed forces for Dick Cheney.[1]

—Janeane Garofalo

Separation of church and state often comes into the sharpest focus when discussing public education. While some argue that religion has no place in the public sphere, especially in schools, others remind us that the religious do not keep their faith in a suitcase that can be dropped off at the threshold of a public institution.

Consider this excerpt from a presidential speech on education:

> Some families have been frustrated to see their children denied even the most private forms of religious expression in public schools. Here is where I stand: I believe the First Amendment does not require students to leave their religion at the schoolhouse door. Just as we wouldn't want students to leave at home the values they learn from religion, we should not require them to refrain from religious expression. Reinforcing those values is an important part of every school's mission.[2]

Unsurprising if it had come from President Bush, whose faith is often the subject of tsk-tsking by the Left. But the president who said this was Bill Clinton, in his book *Between Hope and History.* And there's more:

> I believe the Supreme Court was right a generation ago to prohibit any public authority from creating an official school prayer and making students recite it. But there is absolutely nothing improper about students wanting to reflect upon their faith. Students can pray privately and individually whenever they want. They can express their beliefs in homework, through artwork, and during class presentations, as long as it's relevant to the assignment. They can form religious clubs in high school.

The notion that the far Right is behind the prayer-in-school push is just one of many myths surrounding conservatives and education. Republicans are routinely assailed for their coldheartedness toward education, their poor funding of public schools and educational programs, and their bottom-line approach to schooling— all of which are gross exaggerations, if not factual inaccuracies. Yet, the characterization persists. Noam Chomsky, often a critic of American foreign and domestic policy, has argued that public education is and always has been a bad idea. "Mass education was designed to turn independent farmers into docile, passive tools of production. That was its primary purpose. And don't think people didn't know it. They knew it and they fought against it. There was a lot of resistance to mass education for exactly that reason. . . . The antidemocratic thrust of opinion in what are called democratic societies is really ferocious. And for good reason. Because the freer the society gets, the more dangerous the great beast becomes and the more you have to be careful to cage it somehow."[3]

Public education as *un*democratic? That's a new one. In his 1999 book *Chomsky on Miseducation* he went a step further, insisting that public schools were mere propaganda machines and calling for schools to stop teaching democracy altogether. "Because they don't teach the truth about the world, schools have to rely on beating students over the head with propaganda about democracy. If schools were, in reality, democratic, there would be no need to bombard students with platitudes about democracy. They would simply act and behave democratically, and we know this does not happen. The more there is a need to talk about the ideals of democracy, the less democratic the system usually is."[4]

But Chomsky is not, of course, the only one weighing in. Democrats and liberals have done a tremendous job of associating Republicans and conservatives with a heartless lack of concern for education, an issue that would, on first blush, seem nonpartisan. No one, after all, is suggesting that we *not* educate our children. But if the liberal rhetoric is to be believed, you'd think that's what conservatives wanted. And any attempts by the Right to improve education and access to it are disingenuous and strategic measures designed to improve the bottom line of the party. For example, historian Gareth Davies, in the *Journal of American History* argued that President Nixon's push for bilingual education in the late sixties and early seventies was not the recognition of a new, growing minority of Spanish-speaking Americans, but an underhanded attempt to lure Hispanic voters to the Republican Party. "Richard

Nixon's quest for a 'new Republican majority' sometimes took him in surprisingly liberal directions."[5] But when President Bush's No Child Left Behind (NCLB) law effectively terminated the Bilingual Education Act, NCLB was called racist. Either way, the lesson is: Republicans are horrible people.

New York University history of education professor Jonathan Zimmerman, who considers himself a "nondoctrinaire liberal," is one of the rare college professors to leave his own politics at the door to teach his expertise—and with passion. Because of this, he is a favorite at NYU and has published a number of authoritative books. He discussed the characterization of Republicans as unconcerned with public education in the context of American history. "I think it's mostly unfair. Indeed, one of the most remarkable things about the birth of the common schools was that Americans across the political spectrum supported them. They differed on many details, especially local versus state control, but there was enormous bipartisan consensus about the need for schools themselves."[6] Furthermore, he says that, contrary to Chomsky's take, America gets it right (and always has) when it comes to the basic goals of public education. "I think the simple agreement that everyone should go to school—or at least have the opportunity to do so—is our single greatest achievement. In Europe, people fought for a century about whether the poor should go to school. Why get educated if you don't need it? The American answer was simple: Everyone needs it, because democracy demands it. We govern ourselves; but we can't do that—or do it well—without education."

In the late 1990s, David Horowitz reflected on a *New York Times*/CBS opinion poll revealing that "Democrats enjoy public confidence on most critical election issues, from health care to education to Social Security."[7] But where, Horowitz wondered, did that confidence come from, particularly where education was concerned?

When you add the 40 years of continuous Democratic rule of Congress before Republicans took the House in '94, it's easy to see that Democrats are responsible for everything that's wrong with public schools—at least everything that can be fixed by public policies. Yet according to the poll, Democrats have the public's confidence on education. Education is even perceived as a "Democratic issue." How can this be? Is it because the Democratic slander—that Republicans don't care about education—has some bite to it? Or that Republicans do care but don't have an answer to the failures that Democrats have fostered? Or is it that Republicans don't have programs to rescue poor and minority children from the fate to which Democrats have consigned them?

It wasn't any of those, it turns out. Horowitz suggested it was that Republicans—before Bush took office, that is—didn't know how to best implement their ideas, promising as they were.

Republicans have the programs, but what they don't have is the foggiest idea of how to present them to the American electorate in a way that would win its confidence. They seem clueless about how to fight this political battle. Of course, if the education crisis could be solved by adding more teachers, who would oppose that? The problem is that Democrats have been adding teachers and dollars for decades, while the education crisis has only gotten worse. Republicans have an explanation: You can add all the teachers and dollars you want, but if there is no connection between teachers' performances and their rewards, there is no way the result will significantly improve.

This kind of pragmatic thinking is what has gotten President Bush in trouble with liberals since he took office, and shortly thereafter signed into law No Child Left Behind. After he delivered a rousing and inspirational speech about education at the Republican National Convention in 2000, it's hard to imagine that liberals could accuse him of not caring. "Too many American children are segregated into schools without standards, shuffled from grade to grade because of their age, regardless of their knowledge. This is discrimination, pure and simple—the soft bigotry of low expectations. And our nation should treat it like other forms of discrimination: We should end it."

While it can be said that talk is just talk, No Child Left Behind certainly put Bush's promise into practice. Yet, NCLB is constantly criticized by many on the left for being either bad policy or good policy poorly executed. Zimmerman falls into the latter camp: "No Child Left Behind centralizes a good deal of authority in Washington, but our test 'system,' which is really no system at all, doesn't provide enough information for Washington to exercise this authority in a knowledgeable or reasonable way." Those who oppose NCLB generally do so on such grounds—that it *could* work, but doesn't. But actually, by almost all accounts, it *is* working, in spite of its flaws, which have even some conservatives questioning its efficacy. The Department of Education and the National Assessment of Educational Progress released a report in July 2005 proving the law has actually been incredibly effective. According to the report:

* More progress was made by nine-year-olds in reading in the last five years than in the previous twenty-eight years combined.
* America's nine-year-olds posted the best scores in reading (since 1971) and math (since 1973) in the history of the report. America's thirteen-year-olds earned the highest math scores the test ever recorded.
* Reading and math scores for African-American and Hispanic nine-year-olds reached an all-time high.
* Math scores for African-American and Hispanic thirteen-year-olds reached an all-time high.
* Achievement gaps in reading and math between white and African-American nine-year-olds and between white and Hispanic nine-year-olds are at an all-time low.

* Forty-three states and the District of Columbia either improved academically or held steady in all categories (fourth- and eighth-grade reading and fourth- and eighth-grade math).[8]

In addition to the complaint that NCLB isn't working, the other common criticism is that it is poorly funded by Bush and other Republican lawmakers. Zimmerman discussed this point. "Our single greatest disaster lies in the failure to adequately—or equally—institute this vision. Some of us get educated and others do not, usually because of our place on the class ladder. Horace Mann famously condemned private schools, because he said they would siphon off the most able citizens and impoverish (in every sense) America's common schools. That's more or less what has happened. The private schools and the best public systems prosper, and others don't." But, according to the Department of Education, funding—or lack thereof—is hardly debatable:

President Bush's FY 2007 budget request demonstrates his continued commitment to education, with dramatic funding increases over 2001 for key education programs, including:

* 29% increase in total Federal education funding (from $42.2 billion in 2001 to $54.4 billion in 2007);
* 33% increase in total K-12 funding (from $27.3 billion in 2001 to $36.3 billion in 2007);
* 40.4% increase in total NCLB funding (from $17.4 billion in 2001 to $24.4 billion in 2007);
* 45% increase in Title I (from $8.8 billion in 2001 to $12.7 billion in 2007);
* 68.5% increase for Special Education (IDEA) grants to states (from $6.34 billion in 2001 to $10.7 billion in 2007); and
* Quadrupled funding for reading (from $286 million in 2001 to $1.2 billion in 2007) (a 300 percent increase).[9]

Opposition to No Child Left Behind from the left is particularly puzzling because the law was passed in 2001 with tremendous support in Congress, and in many ways it caters to the traditional approach to public education by the Left, which reflects an ideological pattern of increasing funding and federal government involvement. The House voted 381–41 in favor, with 198 Democrats voting yes and only 6 voting no. Republicans only voted 183–33 in favor. And in the Senate, the law was passed 87–10, with Democrats voting 43–6 and Republicans voting 44–3.[10] In fact, NCLB's chief author was Ted Kennedy, who, as recently as March 2007, was still voicing his support in hopes of securing its impending reauthorization. In a *Washington Post* editorial, Senator Kennedy wrote:

> Five years ago, Congress and President Bush made a bold and historic promise. We pledged in the No Child Left Behind Act that the federal government would do all in its power to guarantee every child in America, regardless of race, economic background, language or disability, the opportunity to get a world-class education. We have made progress toward fulfilling that commitment. Before the act was passed, most states lacked ways to track student progress and teacher effectiveness. Many state accountability requirements had no commitment to improving education for every child. Only four states had approved assessments that tracked and reported the achievement of every group of students in their schools.[11]

Despite such strong ties to Democrats, No Child Left Behind continues to garner criticism for its imperfections, and it seems everyone has a little advice for the Republicans, who are apparently at fault. Neal McCluskey, an education policy analyst at the Cato Institute, wrote, "In education we continue to have this Soviet model, where the government must supply the schools and you get to go to the schools the government gives you—and that's essentially it. Conservatives, who've traditionally opposed big government, have to understand how the market works. They talk about the market a lot, but they never seem to really trust it—or they don't now seem to trust it. They have to get back to saying, 'Why shouldn't our schools run like the computer industry, the automobile industry and all those things we take for granted every day?'"[12] Likewise, Professor Zimmerman has some advice: "Better education costs money. Will money guarantee better education? Of course not. It's a necessary condition, if not a sufficient one. Insofar as Norquist-style 'tax revolt' conservatives fight against raising money for schools, they harm education. If you want quality schools, you'll have to pay. Or stop complaining." And what's a quick way to get the job done, according to Zimmerman? "[Republicans need to] make a simple deal with the Democrats: we'll give you more money if you insist that all teachers are seriously educated in their disciplines of instruction, AND if you insist that all kids must demonstrate real competency in order to advance and graduate." This is the explicit intention and goal of No Child Left Behind, which Zimmerman acknowledges, but he says the program doesn't provide enough money to do so effectively.

True, NCLB is not the darling of every conservative. But it would be too simple to say that the legislation is a dispositive indicator of the Republican position. For many years, conservatives have argued that education is a local issue that should be funded at the state level, with accountability and curriculum determined locally as well. However, that position was lambasted by Democrats who like to equate frugality and healthy skepticism with apathy or heartlessness. However, if one is determined to spend federal funds on education, NCLB responsibly attempts to impose accountability on schools and teachers. Complicating the issue is the complaint by many teachers, who say that the law imposes overly rigid standards on them. For example, the National Education Association criticizes NCLB for not using "more than test scores to measure student learning and school performance."[13] Many Republicans would respond that this is the price one pays for trying to regulate a local issue with a federal bureaucracy. You can't have it all.

Supporters—on the left and the right—of No Child Left Behind, and similar education reforms that favor school choice, criticize policies that look to pour giant sums of money into low-income or failing public schools without demanding anything in return. A number of outspoken liberals are in favor of just such ludicrous proposals, including presidential candidate John Edwards. Upon the unveiling of his proposed education reform, the antitax group Club for Growth, headed by former congressman Pat Toomey, came out swinging against it. Toomey said:

> I guess decades of failed education policy are not enough for John Edwards. One has to wonder, though, how many years will be enough. When will Edwards finally realize that pouring more money into an education monopoly is not going to make our schools any better? When will he realize that the same money can be given to low-income parents to make their own education choices for their children? While John Edwards throws himself at the feet of the teachers' unions, local governments across America are implementing school choice programs with real success. If John Edwards truly cared about education, he would support school choice programs that have a proven track record of working. Unfortunately, Edwards cares more about winning points from his special-interest buddies at the NEA than he does about genuine education progress.[14]

Not only is money insufficient to guarantee improvements in public education, but it is sometimes the case that the best funded schools are the worst producers. Washington, D.C., schools rank very high in per-pupil spending, but rate extremely low when it comes to student performance. Increased spending tends to benefit teachers' unions, one of the Democratic Party's most loyal constituencies, and not the education system. As Peter Brimelow pointed out in *The Worm in the Apple: How the Teacher's Unions Are Destroying American Education,* "historically, as much as 98 percent of [National Education Association] PAC money has gone to Democrats.[15]

So if money is not necessarily the solution to fixing failed schools, what do Republicans propose as an alternative? One suggestion is using public money to send children at failed schools to private institutions through vouchers and other methods that would have a progressive impact on those most in need. Rather than using public money to send poor and minority school children to quality private schools, some of which are parochial, many liberals would rather continue sending these children to the same failed inner-city public schools, where they have little chance of getting the education they deserve. So which is really the party that doesn't care about education?

Other experts have suggested a larger movement to privatize secondary education, which may seem like a radical idea, but thanks to incredible recent failures, it is one that is gaining steam. Yale University academic and political commentator David Gelernter asked, "Do we actually need and want our public schools, or do we keep them around out of fear of the teachers union—and habit, like a broken child's toy we are too sentimental to throw away?"

He went on to explain his rationale. "We know that private schools are perfectly capable of supplying first-class educations. . . . If sending *some* children to private school at public expense is worth discussing, why not sending *all* children to private school?"[16] So even among conservatives there is disagreement about what constitutes the right approach to education. Some prefer the Less Government model. Some prefer the Spend Money, But Impose Standards model. However, *all* Republicans believe that education is important and truly want "no child left behind."

Unfortunately, the myths persist, thanks in large part to

politicians like John Kerry, no stranger to irresponsible statements poorly contemplated. Something Kerry said in October 2006 seems particularly revealing. "We're here to talk about education. But I want to say something before that. . . . You know, education, if you make the most of it and you study hard and you do your homework and you make an effort to be smart, you can do well. If you don't, you get stuck in Iraq."[17] Whether he believes this or not, he was clearly using education as a political punch line, imploring students to take their education seriously, lest they end up in the U.S. Armed Forces. The statement is offensive for many reasons, not the least of which is its crude and callous use of education to make a statement about foreign policy. And yet it's Republicans who are called insensitive.

CHAPTER 5

Republicans Are NASCAR-Loving Rednecks

The Myth of the Hick

Rabbit?! You rednecks eat anything! I ate a squirrel quesadilla but this is where I draw the line.

—*King of the Hill*

Popular comedian Jeff Foxworthy, who headlined the *Blue Collar Comedy Tour* and *Blue Collar TV*, defined "redneck" as "a glorious absence of sophistication."[1] With television shows like *King of the Hill* and pop songs like Gretchen Wilson's "Redneck Woman" crowding the airwaves, the modern redneck is no longer what he was fifty years ago. And he's certainly not what he was a couple of centuries ago. Today, the term redneck can be a source of pride and a badge of honor, connoting a down-to-earth, unpretentious antielitism that prizes the simple things over the latest trends in *Vanity Fair.* Foxworthy, along with other similar comedians like Bill Engvall, Larry the Cable Guy, and Ron White, represent a new redneck contingent: we'll call it "redneck lite." It's all the charm and colorful kitsch of *The Dukes of Hazzard,* without the poverty and illiteracy of *actual* redneckism.

But modern rednecks like Foxworthy were not always thus— that is, they were not always rich and funny. Most historians agree that the term refers to the influx of Scots-Irish Presbyterians in the late eighteenth and early nineteenth centuries into Appalachia and the southern United States. Whether the "red neck" part refers to the red cloths they wore around their neck to protest the Church of England, or to the sunburns they got while working outdoors, among other etymological explanations, rednecks were, essentially, poor white people. They were seen as clannish, lawless, migratory, and mistrusting of the government, and were also frequently called "crackers."

But this group was behind some seminal moments in U.S. history, including the Whiskey Rebellion, and turned up in inordinate numbers to fight in the War of 1812, the Texas Revolution, and the Mexican-American War. Tennessee, in fact, turned out so many volunteer soldiers it was nicknamed the Volunteer State. And during and after the Civil War, like many blacks, this group of poor white southerners was disenfranchised and pushed even further into financial destitution, and became the subject of ridicule and discrimination not only by upper-class white southerners and northerners, but by black southerners, who routinely joked that one was better off having been a slave than a redneck. The popular assumption that today's rednecks have Confederate ties is largely a myth. Certainly, many poor whites fought in the Civil War for the South, thanks to geography, but most were ambivalent about the war, as none were wealthy enough to employ slave labor in the first place, or to benefit indirectly from such a system. Eventually, due to labor initiatives during World War II, rednecks were trained and educated, emerged from poverty and second-class citizenship, and popped up elsewhere, from Pennsylvania to California, and even in Canada.

But what may be the most important legacy of the redneck is America's second-most-watched sport on television, and one with a growing fan base of 75 million Americans: NASCAR. Second only to the NFL in television viewership, NASCAR is a hugely successful business and incredibly popular sport that has become the benchmark of innovative entertainment branding. But NASCAR is often lampooned, or used as a handy one-word stand-in for "redneck," and has become associated almost solely with the Republican voter pool. As the weekend approaches, friends will joke, "What's the race this Sunday? The Hubcaps Make Great Wind Chimes 500?" a one-two punch deriding NASCAR simultaneously for its redneck ties and its fetish for sponsorship.

"It's unlikely that 75 million people are rednecks," said Tony Stewart, the circuit's resident bad boy, and the 2002 and 2005 Nextel Cup champion. And in an explanation more reminiscent of Howard Dean than Jimmy Dean, Stewart goes on to say:

> I think the people who honestly believe that need to come out to California, Las Vegas, and Phoenix. They need to come to Michigan, come to Kansas, to Illinois. We go to areas that aren't the typical [southern] part of the country where everybody thinks NASCAR fans are from. Come to those areas and see the culture around it. It's really cool to go out to California, because when we do our hospitality appearances, you're out there seeing people tailgating all day just like they're going to a football game. It's not an atmosphere that's any different than an NFL game that you go to.[2]

Likewise, Jeff Moorad, co-owner of the Hall of Fame Racing team, and CEO of the Arizona Diamondbacks, says it's simply too popular a sport to paint with a single brush. "I think it's difficult to generalize about the politics of any fan base, NASCAR included.

Politicians are drawn to successful sporting events, whether there's a Republican focus administration or a Democratic one. I assure you and fans alike, politicians of all shapes and sizes will flock to the Daytona 500, and the fans will represent all political affiliations."[3]

NASCAR does have redneck roots, of course, and there is still a palpable pride in that past. Many of the first stock car racers were bootleggers running moonshine through the hills of North Carolina and Tennessee. After Prohibition was lifted in 1933, these runners kept their souped-up cars and turned to racing. But the NASCAR we know today is hardly an underground or unsophisticated operation. And Stewart is right in that its 75 million fans are, demographically, incredibly diverse. Of NASCAR's double life, Lowe's Motor Speedway president H. A. "Humpy" Wheeler recently said, "Are we moonshiners, country music, banjos and Route 66? Or are we merlot and Rodeo Drive?"[4]

Andrew Giangola, NASCAR's head of business communications, provided pages of facts and statistics proving that NASCAR's fans are as diverse as those of any other sport, presenting a compelling argument against the Republican-As-NASCAR-Loving-Redneck myth. He does, however, see NASCAR's infectious popularity as uniquely American.

There's been lots of recent speculation about why NASCAR has become so popular. Some believe NASCAR's growing popularity is because of the universal appeal of the automobile and America's continuing love affair with cars and speed. Some have said in an era of reality programming, NASCAR is the best reality show on TV today: Forty-three courageous, skilled, daring athletes, putting it all on the line each week, with one winner emerging four hours later. Some say the multitudes are drawn to the family atmosphere and tremendous spectacle of a NASCAR event. Americans love big events, and seventeen of the twenty largest sporting events in the country each year are NASCAR races. The sport is an extraordinary traveling road show: Woodstock meets the Super Bowl meets the best state fair you've ever been to, thirty-eight weekends a year. Our fans tell us that a big part of the appeal of NASCAR is that on any given weekend twenty-five to thirty drivers and their teams, through hard work, preparation, and performing in crunch time when it all matters, can win the race. NASCAR fans in surveys say they like that the drivers are "accessible," "down to earth," and "people just like me." If grit, determination, parity, equality, humility, courage, and a direct relationship between work ethic and success, and the rewards that performance brings, are all uniquely American attributes burned into our country's national identity, and also elements distinguishing NASCAR, then I think we would be honored with that characterization.[5]

The stereotype that all NASCAR fans are Republicans is completely inaccurate, according to NASCAR. Of its 75 million fans, 28.2 percent say they vote Republican, versus 26.8 percent who say they vote Democratic, and 10.3 percent who say they vote Independent. (The 34.7 percent that remains represents fans who are not registered voters.) Other numbers go even farther to debunk the myth:

* The average NASCAR fan is more affluent and more likely to have children who are under eighteen than the average American.
* Women make up 40 percent of NASCAR's fan base.
* People of color account for 20 percent of NASCAR's fan base, making NASCAR the fastest-growing major sport among minorities.
* NASCAR has the most Fortune 500 sponsorship of any sport.
* NASCAR races in all corners of the country. Top-tier races take place in or near Boston, Chicago, Detroit, Las Vegas, Los Angeles, Kansas City, Phoenix, and Sonoma, California.

   ❊   There are more NASCAR Sprint Cup drivers from California than any other state in the union.

Giangola also elaborated on the misconceptions about fan experience at NASCAR races:

> Some arrive at the race in a pickup truck. Others helicopter in. Some camp in the infield. Others stay in multimillion-dollar motor coaches. Some enjoy a corn dog from the concession stand. Others nibble on shrimp in the luxury skyboxes. On most weekends, NASCAR is the country's top-rated sports programming. That adds up to a heck of a lot of people watching—some in small apartments, others in huge houses that seem to span two ZIP codes. The point is, the sport's fan base is large, diverse, and growing. It is indeed a cross-section of the entire electorate. As much as it's tempting to create a memorable moniker to sum up NASCAR fans, 75 million Americans are not sum-up-able. It's inaccurate and unfair to describe such a large group of people with a clever catch phase, like "NASCAR Dads." If you have a pulse, you're a candidate to be part of NASCAR Nation. The sensory thrill of an eight-hundred-horsepower racecar firing up its engines and then racing at 180 miles per hour six inches from the next car—closer than you park next to someone at the Home Depot—transcends race, gender or politics.

And even geography. NASCAR recently considered building a new, state-of-the-art track in, of all places, New York City, which is not that surprising considering the sport holds its annual Champions Week there, and televises its awards banquet from the Waldorf-Astoria in Midtown Manhattan.[6]

Indeed, one of the most unlikely NASCAR fans is a Canadian-born mountain climber and University of South Carolina nursing professor named Patrick Hickey, who is one of only 150 people to have climbed the highest peaks on all seven continents. When NASCAR learned that Hickey, a huge Jeff Gordon fan, was climbing Mt. Everest, they choppered a Sprint Cup flag by medevac helicopter to his base camp, and a long, cold, dangerous climb later, Hickey planted the flag on the top of the world. In thanks, NASCAR invited Patrick to meet his favorite driver at the Bank of America 500 at Lowe's Motor Speedway in 2007, where Hickey also sat in on the drivers' meeting and was on the track for opening ceremonies. Hickey's experience highlights NASCAR's unique relationship with its fans, which has helped solidify its place as one of the country's most popular sports. As Hickey put it, "This recent experience has shown me that it's the people's sport. The opportunity to get up close to your driver is amazing."[7] Whereas access to, say, the New York Yankees equipment room, dugout, clubhouse, bullpen, ball field, players, coaches, and front-office personnel *while* they're preparing for a big game is unimaginable, NASCAR fans—even those who haven't climbed Everest—can tour the haulers, visit their favorite driver's pit box, watch crews make final car adjustments, walk the race track, and meet drivers, their pit crews, and NASCAR officials before the races start. NASCAR exists *for* the fans, and not itself. And as for the stereotype that NASCAR is just for hicks? Hickey says, "I think it touches every aspect of American life, rich or poor. Traditionally it's been considered a 'redneck sport,' but I think the recent surge of popularity has shown that it's all levels. I'm a well-educated professor from Canada, and I've been an avid fan for many years."

While NASCAR has without question attracted new fans by being, as Hickey put it, the people's sport, it isn't averse to making money. And it does that very well. NASCAR's business model has been so effective, it secures multimillion-dollar sponsorship deals with some of the biggest names in business, who realize the sport's huge fan base and vast marketing potential. Mindy Kramer, the public relations director for Office Depot, which sponsors Carl Edwards' 99 car, suggested that NASCAR presents unique and sophisticated opportunities to attract a wide variety of customers, unlike any other sport could:

> We've done a lot of things within the sport that have enabled us to target that small business customer. That's our core customer. It's not necessarily Joe Q. Public walking in off the street; it's the person who runs their small business—maybe the mom and pop shop that's got five employees. It's the real estate agent, it's the travel agent, it's the gas station owner, it's the locksmith. That small business owner is responsible for 80 percent of our sales, so how do you reach that person, all the time, in a way that's going to interest and engage them? You have the ability to be in front of millions of fans because the car is our billboard for our brand. And you can bring customers to the track and do hospitality. Likewise, the bigger customers, who have their own sales rep at Office Depot, or maybe they order out of our catalog, or they have their own web site that we set up to order their supplies, are brought in to meet our driver, Carl Edwards, and they get that unique opportunity. You become a baseball sponsor, and you don't get to bring your customers down into the dugout to watch the game. We can go in the dugout. We go out on pit road. Our customer sits on top of our pit box, they go in the race hauler, they see how the cars are made. It's unique. NASCAR's created something for the fan and for the sponsor that no sport out there can match.

While NASCAR obviously appeals to a wide variety of Americans (and Canadians!), it has enjoyed an especially long and meaningful relationship with the armed forces, which also may contribute to the myth that the sport is particularly "red." With cars sponsored by the National Guard, the Air Force, the Marines, the Navy, the Coast Guard, and the Army, prerace flyovers, and elaborate and moving performances of the national anthem, races often seem like a patriotic outdoor stage play. And recently, the military has turned to NASCAR for recruitment. Every division of the armed services has a presence at NASCAR races to actively recruit from among the fans. The Army generates tens of thousands of leads per year through NASCAR.

But it goes deeper. NASCAR has a huge fan base among members of the armed forces, and just because many are now overseas, the interest is not diminished. "The coolest thing is that we'll get pictures back from the troops, and they'll have the drivers' flags hanging off of military vehicles or they'll have the drivers' numbers on their vehicles," Tony Stewart said. "It's neat to see that since there's 75 million fans and a lot of them are in the military, they're over there serving our country and still following what you're doing, supporting you while they're over there defending our country. It's pretty inspiring, seeing how much of a role we play in keeping the troops pumped up."

But it hardly makes sense that an affiliation with our armed services would create such an enduring and adhesive association with Republican politics. After all, patriotism isn't partisan. "A true *man* is not proright or proleft. He is pro–our country," said Bubba the Love Sponge, a popular shock jock and satellite radio host based in Florida, and a good friend of Tony Stewart. His brand of humor is the raunchy kind, featuring segments like the "M.I.L.F. Search," the annual "Shit Your Pants" contest, and frequent interviews with porn stars. But unlike Howard Stern, his friend at Howard 101, Bubba speaks to the "redneck" listener: blue-collar workers, long-haul truckers, outdoorsmen. He was arrested in 2001 for killing a pig on the air in a segment called "Bubba's Road Kill Barbecue." "We represent the average, hard-working, ass-kicking man in America," he said.[8]

But on the Tucker Carlson vs. Jon Stewart skirmish on *Crossfire,* Bubba took an unpopular position for an entertainer, albeit a predictable one for his market, lambasting the sacrosanct Stewart and aligning with Carlson, whom he also describes as a friend. "Tucker all the way. [He's] a real dude, and is the same on and off the air, unlike Jon Stewart." When we asked which was sexier, a woman holding a shotgun or a woman holding up a peace sign, he replied, "Shotgun, because she can do a few things with that gun. One, she can protect you from her husband that might be mad because you got caught with her. And secondly, she could also go out hog hunting and get me some nice ribs to grill." Surprisingly, though, this redneck is a Democrat, and if his audience numbers are any indication, he is not the only liberal redneck out there. In fact, Bubba ran as the Democratic Party candidate for sheriff of Pinellas County, Florida, in 2004 and received 30 percent of the popular vote.

When we asked if he and his friend Tony Stewart ever clashed politically, he said, "Tony is a conservative from Indiana. I used to be a conservative from Indiana. When Tony stayed at my house for about a week just prior to the Daytona 500 it was a topic that I figured didn't need to be brought up. Tony is a very good debater. Perhaps that's a topic we should bring up the next time we have him in the studio."

So while it holds that not all rednecks are Republicans, with Bubba as exhibit A, it should also hold that not all Republicans are rednecks. Such clarifications might seem redundant and obvious, but then again, someone recently asked, "Do rednecks really eat possum?" on the Yahoo! Answers website. (Answer: people in many parts of the world, including the American South, eat possum. And it's excellent!) If you secretly fantasize about barreling down a dirt road in a Ford F-150, Lynyrd Skynyrd blaring through the speakers, bandanna hanging from the rearview and six pack of Miller Lite on the seat, and you're wondering if *you* might be a redneck, follow one of Jeff Foxworthy's general rules: "If you've ever given mouth-to-mouth resuscitation to a dog . . . you might be a redneck."[9] But, remember—you might *not* be a Republican.

CHAPTER 6

Republicans Hate the Planet

The Myth of the Reckless Conservative

Everybody wants to save the earth; nobody wants to help Mom do the dishes.[1]

—P. J. O'Rourke

If Republicans are all evil, SUV-driving, endangered-species-hunting, ocean-polluting, forest-raping planet-killers, then liberals are the masters of absurd, hyperbolic declarations. The best one in recent times comes courtesy of Pulitzer Prize–winning *Boston Globe* journalist Ellen Goodman: "Let's just say that global warming deniers are now on a par with Holocaust deniers."[2] Similarly, Democrat Robert F. Kennedy, Jr., said of politicians who have failed to confront global warming to his liking at a Live Earth Concert, "This is treason. And we need to start treating them as traitors."[3] Suddenly, skepticism over whether inconveniently bad ski seasons are caused by humans—and foreshadow the coming apocalypse—is akin to denying the worst genocide in human history and providing aid and comfort to Al Qaeda.

Although not all proponents of the global warming theory are quite as extreme (or offensive), the rest generally share some penchant for paranoia and advocate the certainty of a global climate cataclysm merely because they cannot recall balmy days in January when they were kids. Astonishingly, anecdotes and impressions seem to constitute a large measure of the evidence people cite when fervently asserting their global warming arguments. The "expert" declarations are usually handed down during an uncharacteristically warm day in midwinter, when someone says with an indignant huff, "And there are still people who don't believe in global warming!" When it snows in April, however, as it did in 2006 and 2007 throughout the country, the statements are not rescinded, nor are the science-by-impression methodologies questioned. Despite the vast complexity of this sensitive issue, it seems as though many on the left love to play scientific expert and cast skeptical conservatives as environmental grim reapers.

In reality, Republicans have a rather distinguished history of implementing environmentally protective policies, despite popular opinion to the contrary. The legacy extends all the way back to the first Republican president, Abraham Lincoln, who set aside land that eventually became Yosemite Park.[4] Republican president Theodore Roosevelt established the national park system, which has preserved hundreds of thousands of acres of land. Republican president Richard Nixon established the Environmental Protection Agency and signed the Clean Air Act, the Clean Water Act, and the Endangered Species Act.[5] The 104th Republican-led Congress passed fourteen pieces of major environmental legislation, more than the previous four Democratic-led Congresses combined. President Bush has committed billions of dollars to environmental initiatives and has called for billions of dollars in tax incentives to encourage the use of new, environmentally favorable technologies and energy.[6] Bush also agreed to the G8 aim of halving emissions by 2050.[7] Al Gore even praised the environmental accomplishments of another Republican president, Ronald Reagan, in protecting the ozone when he said that President Bush should follow Reagan's lead in tackling environmental problems.[8] Frustratingly, but not surprisingly, these accomplishments go largely unnoticed.

So, if Republicans are responsible for so many environmental advances, why are they so convincingly cast as the pillagers of the Earth? The Council of Republicans for Environmental Advocacy points out that two of the nation's largest environmental groups, the Sierra Club and League of Conservation Voters, claim to be nonpartisan, but give the overwhelming number of their endorsements and campaign donations to Democrats. Combined with the media's general political slant, it is not surprising, therefore, that the Republican environmental position is an easy target.[9]

Newt Gingrich, who has always been a conservationist, once taught a college class on environmental studies, and recently authored the book *A Contract With the Earth,* explained one reason the Right is so often associated with antienvironmental policy, despite a long history of just the opposite. "The leading environmental groups on the Left—particularly the Sierra Club and the League of Conservation Voters—began to equate the environment with litigation, regulation, taxation, bureaucracy. . . . And you were either for their solution or you were against the environment."[10]

At the same time, it would be an oversimplification—and an inaccuracy—to say that Republicans take the same position on global warming and the environment as most Democrats. It is true that Republicans have generally been more resistant to passing sweeping regulatory legislation, particularly in the international arena, and that Republicans tend to approach the issue with a healthy dose of skepticism, which is not the same as indifference or denial. Science supports this skepticism, because establishing the facts for a planet as large as ours, and with as many variables as ours, is not easy. Furthermore, and perhaps most important, the emerging consensus is still, well, emerging. As recently as May 1975, a headline in the *New York Times* reported, "Scientists Ponder Why World's Climate Is Changing; a Major Cooling Widely Considered to Be Inevitable."[11] Pardon us for being a bit confused, but it seems strange given the clear "consensus," that only thirty years ago temperatures were *dropping,* not rising.

While many global-warming alarmists are very quick to point to "the consensus," anyone researching this issue quickly discovers the sheer volume of information that exists and the wide variety of opinions. It seems as though every week another article appears, questioning or refuting the alleged "science" we hear. Journalist James Taylor said, "Many of the assertions Gore makes in his movie, *An Inconvenient Truth,* have been refuted by science, both before and after he made them. Gore can show sincerity in his plea for scientific honesty by publicly acknowledging where science has rebutted his claims."[12] In October 2007, CNN meteorologist Rob Marciano stated that "there are definitely some inaccuracies" in Gore's film, and "the biggest thing I have a problem with is this implication that Katrina was caused by global warming." Marciano pointed out that the Oscars "give out awards for fictional films as well."[13]

Finally, Dr. William Gray, a renowned meteorologist whose hurricane predictions are widely cited, acknowledges that global warming is taking place but attributes it to the natural cycle of ocean salinity. In a speech immediately following Al Gore's receipt of the Nobel Peace Prize, Gray said, "The human impact on the atmosphere is simply too small to have a major effect on global temperatures. . . . It bothers me that my fellow scientists are not speaking out against something they know is wrong . . . but they also know that they'd never get any grants if they spoke out. I don't care about grants."[14]

In fact, there does not even seem to be a consensus on whether there is a consensus. Even Naomi Orsekes, a professor at the University of California San Diego who writes often on global warming, admits that "there is real debate about what I call 'tempo and mode'—how fast changes are happening, and how worried we should be about them. There is certainly a range of expert opinion about the question of worry."[15]

Richard Lindzen, a professor of meteorology at MIT, has discussed exactly what has been proven so far. "There is little argument that levels of CO_2 in the atmosphere have risen from 315 ppmv when we began systematic measurement in 1958 to about 380 ppmv today. There is also relatively little argument that pre-industrial levels were about 280 ppmv . . . and there is widespread agreement (although with appreciably greater uncertainty) that over the past century there has been net warming of between 0.5 and 0.75C."[16]

Most scientists would probably even agree with the Intergovernmental Panel on Climate Change (IPCC) report, which is the most frequently cited report on global warming. It claims that "most of the observed increase in globally averaged temperatures since the mid-20th century is very likely due to the observed increase in anthropogenic greenhouse gas concentrations."[17] However, the major disagreement, according to Lindzen, lies in whether "our present limited knowledge warrants deep concern or not."[18] He thinks not. Regarding those who are quick to claim consensus, Lindzen says, "Their intellectual insecurity when confronting such a complex issue is relieved by being told that all scientists agree with whatever propaganda they are fed. Under the circumstances, they are made to feel that in going along with the propaganda, they are displaying intelligence and acquiring the right to consider anyone who does not either stupid or hopelessly corrupt."[19] Lindzen also discussed the difference between the U.S. perspective and the European one. "In the U.S., those who support state planning and bureaucratic control look at global warming as a dream come true. Those opposed to state planning and bureaucratic control have been suspicious of the issue from the beginning. In Europe, there has been little partisanship. However, in Europe, all parties are largely committed to state control."[20]

Like most problems that the world faces, large and small, the question ultimately becomes, What do we do about it? The most politically popular solution has been the Kyoto Protocol, which the United States has not adopted. Nations that have ratified the Kyoto Protocol are committed to either reducing their greenhouse emissions or trading for credits if they do not reduce emissions.[21] Although Republicans have taken the brunt of the criticism for failure to pass the Kyoto Protocol, people tend to forget that the Senate rejected the Kyoto Protocol on July 25, 1997, by a vote of 95–0.[22] George W. Bush has been the subject of constant criticism for not later submitting the treaty for ratification, despite the fact that the Protocol still contained exemptions for developing nations like China and still would have imposed the same heavy economic burden on the United States. As James Inhofe, former chairman of the Senate Environment and Public Works Committee, rightly stated, "Symbolism does not solve a supposed climate crisis,"[23] a sentiment with which Professor Lindzen agrees. "Kyoto is purely expensive symbolism," says Lindzen, that "would have little impact on climate. . . . Frankly, this would be almost as true even if India and China agreed to join what for them would be an economic suicide pact."[24]

While the U.S. government has not been as vigilant and active as scientists like Professor Orsekes would prefer, she says that the "business community now recognizes that climate change is a *business* issue—with both perils and opportunities at stake."[25] Where Republicans tend to differ from someone like Orsekes, however, is in the belief that the government should be the driving force behind change. Private businesses seizing the initiative to curtail global warming and implement environmentally sound business strategies is precisely what many Republicans will applaud. In fact, Enron, which is often associated with conservative, corporate greed, "had been one of the most intense lobbyists for Kyoto" due to the opportunity for profit in emissions trading.[26] Incidentally, the link between Enron and the Republican Party is something of a red herring, a veil to hide the company's real allegiances, which mainstream media aren't talking about. Enron CEO Ken Lay *did* personally contribute to two presidential campaigns—$11,000 to be exact. To President Clinton's, that is. He also gave Al Gore $13,750 for his 2000 campaign. During Clinton's two terms, Lay and Enron gave about $900,000 to the DNC.[27]

Kyle Smith of the *New York Post* weighed in on the government versus business debate in an October 2007 op-ed where he argued that "a greener world is being built by private capital, not decreed by the Capitol." He explained, "GM, for instance, has spent more than a billion dollars developing clean hydrogen fuel cells. An affordable electric car, the Chevy Volt, is due in 2010, and though such cars run on household power derived from our coal-burning power grid, they are still cleaner than gas-powered ones, and they're a huge geopolitical step forward. We have coal right here. It's been nice knowing you, Middle East. Drop us a card when you've stopped being insane." In a classic promarkets appeal, Smith acerbically lamented, "Maybe government will fix global warming. And maybe it'll also give us time travel, the ability to raise the dead and plenty of leg room in coach."[28]

Where Republicans also tend to differ from many Democrats on the environment is in prioritization. Only a fool would say he didn't care about the environment. However, on a planet with finite resources and seemingly unlimited problems, the money and energy that we throw at problems must be prioritized according to importance, imminence, and potential for impact. Danish economist Bjorn Lomborg, who heads the Copenhagen Consensus and authored *Cool It: The Skeptical Environmentalist's Guide to Global Warming*, explained this delicate issue at the annual TED (Technology, Entertainment, Design) Conference. He listed ten categories of the largest problems facing the world. Global warming ranked second to last in terms of issues that society should be devoting resources to fixing, simply because it will cost a great deal of money to do a very small amount of good.[29] Lomborg has also pointed to studies showing that warmer temperatures may reduce cold-weather-related deaths. Lomborg believes global warming is real but believes its effects have been exaggerated. Although he supports forms of taxes and public policy to deal with the problem, he says that the best strategy is to increase wealth in other countries so that communities can shore up coastlines and buy air conditioners. He says that even if the United States were to join Kyoto, it would merely postpone rising sea levels by only a few years. "I don't think our descendants will thank us for leaving them poorer and less healthy just so we could do a little bit to slow global warming. I'd rather we were remembered for solving the other problems first."[30]

Another problem the Left faces in championing global warming is the issue's ambassadors. Al Gore is an able and somewhat convincing spokesperson for the cause, but many others are not, and Democrats who want to make global warming a serious agenda issue are right to be worried. After all, who could doubt the sincerity of our representatives in Hollywood, like Leonardo DiCaprio, who triumphantly announced in 2007 that for the first time ever the Academy Awards had gone totally green? (Right. And, for the first time ever, the authors of this book have implemented checkpoints in their apartments to avert terrorism.) Hosting concerts has also become a very popular method of saving the planet, along with cross-country tours by rock stars and celebrities. Pop singer John Mayer boasted that touring is, essentially, carpooling, never mind that it's carpooling in a gas-guzzling, road-hogging behemoth.[31] Sheryl Crow's "Virtual March" across the nation commenced with the rocker's suggestion that people limit themselves to one sheet of toilet paper when using the bathroom, an idea that was quickly mocked and later prompted Crow to insist she was just kidding.[32] In an "oh, well!" interview with the *Boston Globe,* Henry Garza of the band Los Lonely Boys discussed his penchant for eco-unfriendly toys. "I have a motorbike, a Harley-Davidson Sportster. I have some cars that aren't environmentally sound, but I like 'em. My favorite's a '69 Judge GTO." The last time he recycled? "Some cans when we were out fishing three weeks ago. We don't have recycle bins on the tour bus." And does he think global warming is real or a myth? "Real. I've seen the weather change. Big storms all over Texas. I've seen stuff in the sky I never saw as a kid."[33] Incidentally, the band made these remarks while performing at Boston's EarthFest concert. And these are the folks who are trying to convince us to join the cause?

It's not only the spokespeople and the bizarre propositions that hinder the environmental movement. It's the audience that environmental activists are targeting, too. Wittingly or otherwise, the media has turned "going green" into an incredibly elitist economic issue that makes it all but impossible for lower- and middle-class Americans to both identify with the cause and find ways to make meaningful changes. In September 2007 *People* implored its readers to "Get Christina [Aguilera]'s Glamorous, Eco-Friendly Dress!" for a mere one hundred dollars. "Not only is she well-dressed and comfortable, but she's also going green!" The dress, which sounds like something cooked up in Biosphere 5, "is part of Gypsy 05's first 'Go Green' line, made from organic fabrics, natural dyes and is produced in a solar-powered factory." In case you need an extra push to blow one hundred dollars on an outfit you can probably also eat, "Other stars who own this long and elegant dress include Lauren Conrad and Denise Richards."[34] In February 2007, the *New York Times* published a story called "Making Your Second Home Green" and described the noble efforts of husband and wife James and Kathleen Seligman, whose *second* home, in Three Rivers, California, dubbed "Kaweah Cottage," would have "double-paned windows, nontoxic cotton insulation, energy-efficient appliances and clay-based wall coverings." But not everyone can afford a second home, or the luxury of turning it green. By the article's own admission, "Building green still carries a premium. 'You are not going to find the price-sensitive shopper in our stores,' said Lisa DiMartino, the vice president for marketing of Environmental Home Center, a green-home retailer with stores in Seattle and in Portland and Bend, Oregon. 'These are materials that are durable. You are going to pay for that. But the cost in the long run can be less than other products you are going to have to replace. Wool carpets can look great for 20 years. Synthetic carpets will need to be replaced.'"[35]

Indeed, it would seem that for the media, stories on the environment's ever-looming crisis have become a readily available and virtually bottomless source of material. In 2007, the *Boston Globe* devoted months to a special series called "Warming Where We Live," featuring articles like "As Frost Fades, Berry Rivalry Heats," "In Mosquito, A Tale of Climate Change," "Carbon Confusion," "US Lags on Plans for Climate Change," and "Winter Warm Up Costing New England Region."

But that's nothing. In the course of just four days in October, between the eighteenth and the twenty-second, the *New York Times* reported on nearly a dozen different stories, including: "New Coast Guard Task in Arctic's Warming Seas," "Inch by Inch, Great Lakes Shrink, and Cargo Carriers Face Losses," "The Future Is Drying Up," "Save the Planet: Vote Smart," "Recycling the Whole House," and "Members of New Group in Britain Aim to Offset Their Own Carbon Output." The quickly expiring planet has become the twelve-car pile-up of news stories.

Even worse, some on the left are trying to politicize natural disasters—tragic ones like Hurricane Katrina and the 2007 wildfires in California, for example—for their own partisan benefit. Ultraliberal senator Barbara Boxer, Democrat from California, showed an unbelievable lack of sensitivity when she implied that President Bush was somehow to blame for the fires that forced hundreds of thousands to evacuate, contending that the continued need for the National Guard in Iraq was hurting us at home.[36] Likewise, Senator Harry Reid, Democrat from Nevada, blamed the fires on global warming (essentially, on Republicans). Even the reporters he said this to seemed surprised.[37] How are we to get behind the messengers when the message is either offensive or absurd?

Newt Gingrich's book *A Contract With the Earth* rightly demands that a primary goal of modern conservation efforts must be objectivity, for it's this very politicization that undermines both the message and the messengers. He writes:

> To achieve a fully functional and ultimately sustainable world, we must forge a cooperative working partnership among scientists, entrepreneurs, and our nation's citizens. To accomplish this, an empirical standard of objectivity should be reaffirmed. Polarized political factions have spent decades fighting over the meaning of scientific findings often distorted by the media. Despite many challenging environmental problems, there is reason for optimism, but today's science will not save us; we must strengthen our investments in science and technology to enlarge our environmental tool kit and prepare for any outcome. Good public policy requires accurate, objective science and a trustworthy and transparent process of dissemination. We must return to a civil society where candid discussion, debate, and disagreement result in rational compromise and consensus.[38]

In *The Conservative Mind*, Russell Kirk, describing the political philosophy of Edmund Burke, said, "If men are discharged of reverence for ancient usage, they will treat this world, almost certainly, as if it were their private property, to be consumed for their sensual gratification; and thus they will destroy in their lust for enjoyment the property of future generations, of their own contemporaries, and indeed their very own capital."[39] Such perspective does not necessarily validate Republican environmental policies as "progressive." However, it does provide a window into why the liberal ambassadors who champion global warming are less than ideal spokespeople.

Most secular nature-purists see global warming as Mother Nature's punishment for the evil machinations of capitalism and modernity. Many of these people, while decrying our overuse of modern comforts, epitomize excess consumption with their private jets and entourage of SUVs. Hollywood has done immeasurable damage, consuming disproportionate resources for "sensual gratification," while lambasting those who claim to take moral stances on other social issues. Of course, saving the environment has suddenly become a moral issue (although disposing of Saddam Hussein was not). Champions of this cause would probably agree, however, that public opinion is not sufficiently unanimous—or motivated—to adequately tackle the problem. Perhaps the public, whether in middle America or on the coasts, would take the problem more seriously if we could take the messenger more seriously.

Still, even a comical messenger does not totally negate a serious message. We should all approach this issue with an open mind and do our best to preserve the environment in a rational, cost effective manner. After all, it is our children's world, and we should try to save it . . . one Hollywood awards ceremony at a time.

CHAPTER 7

Republicans Are Stupid

The Myth of the Dumb-Ass Conservative

My guess is more reporters probably vote Democrat than
Republican—just because I think reporters are smart.[1]

—Jerry Springer

Republicans and the politicians they elect are often ridiculed and
called "stupid" by the media, Hollywood, Democrats, college students who wear T-shirts, and hordes of drivers who feel their back
bumpers could use some sprucing up. Some of the better slogans
are pretty funny:

"If you can read this you're not the president."

"Vote Republican. It's easier than thinking."

"Somewhere in Texas a village is missing its idiot."

"My kid is an honor student. My president is a moron."

"Bush-Cheney: We're Gooder!"

"I think, therefore I vote Democrat."

It isn't clear where the myth comes from, or why it endures, but it almost always goes unchecked. Ellis Weiner wrote a scathing diatribe against well-known conservative pundits on The Huffington Post in 2007, calling Bill Kristol, Charles Krauthammer, David Brooks, and Fred Barnes "the Usual Gang of Idiots."[2] In the same post, he wrote "To assist them, they have the services of exactly the kind of spokespersons such people deserve: the neighborhood saloon loudmouth Rush Limbaugh, Sean 'The Boston Terrier of Indignation' Hannity, the self-parodying O'Reilly, the vile Coulter, with assorted nudniks like Glenn Beck and Dennis Prager to come in off the bench in case, against all odds, there's a shortfall of teh stoopid [sic]. Oh, and Fox News, as dependable as Pravda and easily as accurate, unswerving in its dedication to cheering on Chimpy."

Even the more polished and polite liberals regularly take pot shots. Democratic presidential contender Barack Obama called Republican national security policies "tough and dumb" while on the campaign trail in October 2007.[3] Time magazine writer Margaret Carlson once said on CNN's Capital Gang that "the only thing that could explain this love of tax cuts is a lowered IQ."[4] The New York Times called the Republican Party's "Contract with America" a "politically stupid" strategy, despite the fact that it led to the first Republican Congress in decades.[5]

When did this happen? Though the majority of catchy slogans (certainly the funnier ones) focus on Bush the younger, it would seem Republicans have been stupid for decades, so this can't be pinned squarely on the president. In fact, in ancient times—or at least 1950—writer Lionel Trilling famously called conservatism "irritable mental gestures which seek to resemble ideas."[6] Ronald Reagan, before he died and became sacrosanct, had long been the butt of liberal jokes. During his campaigns and presidency, liberals liked to insist, "Come on, he's an *actor*," as evidence of Reagan's stupidity, and have since used the same rhetoric for Charlton Heston and Arnold Schwarzenegger. (That hasn't stopped liberals from applauding Ben Affleck, Tim Robbins, and Alec Baldwin for their political wisdom.)

So if Republicans have always been stupid—surely Jefferson Davis, when alone with his buddies, called Lincoln a dumbass—the question isn't when, but why? What is it about conservatism—which boasts some of the smartest people in history—that lends itself to the myth of the dumb Republican?

Maybe it's the way Republicans talk. After all, Dan Quayle said some *really* stupid things, but then so did Bill Clinton: "It depends on what the meaning of the word 'is' is."[7] Al Gore was also a wealth of missteps: "It was clear to me that men and women were equal—if not more so."[8]

And no one dares call them stupid.

Is it an issue of education, then? President Bush was educated at Yale and Harvard. His father also went to Yale. Dan Quayle earned degrees at DePauw University and Indiana University Law School. Colin Powell graduated from City College of New York and George Washington University. Condoleezza Rice earned degrees from the University of Denver and Notre Dame, and is a Stanford fellow at the Hoover Institute.

And, as Ann Coulter noted in her book *Slander,* some of the academic accomplishments of those on the Left are less than stellar. Al Gore's sophomore college report card featured a D, C-, C, C, C+, C+ and B-, placing him in the bottom fifth of the class for two years in a row. As a 2000 *Washington Post* story put it: "His generally middling college grades at Harvard in fact bear a close resemblance to the corresponding Yale marks of his presidential opponent, George W. Bush, whose studiousness and brainpower have been more open to question during this campaign. . . . For all of Gore's later fascination with science and technology, he often struggled academically in those subjects. The political champion of the natural world received that sophomore D in Natural Sciences 6

(Man's Place in Nature) and then got a C+ in Natural Sciences 118 his senior year. The self-proclaimed inventor of the Internet avoided all courses in mathematics and logic throughout college, despite his outstanding score on the math portion of the SAT."[9] Gore would later enroll in—and fail to complete—both divinity school and law school. Yet, the Nobel Peace Prize–winning, global-warming genius was described by *U.S. News & World Report* as "very smart . . . almost too smart."[10] Yeah, too smart like a dropout.

So if it's not an issue of education, maybe it's that liberals are simply better read. In response to an Associated Press–Ipsos poll that said that liberals read books in greater numbers than conservatives, former Democratic representative from Colorado Patricia Schroeder suggested it was because liberals are inherently smarter. "The Karl Roves of the world have built a generation that just wants a couple slogans: 'No, don't raise my taxes, no new taxes. . . . It's pretty hard to write a book saying, 'No new taxes, no new taxes, no new taxes' on every page."[11] On the other hand, according to Schroeder, liberals "really want the whole picture, want to peel the onion." But weren't we supposed to believe that Rove was the evil genius behind all the cunning and strategy that got President Bush elected? An AP story noted that, "Rove . . . is known as a prodigious reader. White House spokesman Tony Fratto said Schroeder was 'confusing volume with quality' with her remarks. 'Obfuscation usually requires a lot more words than if you simply focus on fundamental principles, so I'm not at all surprised by the loquaciousness of liberals,' he said."[12]

If certain studies are to be believed, conservatives are dumber than liberals because liberals have more nuanced cognitive abilities. *Nature Neuroscience* published the results of a study in which participants were asked to press a button when shown one letter (either a

W or an M), and not to press a button when shown the other. The study found that conservatives were more likely to make "errors of commission" (which presumably means that they just kept hitting the wrong button), whereas liberals were associated "with greater accuracy," and were "more responsive to informational complexity, ambiguity and novelty."[13] Only on Sesame Street are Ws and Ms considered complex information. To put it in dumb Republican terms, the study essentially likened a conservative to a dog who could indeed sit on command, but performed the same action when told to stay, roll over, come, and fetch.

Nonetheless, the ever-impressed media jumped on the findings. The *Los Angeles Times* wrote that the study "suggests that liberals are more adaptable than conservatives" and "might be better judges of the facts."[14] Similarly, the *Guardian* proudly proclaimed that liberals "are more able to handle conflicting and unexpected information."[15] But William Saletan, a writer for *Slate,* was not fooled. Criticizing the study, he wrote in an article called "Rigging a Study to Make Conservatives Look Stupid," "You've manufactured a tiny world of letters, half-seconds, and button-pushing, so you can catch us in clear errors and keep out the part of life where our tendencies correct yours. And now you feel great about yourselves. Congratulations. You haven't told us much about our way of thinking. But you've told us a lot about yours."[16]

So if Republicans aren't dumber because of brain capacity, reading proclivity, the way they talk, or a lack of education, maybe it's something a little less obvious. In fact maybe it's something that is downright controversial.

American liberal arts colleges are rife with left-wing bias (it's even in the name), so much so that some scholars and critics are calling for sweeping reform. So with a growing number of young conservatives populating the better U.S. universities, could it be that Republicans are stupid *because* they went to college?

Penn State literature professor Michael Bérubé's book, *What's Liberal About the Liberal Arts?* was reviewed in the *New York Times* by Boston College political science professor Alan Wolfe, who praised Bérubé's efforts to prove that the myth of liberal "bias" on college campuses is a conservative ploy to control higher education. Wolfe summarizes Bérubé, contending that "without the University, and its ability to influence the minds of young adults, conservative success is transient, and conservatives know it."[17]

Bérubé takes aim at right-wing academic David Horowitz, a former liberal activist and author of *The Professors: The 101 Most Dangerous Academics in America.* Wolfe and Bérubé do not necessarily disagree with Horowitz's claims that college campuses are stacked with left-wing professors. In fact, in a book that attempts to prove that liberal bias at universities is merely an allegation of victimization by conservatives, they admit: "Left-wing domination of academia is so obvious a fact that Bérubé never tries to deny it. He knows that his own field 'is so pervasively liberal-left that smart young conservatives will shun it altogether.'"

Perhaps this is precisely what happened to orthographically challenged Quayle, Yogi Berra of vice presidents, who once said, "I've never professed to be anything but an average student."[18] He wasn't stupid—he was shunning!

The stereotype that conservatives are stupid manifests itself with regularity on college campuses and frequently comes from professors themselves. Duke University's philosophy chairman, Robert Brandon, in explaining the lack of political diversity among faculty, said "If, as John Stuart Mill said, stupid people are generally conservative, then there are lots of conservatives we will never hire."[19]

But it's not just promoting this myth that makes college a tricky place for young conservatives. It's the subtle (and often not-so-subtle) ways in which some professors try to pass on their liberal beliefs to their students, who they assume are too dumb and impressionable to realize what's happening. NYU politics professor

Bertell Ollman, a well-known Marxist, if there's been such a thing since the advent of the Model T, told his graduate students that patriotism was an instrument used by the state to confuse and manipulate its citizens. On the first day of a graduate class called Communication and Political Propaganda, NYU media professor Sal Fallica casually described liberals and conservatives as "anti-war" and "Bush apologists," respectively. The odd spontaneous debate on the immorality of capital punishment in an undergraduate art history class is nothing out of the ordinary. In yet another NYU graduate course, a visiting professor decided that the best way to handle President Bush's re-election in 2004 was to ask the class the probing and intellectually rigorous question, "So how the hell did this happen?"

Stanley Fish, a prominent literary scholar, author, and professor, wrote a revealing piece in a *New York Times* blog condemning just this kind of behavior by professors on college campuses. When a subcommittee of the American Association of University Professors handed down a new report outlining just how political professors can get in the classroom, Fish wrote that "the report's authors validate the very accusation they are trying to fend off, the accusation that the academy's leftward tilt spills over into the classroom. No longer writing for the American Association of University Professors, the subcommittee is instead writing for the American Association of University Professors Who Hate George Bush (admittedly a large group). Why do its members not see that?"[20]

Hudson Institute president Herb London, who ran for mayor of New York City in 1989 and governor of New York in 1990, is a pro-life Jewish conservative who knows something about academic intolerance. He founded the Gallatin School of Individualized Study at NYU in 1972, and was its dean until 1992, and says that one of his goals in creating the program was to find a place for a broad range of intellectual beliefs among both faculty and students. But, he says, "Over the last thirty or forty years there's been a movement toward orthodoxy, and I find that repellent. Where we once blacklisted the Left, we are now graylisting the Right on college campuses. Being a college professor shouldn't mean having the freedom to say *anything*, but the freedom to talk about the things you know, the things in which you are an expert. The conservative professor today is regarded as a pariah. College administrators don't fully understand that diversity is not just about race or geography, and they're not interested in cultivating an intellectual diversity. Why can't someone be a born-again Christian or oppose abortion? It is impossibly difficult for a conservative to get a job on a college campus and obtain tenure."[21]

Horowitz's solution is to establish an Academic Bill of Rights "that stresses intellectual diversity, that demands balance in reading lists, that recognizes that political partisanship by professors in the classroom is an abuse of students' academic freedom, that the inequity in funding of student organizations and visiting speakers is unacceptable, and that a learning environment hostile to conservatives is unacceptable."[22]

Until then, conservative college students will likely continue shunning, and liberals will likely continue ridiculing Republicans of every age for all kinds of intellectual crises—from hitting the W button instead of the M, to misspelling a word. Maybe one day the internet will finally bring these poor, dumb Republicans up to speed. We'll get Al Gore right on it.

CHAPTER 8

Republicans Are Intolerant

The Myth of the Closed-Minded Conservative

You sons of bitches. I just hate you. I hate you to the depths of my soul. I will hate you when I'm dead. I will hate you a million years after I'm dead. I will still hate you. My hate will be a star in the firmament that will shine down on your Republican asses forever.[1]

—Mike Malloy, *The Mike Malloy Show*

The fringe website RepublicansHateAmerica.com is a crude and typo-ridden celebration of all things, well, *not* Republican. It's not accurate to classify the site as liberal, as there are no actual positions being espoused here. It's a disturbingly angry and incredibly disjointed collection bin of sorts for recycled, unrelated, anti-Republican *stuff*. Here, if you can manage to navigate the poor layout, you can buy your "Gross Old Pedophile" bumper stickers, or your "Republicans Hate America" thong. You can calculate your "Republican Age," which, mocking the prolife position, tells you how old you are in embryonic terms. (The authors of this book are 348-month-old embryos, as it turns out.) You can peruse uniquely categorized lists of Republicans—lists like "Pro-Torture Republicans" and "Pro-Lynching Republicans." According to the "About" section of RepublicansHateAmerica.com, the site's mission is lofty (and misspelled): "This sites [sic] purpose it [sic] to give examples of how Republicans want to change our great country by any means possible and will."[2] Those examples, at least according to the site's two contributors "jmk" and "Frankie," are numerous (and also misspelled): "Many people on the right do not deny that why want [sic] to change this country: examples are: fascist religious beliefs, elimination of free public education, removal of science (evolution), abolition of all social programs, civil rights bases [sic] on supernatural beliefs, etc. This blog is a collection of news stories and other events in which one can truly see how these people cannot stand our country and want to change it for their own specific ideals only." While it's hard to understand exactly what is being said here, if anything is clear from RepublicansHateAmerica.com, it's only that "jmk" and "Frankie" hate Republicans. All of them. With a vengeance.

Websites and blogs like this one are rampant, and some are even more vitriolic. A quick scan reveals an incredibly fervent and vibrant anti-Republican strain both in America and abroad. Like RepublicansHateAmerica.com, very few actually outline what they are *for*, or offer any kind of constructive criticism, which in turn lends these portals an air of extreme embitterment and hostility that at the very least seems irrational, and at worst borders on lunatic. Radio is another sanctuary where angry ranting and raving takes the place of actual criticism. Onetime Air America talk-radio host Mike Malloy, who refers to President Bush as "Giggling Killer" and Laura Bush as "Pickles," classified Republicans—yes, all of them—thus: "Republicans are vile. All Republicans are liars, cheats, sneaks; they are deceivers. They are immoral, and they have no ethical structure whatsoever. I don't care if they're members of Congress or your momma. If they are Republicans, they are thugs. They support mass murder. They support the destruction of this country."[3]

Yet, despite this kind of vitriol, it's Republicans who are labeled intolerant, hate-filled, and narrow-minded. And Americans—particularly religious ones—who dare to vote Republican are immediately called any number of bad names by the Left. Glenn Beck, CNN Headline News pundit and radio personality, said in defense of the conservative voter, "I don't believe that America is as stupid or as bigoted as the media always wants us to be. America will look at a guy whose values they share. If he shares values with the American electorate and he actually lives them, what church he goes to won't make a difference to most Americans, just as I, being a Mormon, won't vote for [Mitt Romney] just because he's Mormon."[4]

Joe Conason, author of *Big Lies: The Right-Wing Propaganda Machine and How It Distorts the Truth,* wrote about supposed Republican intolerance during the 2004 national convention in New York City in an article titled "A Gay Old Time for the GOP."[5] In it, he described a problem the Republican Party would face during its bid for re-election. "To feign tolerance and diversity is a challenge for a party whose platform denies basic rights to the gay and lesbian minority, but the President's political strategists believe that four days of big-tent rhetoric can buy four years of narrow-minded government. If the G.O.P.'s 2000 convention took on the ridiculous trappings of a multicultural minstrel show, this year's spectacle might be called 'Queer Eye 2004.'" Later, he wondered, "Are the Republicans trying to fool independent voters by pretending to endorse a modern inclusiveness they abhor? Or do Messrs. Schwarzenegger, Giuliani and Cheney represent a sophisticated leadership that merely pretends to detest homosexuality so the rubes will remain Republican?" Here, for Conason, the attempt by Republicans to present a more inclusive attitude toward homosexuality, albeit while opposing gay marriage, is either an act or a strategy. Either way, Republicans are still, of course, intolerant. (And stupid, but we covered that in the last chapter.)

Dennis Prager pointed out the baselessness of so-called liberal tolerance as well as the liberal penchant for rampant hyperbole in an article for Townhall.com in 2007:

> Liberals not only believe that conservatives are philo-sophically imperfect, but they often believe that conservatives are bad human beings. . . . Howard Dean has said that conservatives don't care about children who go to bed hungry. Liberals yearn for a world without conservatives at least as much as most believing Christians want a world without non-Christians. The difference is many liberals are immeasurably more likely to impose their views on others than Christian Americans are. Liberal judges impose their views—e.g., on same-sex marriage—on society. And liberal educators force young students to watch Al Gore's "An Inconvenient Truth," the former vice president's hysterical beliefs about impending doom—and offer no countering viewpoint.[6]

Conservative positions on various social issues tend to lend misplaced credibility to the myth of the intolerant Republican, but its persistence is frustrating. Positions on gay rights, minorities, immigration, abortion, and even the war are routinely painted as coming from intolerance, not ideology. Yet Democratic positions on these same platform issues, which are just as "extreme" if one is on the opposite side, are supposed to represent tolerance and inclusion, regardless of who is being excluded in the process. According to Democrats, prolife Republicans don't value life, they hate women. Anti–gay marriage Republicans don't value the religious connotations of marriage, they hate homosexuals. Anti–affirmative action Republicans don't value equal opportunity, they hate blacks. Prowar Republicans don't value freedom, they hate Muslims. And so on.

But in fact it's the Left that has become—both ideologically and politically—so intolerant of those outside itself that many have started calling liberalism a religion. Ann Coulter's book *Godless: The Church of Liberalism,* for one, discusses the hypocritical and problematic liberal hostility toward God, and specifically toward Christianity, and its simultaneous embrace of its own pseudoreligious importance. Likewise, Jonah Goldberg of *National Review* described liberalism as a dangerous total philosophy of life. "There's that basic conflation of morality and an attitude that Eric Voegelin would call a political religion, where you make your politics into a religious orientation, which says that there's no room for those that disagree, except to call them the enemy."[7] In contrast, conservatism allows for far more individual freedom of expression, of idea, of practice, and of action, according to Goldberg. "Conservatism and most forms of libertarianism are partial philosophies of life. Conservatism does not tell you what kind of clothes to wear. It doesn't tell you what kind of movies to like, necessarily. It doesn't tell you what kind of people to marry. Conservatism, rightly understood, describes a very specific and very limited sphere of life. Liberalism, alas, does not do that. It tells you how to be, what to buy. You have to wear progressive clothes, drive progressive cars, have progressive attitudes about what kind of toilets you use."

Indeed, it seems as though there is no safety zone around a liberal. Politics are taken so personally that liberal intolerance for anything *not* liberal has merely become a mark of conviction, and not of the kind of antiquated, wayward, and cancerous irrationality that characterizes intolerant Republicans. It's a wonder the country is not more outraged. This kind of liberal "conviction" propels incredibly offensive anti-religious rhetoric. Bill Maher said of conservatives in 2004 on his television show, "When they talk about values, they're talking about things like going to church, voting for Bush, being loyal to Jesus, praying. These are not values."[8] This kind of liberal "conviction" has also given birth to some of the most classist and elitist rhetoric this country has ever produced.

Popular author Ayelet Waldman wrote on her personal blog in November 2004:

> I'm am [sic] so goddamn sick of these "red-staters." This website pretty much expresses everything I feel about those cretins: www.fuckthesouth.com. *We* are the real Americans. Everett Moran, standing brave and resolute in the face of bigotry, is a real American. George Soros, devoting his life and his fortune to serving those less fortunate than he is, is a real American. The citizens of California who have donated their own money to support stem cell research, to compensate for the cowardice of our Taliban government, are real Americans. The rest of them? The ones that destroy the Constitution in service to their narrow-minded and zealously self-centered agendas? Those pinheads sure as hell aren't Americans. Secession. That's what we need. Let them take their scrub-farms and stipmalls [sic] and get the hell out of our country. We'll open our doors to immigrants, to the brilliant and open-minded of the world. And we'll leave them eating dirt and handling snakes."[9]

This is the kind of stuff Republicans would be hanged for. Incidentally, Ayelet's favorite website, www.fuckthesouth.com, is an insane—yes, *insane*—page-long diatribe against southern Republicans. The author seems unaware that Civil War southerners (see "We should have let them go when they wanted to leave") were Democrats, or that being called "arrogant" isn't a compliment (see "You wanna talk about us northeasterners being fucking arrogant? Arrogance is the fucking cornerstone of what it means to be American"). A particularly perplexing section targets, of all people, Floridians in climatological crisis: "And the next time Florida gets hit by a hurricane you can come crying to us if you want to, but you're the ones who built on a fucking swamp. 'Let the Spanish keep it, it's a shithole,' we said, but you had to have your fucking orange juice."[10]

Fox News commentator and author Bernard Goldberg once described his brand of politics as "old-fashioned liberal," and denounced today's Left as, well, mean. "I'm a liberal the way liberals used to be when they were like John F. Kennedy and when they were like Hubert Humphrey. When they were upbeat and enthusiastic and mainstream. I am not a liberal the way liberals are today, at least as exemplified by Al Franken and Michael Moore, where they're angry, nasty, closed minded, and not mainstream, but fringe."[11] It's safe to assume Goldberg would include www.fuckthesouth.com in that category. One would hardly call the site "upbeat and enthusiastic and mainstream." Hating Florida, after all, is hardly mainstream. In fact, John F. Kennedy loved Florida and Florida loved him back (see "Kennedy Space Center"). Tampa renamed Florida State Road 60 "Kennedy Blvd" in 1964 by unanimous vote. The Kennedys had a compound in Palm Beach until 1995, where John would spend holidays as a child.

But it's not just a matter of sites like www.fuckthesouth.com and fringe liberals like this being nasty and closed-minded, or the obvious hypocrisy of characterizing conservatives as intolerant. It's that the Democratic machine seems to have no place for dissidents, whereas conservatism rightly allows for a far greater intellectual and ideological diversity (witness Rudy Giuliani, Michael Bloomberg, Arnold Schwarzenegger). Political commentator David Horowitz pointed out the cases of former Pennsylvania governor Bob Casey, a Democrat, and former Harvard University president Lawrence Summers, who were turned against quite abruptly by the Left when they foolishly voiced a stray opinion—Casey for being prolife and Summers for wondering if there was a reason men outnumbered women in high-end science fields. "The conservative coalition is far more diverse than the liberal coalition. The liberal coalition has a party line, and you pretty much have to agree. As you know, they wouldn't let Governor Casey of Pennsylvania speak at the convention because of his politically incorrect stance on abortion. I think the Larry Summers incident was a show of how powerful the totalitarian impulse is on the Left. Summers was brought to his knees because he dared to raise a question that was considered politically incorrect, which just shows how intolerant the Left is."

The kind of intolerance used continually to describe the Right seems now the sole property of the Left—yet the stereotype persists. *National Review*'s Jay Nordlinger explained the phenomenon as a matter of exposure. "I think conservatives are more used to being around liberals, because liberals have dominated everything in our lives, especially our schools. I think it was John Podhoretz who once said that all conservatives are bilingual. They speak both conservative and liberal. But liberals don't have to be bilingual. They can go a long time without brushing up against someone who's conservative. A *National Review* colleague of mine was recently at a social gathering, and she told the person she'd just met that she worked at *National Review*. The person immediately turned on her heel, leaving my colleague with her drink in her hand and her mouth agape. I'm not sure a conservative would ever do that (turn on his heel)—not because we're so pure and good, but because we've always had to live as a minority, in a sense, and get along with other people. They find out you're conservative, they turn up their noses, or check for horns and a tail."[12]

If there's one place where the horn-and-tail check is performed with more regularity and suspicion, it's Hollywood, of course, where the entertainment industry is perhaps the most stacked and slanted group of laborers in the country. That Hollywood is overwhelmingly liberal is not cause for concern—they're allowed. And the liberal intolerance of conservatives in Hollywood doesn't prove, of course, that the Right is more tolerant—but the discrimination against conservatives (as well as against people of a faith other than Scientology) is disturbing and worth noting, especially since it's rarely discussed or even acknowledged by the very liberals who hypocritically point to conservatives as alarmingly closed-minded. "If you were to keep one secret in Hollywood, it would be that you are a registered Republican," said Randy Douthit, producer of *Judge Judy*, and creator of *Crossfire* and *Capital Gang*. "Presidents of networks, CEOs of studios, movie stars, and other powerful celebs become livid when they discover you are on the 'other side.' Your contract may not get picked up. If your show is on the fence, it is more likely to be canceled. You may not get a decent promotional budget even if you have a successful show, once they discover you as the 'enemy.' If the company newsletter reports about other comparable shows, but not your own successful program, you do start to wonder. Washington and Hollywood have many things in common: money, power, ego. But Washington has a balanced Republican-Democratic count compared to an almost nonexistent Hollywood Republican contingent. Just ask Barbra Streisand."[13]

A number of high-profile and less-than-high-profile celebrities have been open about their conservative politics, and with mixed results. *The View*'s resident conservative Elisabeth Hasselbeck had to endure near-daily harassment by one-time host Rosie O'Donnell, and occasional public snubbings by liberal celebrity guests. In a *Wall Street Journal* article called "Rebels with a Cause," reporter Bridget Johnson discussed the problems Hollywood Republicans face. "According to actor Mark Vafiades, president of the Hollywood Congress of Republicans, Hollywood Republicans do suffer discrimination, sometimes losing work for their political views. 'We hear the stories all the time,' he says, noting that while it's hard to prove, it's kind of obvious when actors get cut from auditions right after the subject of politics is brought up."[14]

According to the *New York Post*, which loves "outing" conservative celebrities in Hollywood, in October 2007 actress Patricia Heaton held an "F.O.A.: Friends of Abe" party for her Republican friends in Beverly Hills. "Joining the 'Back to You' star and her husband, David Hunt, were Jon Voight, Gary Sinise and Bruce Boxleitner with his wife, Melissa Gilbert. 'She's an ardent Democrat, but she said that because all those years she was SAG president she dragged her husband around to all those Democrat events, Melissa felt she had to come to F.O.A.,' said our source."[15] But the event was still, apparently, hush-hush. "They were really keeping this event quiet, as they didn't want the power elite in Hollywood to get wind of it."

Elisabeth Hasselbeck—along with actors Ron Silver, Rick Schroder, Stephen Baldwin, Bo Derek, Angie Harmon, and Rip Torn, appeared at the 2004 Republican National Convention in support of President Bush. Rumored Hollywood Republicans also include Heather Locklear and James Woods, who once said to Jay Leno in 2001, "I love George Bush right now and I always have. I'm the only guy in L.A. who voted for him."[16] But interestingly, when it comes to political celebrities, Johnson's story points out, "A 2002 poll by *The Hollywood Reporter* found the least-admired political celebrities to be Jane Fonda (11.8%), Charlton Heston (10.8%), Alec Baldwin (10.6%), Barbra Streisand (10.5%) and Rosie O'Donnell (9.2%)—four liberals and just one conservative in the publicity doghouse."

The kind of intolerance conservatives are often accused of is not limited to the hills of Hollywood, however. Political pundit and columnist Tucker Carlson says it's almost ubiquitous. "I lived in Washington D.C. for about twelve years and everyone there and everything there is center-left. Everybody who summers in nice places you'd like to visit is pro-choice, and they despise anybody who takes religion seriously."[17]

Indeed, many Republicans and conservatives spend a good amount of time convincing liberals either that they're not the *kind* of Republican they despise, or that, with apologies, they are *exactly* the kind of Republican they despise. Republican political strategist William O'Reilly explained the near-constant conservative dilemma:

"Well, the thing is they insist that these Republicans aren't really

Republicans. They want to believe that it's the individual, not the party, that's implementing the good policy. They really don't want to believe that maybe the ideology has something to do with it. But you have to do what it takes. The first thing you have to do in a place like New York City is convince voters that you're not 'one of those Republicans.' I have no idea who 'those Republicans' are or where they are, but you have to convince people you're not one of them." Republicans are damned if they do and damned if they don't.

Many on the right have examined this mischaracterization from a philosophical point of view and blame the myth of the intolerant Republican on a misunderstanding of conservative dogma, or what is actually a lack of dogma. Conservatism is constantly misinterpreted as being a rigid system of rules and regulations, but this view is both incredibly unfair and completely inaccurate. "For all of these clichés and stereotypes about how conservatives are dogmatic, how we believe in certainty, how we have a tight-bound, orthodox, intolerant view of the world, the reality is that conservative dogma remains unsettled," says Jonah Goldberg. "There's been this fight since the 1950s among conservatives between those who emphasize virtue and those who emphasize freedom. And that argument has not been settled. [Libertarian philosopher] Frank Meyer tried to settle it. It cannot be settled essentially to anyone's satisfaction. And so we have these arguments and will always have these arguments about where the tradeoffs should be. When does virtue intrude upon freedom? And when does freedom intrude upon virtue?" For all of conservatism's perceived sobriety and severity, there is still room for ideological debate. But on the Left, as Goldberg points out, it's a different story. "Liberals, on the other hand, have settled their dogma. The original understanding of dogma is something that seems good. They've mistaken their dogma for reality, which is why they constantly talk about pragmatism, and why they constantly talk about getting beyond labels, getting beyond ideology. They think all the important arguments have been settled already." This accounts for the ritual banishment by liberals of liberals who try to open these arguments again, like Governor Casey. *You can't be pro-life, Mr. Casey, because we've already decided to be pro-choice. Get on board, or get out!*

The fallout after September 11 and the ensuing war against terror brought out another kind of rhetoric that has also gone largely unchecked. While the country gathered in unanimous support of President Bush just after the terrorist attacks, the Left very quickly took up the myth of the intolerant Republican as its weapon of choice in attacking those who remained in favor of the war. For attempting to implement stricter security measures on airplanes and other mass transit, and through legislation like the Patriot Act, Republicans like President Bush were painted by the ACLU and much of the Left as pro-American, anti-Muslim racists who were using September 11 as an excuse to act out their life-long dreams of eradicating the world's problem races in favor of a new Aryan nation. In fact, Bush and his cabinet members were routinely compared to Hitler and the Nazis, an analogy that should deeply offend not only Republicans and Jews, but all life-loving citizens of the world. Keith Ellison, Democrat of Minnesota and America's first Muslim congressman, compared Bush to Hitler, and insinuated in a speech before three hundred members of the Atheists for Human Rights that Bush was responsible for the September 11 attacks. "It's almost like the Reichstag fire, kind of reminds me of that. After the Reichstag was burned, they blamed the Communists for it, and it put the leader of that country in a position where he could basically have authority to do whatever he wanted."[18]

Cindy Sheehan compared Donald Rumsfeld to Hitler and Stalin.[19] British singer-songwriter Morrissey said, "For non-Americans, the United States is suddenly not a very nice place to visit because US immigration officers—under the rules of Bush—now conduct themselves with all the charm and unanswerable indignation of Hitler's SS."[20] Political writer Dave Lindorff wrote in a column for

Counterpunch, "It's going a bit far to compare the Bush of 2003 to the Hitler of 1933. Bush simply is not the orator that Hitler was. But comparisons of the Bush Administration's fear mongering tactics to those practiced so successfully and with such terrible results by Hitler and Goebbels on the German people and their Weimar Republic are not at all out of line."[21] But even before the atrocities of September 11, American Republicans were being compared to the most heinous regimes the world has ever seen. Jesse Jackson famously said in 1994, "In South Africa, the status quo was called racism. We rebelled against it. In Germany, it was called fascism. Now in Britain and the US, it's called conservatism."[22] There are literally hundreds of examples.

President Bush and countless other high-profile Republicans have been so outspoken and clear about their respect for the Muslim community that it's a tragedy that Republicans are painted as intolerant and hate-filled, as that can only stifle efforts to build better communication with Muslims. Little is made of President Bush's very vocal criticism of the Danish cartoons that mocked Muhammad, a subject he was not at all obligated to address. In a statement released after Bush's denouncement of the Danish cartoons, the Muslim Public Affairs Council said it "commends the Bush administration for publicly condemning the Danish publication of a series of cartoons depicting the Prophet Muhammad as a terrorist and called on other American religious and political leaders to follow suit in order to calm rapidly expanding tensions." Liberals, however, criticized Bush's actions for their perceived disregard for free speech—even though neither Bush nor his administration tried to prohibit anyone from publishing the cartoons. Most newspapers decided on their own not to reprint them.

In fact, Bush's oft-stated respect for Islam has won him favor in the Muslim-American community. MuslimRepublicans.com is a website dedicated to giving conservative Muslims a voice. "Due to the onslaught of the liberal media, and often times our own communities, we have not been able to voice our opinions, communicate and share ideas. MuslimRepublicans.com aims to change all of that and provide a home for conservative Muslims who believe in the ideals of the Republican Party, are members of the Republican National Committee and want to work toward having more Republicans elected to office."[23] In June 2007, President Bush rededicated the Islamic Centre of Washington in a move to help assure Muslim Americans that the United States will protect Islam from religious discrimination.[24] In keeping with his continued message that everyday Muslims are not the radical extremists responsible for worldwide terrorism, he appointed the first U.S. envoy to the fifty-seven-nation Organization of the Islamic Conference, to help maintain a meaningful relationship with Islamic countries.[25] Time and time again, President Bush has denounced harassment and violence against Muslim Americans, he has worked to broker Muslim understanding and support, and he has remained absolutely committed to distinguishing between the enemy he is fighting abroad and the religion of Islam itself.

Regardless of how supportive Republicans are of Muslims the world over, and regardless of how supportive Republicans are of other religious groups, and regardless of how open and inclusive Republicans are of those with differing ideological viewpoints, the myth of the intolerant Republican seems indelible. And the unabashed and ubiquitous intolerance of the Left for anyone of the ideological opposition may become a permanent fixture.

Talk-radio host Laura Ingraham, discussing the supposed tolerance of liberals, may have said it best: "They are non-judgmental unless you disagree with them on Iraq, abortion, or recycling—then you're worse than Saddam (whom they routinely describe as merely 'a bad guy')."[26] Again, liberal intolerance doesn't prove conservative tolerance, but where the Left is routinely said to have conviction, the Right is inaccurately painted as a bunch of raging zealots and uncultured phobics.

In March 2003 the Dixie Chicks, an antiwar American pop-country group, told British audiences at a concert they were ashamed that President Bush was from Texas, their home state. Facing massive outrage when they returned to the States, as well as declining ticket and record sales, eventually lead singer Natalie Maines apologized for disrespecting the president. But Bush, who was under no obligation to respond at all, or could have responded with equal vitriol, instead simply said, "The Dixie Chicks are free to speak their mind. They can say what they want to say. . . . I want to do what I think is right for the American people, and if some singers or Hollywood stars feel like speaking out, that's fine. That's the great thing about America."[27] Who sounds like the intolerant one?

CHAPTER 9

Republicans Aren't Cool

The Myth of the Out-of-Touch Conservative

On July 17th, a group of artists gathered in Tompkins Square Park, the East Village's historic anarchistic hub, and held a peaceful demonstration—posing for these photos to illustrate their reaction to the coming invasion of the khaki-wearing, polo-shirt-gut-hiding, palm-pilot-jabbing, SUV-driving, self-satisfied-smirking Republican hordes.

—www.NewYorkCool.com[1]

"Cool" has long been considered a prized commodity on the left, by the Democratic party itself, and by the voting bloc it serves. Since the advent of the audiovisual era, when the first liberal saw his own blurry likeness on a black-and-white television set, "cool" has been a significant factor in portraying the Left as smarter, more cosmopolitan, debonair, edgy, or decidedly hip. After all, what's cooler than getting Marilyn Monroe to sing at your birthday party? What's hipper than a sax-playing president? Who's more "interesting" than the counterculture baristas, tattoo artists, film students, and underground music aficionados whose seeming mission in life is to make you feel hopelessly out of touch?

Republicans, on the other hand, have been locked out of popular culture for decades, thanks to the liberal portrayal of them as boring, unfunny, mainstream, and, well, conservative. Watchblog. com summed it up with a 2004 post that read, rather matter-of-factly: "Democrats are hipper than Republicans. They were the popular kids in school and ridiculed future Republicans as nerds, rubes or hicks. The roles haven't changed much. At a Democratic rally you see Bruce Springsteen and some really cool stars. Republicans are lucky to get the Gatlin Brothers, or other refugees from the geriatric ward."[2] If the Left is a bastion of coolness, the Right is a never-ending sales conference at the White Plains Hyatt.

But what's really behind this stereotype? Just how cool and liberal is pop culture? After all, for every Kanye West, Ben Affleck, and Coldplay (who rate undeniably high on the "cool" scale—just ask any sixteen-year-old), there's a Rosie O'Donnell, Barbra Streisand, and Barry Manilow. (Is there anyone less cool than this trifecta of talent?) And on the flip side, is the so-called establishment—yawn—really that conservative? A deeper analysis may give liberals reason to clutch their vintage Sex Pistols T-shirts a little tighter.

Popular culture is a vast entity, especially in a country like America, whose size alone makes it a veritable megamall of cultural consumption. And politics has shrewdly tapped into nearly every marketable aspect of cultural production. Politics and pop culture make an enviable couple, one that has enjoyed a long and mutually beneficial relationship since Caligula asked for his first lap dance. "I think the connection between politics and entertainment is a basic and psychological one, and it boils down to narcissism, and feeling that you personally, the individual, are the most important person in the world," said ex-VJ "Kennedy." "It's about needing a platform on which to show other people just how important you are. Both politics and entertainment share the common goal of seeking power and fame in varying degrees, and therefore narcissists who seek power and fame are commonly drawn toward each other. So, basically, politicians and celebrities love sniffing each other's butts."[3]

But there's a difference between pop culture that *uses* politics (for laughs, record sales, box office returns, and viewership) and pop culture that *deals with* politics on an ideological level. As leftist-turned-conservative culture critic David Horowitz argued, "Pop culture kind of spits every now and then at the Republican Party, but it doesn't deal with the Republican Party," he said. "There are left-wing shows, like *The West Wing*. And there are left-wing films like *The American President*. But Bush went on *Oprah,* and he was loved on *Oprah*. I don't think that it's so cut-and-dry. We know that the Hollywood acting community is pretty left, but not all of them. And they mouth off every now and then. But that's very different from having films in which the Republican Party is portrayed as a white Christian party all the time. I don't think the Republican Party or the Democratic Party figure significantly in popular culture at all."[4]

It's true—few television shows, movies, novels, and musicians explicitly focus on party politics (probably because real politics in action is exceedingly boring), though they may depict politicians or comment every now and then on political views. But pop culture, which is, by definition, a mainstream entity, has always represented pervasive American viewpoints in a largely populist way. So conservative views that are held by a majority of Americans will be reflected in all aspects of American culture—cool or uncool as they may be. The same is true of liberal views. For example, successful sitcoms have always reflected the prevailing conservative idea of what a "family" should be. Whether that family is headed by a bigot like Archie Bunker, or a Jewish woman and a gay man like Grace Adler and Will Truman, the idea is that a family is a unit of people who continually come together to solve problems, who rely on one another for counsel, leadership, loyalty, companionship, and support. As Horowitz put it, "There's a conflict, and they come together. And they're very—I hate to use words like pro-family—but families are really important. A lot of the most successful comedies, like *Everybody Loves Raymond* and *Frasier* are completely nonpolitical and their values are pretty traditional, if you like. If you object to seeing a gay person on the screen, then you'll find pop culture very left, but if you think about it, the subtext message—it's not overtly said—is very strongly law-and-order, beat-the-enemies, Americans-are-great, families-are-good. It's all conservative."

Television is a fantastic lens through which to view American values, and it seems to take that responsibility quite seriously. After all, there's a ton of money at stake. So conservative views about law and order, justice, and right and wrong are reflected in many of the talk shows that are some of the country's most popular. *Dr. Phil*, for example, one of Oprah's successful spinoffs, features Dr. Phil McGraw dishing out daily doses of conservative values to his guests in need. He routinely talks about God and the importance of family, and he often goes after the bad guy in need of rebuke—the cheating husband, the fraudulent businessperson, the mother with an addiction problem. While his is not an explicitly political show, it's hard to ignore its political message. Likewise, the *Law & Order* series and its offshoots prove that Americans have an insatiable appetite for witnessing the hands of justice at work. As Horowitz noted, "An aspect of popular culture that is entirely ignored by conservative critics is all the cop shows. All the cops-and-robbers shows as it were—and there's a ton of them—are about good guys and bad guys. And from the get-go that's conservative right there. Then there's the reality cop shows." Indeed, the longevity and popularity of television shows like *COPS,* which has been on the air for almost twenty years, reaffirm the relevance of law and order to everyday Americans.

Similarly, judge-and-jury reality shows like *The People's Court* and *Judge Judy* are also compelling enactments of good prevailing over evil that we can't seem to get enough of. Premiering in 1996, *Judge Judy* has brought in the highest ratings of any court show in history,[5] and has been nominated for an Emmy ten times. Randy Douthit is the show's executive producer, as well as the creator of *Capital Gang* and *Crossfire,* and the original executive producer of *Larry King Live.* While he admits the show promotes a law-and-order message, he contends it's more "American" than political.

> Judge Judy's adjudicating of a small claims case follows the same storytelling path of most trial shows. She lays out the conflict between two parties, dissects their stories according to law and common sense, discovers the truth, and then gives a verdict. The good guy wins; the bad guy loses and gets a scolding as a bonus. Perhaps some people perceive *COPS* and *Judge Judy* as entertainment for the red states. However, ratings would reflect a healthy mix of both red and blue states. Judge Judy takes a point of view that requires people to be responsible for their own action. That may not be a far-left theory, nor is it exclusively conservative. Taking responsibility belongs to Middle America. It requires people to better themselves without blaming others for their shortcomings. Shows that promote ideals that are wrapped in the American flag, or dressed in police uniforms represent proud Americans, left, center, and right.[6]

Though Douthit's point is a salient and optimistic one—taking responsibility for one's own actions should belong to everyone—those ideals are more often aligned with the Right than the Left.

But it's not only the small screen that reflects more conservatism than liberals would have you believe. Film, where artistic freedom is perhaps a bit more generous, has also been a funnel for conservative ideology as much as it has for the counterculture, even if not in immediately recognizable ways. While it's true that good prevailing over evil is not exclusively conservative, movies that enact this kind of triumph, like superhero movies, war movies, or horror and action films where the villain meets a horrifically graphic end, are hardly liberal story lines. Judd Apatow has made a name for himself by writing and directing comedies in which the focus may be on gratuitous sex, but the protagonists are decidedly (and often hilariously) conservative. *The 40-Year Old Virgin,* for example, chronicles the conflict between one man's friends, who want him to finally get some action, and his desire to get over his insecurities and find true love. In another Apatow film, *Knocked Up,* a twenty-something television executive's life is thrown off track when she accidentally gets pregnant. Despite all she has to lose by having a baby, she barely considers having an abortion, and in fact, the word "abortion" is never uttered in the film. (Although one of the father's friends suggests he take her for one. "I won't say it, but it rhymes with shmashmortion.")

David Horowitz sees this conservative strain throughout many Hollywood films. "It's a mixed bag, Hollywood, when it comes to good and evil and foreign policy and things like that. *Saving Private Ryan* was a very patriotic film. Every picture about the military after the Vietnam War was negative, until *Officer and a Gentleman.* In the film *Cinderella Man,* the guy pays back his welfare money, the money he took when he was at the bottom of the barrel. He got money from welfare and it's a humiliation. When he made it, he paid it back. What's liberal about something like that?" Even the old westerns of decades ago have their modern-day counterparts where the go-it-alone cowboy-type saves the day. "Have you seen *Spider-Man?* He beats bad guys, he's a loner, he's pretty much the silent type. That's still the iconic hero. It hasn't changed. And men are men in films; women are women. They don't go by Women's Studies precepts. There are a lot of films, but if you look at the blockbuster movies, they're pretty traditional."

Byron York, White House correspondent for *National Review,* doesn't see Hollywood productions as liberal, but as nonpartisan. "Hollywood is certainly dominated by liberals, but I think a lot of what is produced by Hollywood is basically apolitical, or at most very subtly political. For every *Brokeback Mountain* there is a *Wedding Crashers.* What does that say? It says that Hollywood loves making its point but that it also loves making money. I think Hollywood types were more overtly political when they had their guy in the White House. I was surfing the other night and saw *The American President* with Michael Douglas and Annette Bening, which was made in the Clinton years. Absolute dreck. There was also *Air Force One* and *The West Wing*—all were portrayals of really great liberal presidents, which Hollywood believed it had in Clinton. Now, we have *Fahrenheit 9/11,* and the only way Hollywood can portray the presidency in fiction is in a fantastical way, with Geena Davis as the president."[7]

As much as television and movies define what's cool in America, so do professional sports. With presidents who run baseball teams and baseball players who become senators, the overlap is and has always been a prominent one. And nothing has brought politics and sports together like the steroids scandal that has hung like a cloud over nearly every professional and amateur sport for the past five or ten years. It's no coincidence that the first serious examination of this problematic social issue has come at the behest of conservative lawmakers—and athletes themselves. Former New York Mets and New York Yankees pitcher Al Leiter, a well-known conservative, explained it thus: "We have a Republican president who owned the Texas Rangers. And I've been to the White House, I've met with him a couple times, I've been in the Oval Office. He loves the sport and his tie to the sport is really close—and he's got a pretty good fastball. He sees the cultural, family values that have blossomed from the great sport of baseball. And as a result of the steroid issue,

Congress really wants to make an example out of Barry Bonds. Senator Jim Bunning told me straight up, along with Senator Orrin Hatch, 'Yes, we care about baseball. We care about *all* sports. But mostly we want this changed at the high-school and college levels. Because we know the ramifications, we know how much kids look up to you guys.' So I left thinking that this was a cultural thing. They wanted the legislation. They were serious about it."[8]

Baseball, in particular, represents America's long-held belief in tradition, community, and preserving what is good and right. In this way, many consider it a "conservative" sport. George Will, a syndicated columnist who writes often about baseball, explained, "Baseball fans are backward-looking. They look back to baseball as it was when they were young and fell in love with it. You have reference to the soldiers playing a game of 'base' at Valley Forge in 1777. It is therefore as old as the republic. And it is the game of the long season, and it generates an enormous sediment in terms of numbers and memories and episodes, and that makes for an interest in the past, which is really the beginning of conservatism."[9]

There are also far more noticeable (or vocal) conservative athletes, coaches, and former athletes than there are liberal ones. Jim Bunning, Lynn Swann, Curt Schilling, Jason Sehorn, Joe Gibbs, Mike Piazza, Tom Glavine, Todd Zeile, J. C. Watts, Steve Largent, Tom Osborne, Jim Ryun, Ben Nighthorse Campbell, Steve Young, Brent Jones, John Elway, Karl Malone, Greg Anthony, Arturs Irbe, and Judy Martz are just a few. In fact, there are so many Republican athletes that it prompted John Solomon to ask, "Why Are All Jock Politicians Republicans?" in a 2001 article for Slate.com, writing, "If there's one congressional faction unfazed by Washington's frequent calls for bipartisanship, it's the jock caucus. That's because it's all Republican. . . . Republicans aren't throwing a shutout just in Washington. They have far more prospects in their farm system of state and local offices, and they have a number of athletes ready to be drafted."[10]

Does this mean sports are conservative? Probably not. It most likely suggests that successful people who earn large salaries grow to have an interest in protecting those salaries—and that conservative economics present the best opportunity to do so. Jeff Moorad, CEO and managing partner of the Arizona Diamondbacks, considers himself a moderate Republican. ("I have many friends on both sides of the aisle, and I've always prided myself in understanding as much about an issue as I can."[11]) As he put it, "Remembering back to my days of representing players, there are a few things that impact political egocentrism most significantly, and one of them is when an athlete writes a big check to the IRS for the first time. I would say the explanation doesn't really run much deeper than that." And from personal experience, Moorad knows what time and circumstance can do to a person's politics: "I grew up admiring JFK, but have come to be a great admirer of Ronald Reagan. The reason? Maturity, age, and an appreciation for results."

The rise in popularity of NASCAR—it's second only to football in television viewership—has some contending that sports are increasingly appealing to red-state voters. Though NASCAR has undeniable roots in the South, and is presumably populated by conservative drivers, team owners, and executives, that's not necessarily the case for its fans. NASCAR research points out that fans are almost equally divided down party lines. Tony Stewart, two-time Sprint Cup champion, discussed the popularity of NASCAR in terms that may surprise liberal sports fans in the Northeast who like to make fun of "those NASCAR hicks." "Our only rival is the NFL, basically. And I think if the NFL wasn't primarily a winter sport they wouldn't be number one right now. Obviously we'd love to be the number one sport in the United States, but to be a summer sport where everybody's out during the majority of the summer, I'm really proud of where our sport's at now. The growth of football and baseball and basketball hasn't necessary tapered off, but it's started to level off, and our sport is still climbing at an astronomical rate."[12]

* * *

In addition to the myth that popular culture is the sole domain of liberals and that conservatives are out of touch, there is the myth that the Republican leadership is the invisible velvet rope keeping those few conservatives who may be curious out of the liberal VIP room of "coolness." Thanks to indelible counterculture mileposts like Haight-Ashbury and Woodstock, conservatives have inaccurately been labeled "the establishment" by liberals who cling to the romanticism of rebellion and revolution that they can no longer inspire. But what's missing from this interpretation is the reminder that those running the country during Haight-Ashbury and Woodstock were liberals. Tucker Carlson, host of his eponymous television show on MSNBC, discussed the misconception. "Well, you know, that's a canard. At the time I grew up, in Southern California and then in New England, everybody in authority was liberal—everybody I dealt with in positions of authority was liberal. And the dumb pieties of the day, like Woodstock, for example, were for liberals. And they were the ones in charge!"[13] Furthermore, he sees popular culture as an extension of that generation's angst with the liberal leadership of their time. "American pop culture has been in the exclusive control of baby boomers who never got over 1966. They were the ones telling dad, the pallid bourgeois commuter, to go fuck himself. And they were rebelling against their parents' generation. But it's an America that I never experienced, the one where conservatives have been the establishment. There has not been a conservative establishment that I can remember."

Moreover, there's evidence that the traditional answer to the establishment—the counterculture—is becoming more conservative. With outcrops of so-called goth Republicans and punk Republicans all over the country, popular culture's blue sheen is taking on a decidedly red tint. In 2004, *New York Times* writer Warren St. John discussed the seemingly oxymoronic emergence of punk conservatives in a story called "A Bush Surprise: Fright-Wing Support." (It would seem a remarkably *out*-of-touch suggestion that punk-music fans are, in some way, frightening.) St. John writes, "With his mohawk, ratty fatigues, assorted chains and his menagerie of tattoos—swallows on each shoulder, a nautical star on his back and the logo of the Bouncing Souls, a New York City punk band, on his right leg—22-year-old Nick Rizzuto is the very picture of counterculture alienation. But it's when he talks politics that Mr. Rizzuto sounds like a real radical, for a punk anyway. Mr. Rizzuto is adamantly in favor of lowering taxes and for school vouchers, and against campaign finance laws; his favorite Supreme Court justice is Clarence Thomas; he plans to vote for President Bush in November; and he's hard-core into capitalism."[14] Rizzuto, who also founded a website called Conservative Punk, explained that punk and capitalism actually go hand in hand: "The biggest punk scenes are in capitalist countries like the US, Canada and Japan. I haven't heard of any new North Korean punk bands coming out. There's no scene in Iran."

Groups like Rizzuto's might have emerged even sooner had the Left practiced its own creed of inclusion and tolerance. In the same story, conservative talk-radio personality Andrew Wilkow commented on the problems punk conservatives faced in coming out, as it were. "It turns out there are a lot of people who like a certain music and like to dress a certain way, but who want to think for themselves politically. They were being told by their favorite bands they couldn't think this way, but they did, and they still liked the music." With other conservative punk groups like GOPunk, Anti-Anti-Flag and Punkvoter Lies, perhaps it's true that this is no longer your grandfather's counterculture.

Whether popular culture is more liberal or more conservative is debatable. And, as others have suggested, it's likely that pop culture is far less concerned with politics than it is with entertaining. This hasn't stopped liberals, however, from possessively co-opting the American zeitgeist, at least where it's considered "cool." But with larger-than-life influences like television, Hollywood celebrities, athletes, and the media, what is done and said on the national stage affects what happens at the voting booths. Whether it's Mel Gibson or the Dixie Chicks, pop culture speaks to deep-seated and long-held beliefs and values that help to shape and define American politics. For that reason, some feel as though Republicans should get more involved in the national pop culture discourse, even if it means convincing Americans that pop culture isn't all that liberal.

As Brian C. Anderson, author of *South Park Conservatives*, said, "I think the right has had a largely antagonistic attitude toward pop culture—and pop culture, until quite recently, has had a largely antagonistic attitude toward the right. I'd love to see Catholic filmmakers, libertarian novelists (many sci-fi writers are libertarian), and lots more."[15] According to David Horowitz, "The Republican Party ignored the popular culture for many, many years. I think 'South Park Conservatism' is a real phenomenon and it's only recently that conservatives have paid any attention. And conservatives still make huge mistakes. They mistake Hollywood idiots for Hollywood. Hollywood pictures have changed dramatically in their view of the military over the last few years. Conservatives really aren't very much in the popular culture. They don't compete, and I think it's a mistake. It's not like it's an individual choice. There's something characterological there. Conservatives don't choose those professions much. I think conservatives feel like outsiders and then project it."

There are, in fact, indications that Republicans are getting sick and tired of the stereotype that they can't "hang" like the Left can: John McCain held a fundraiser in 2007 at Marquee, one of New York City's hottest nightclubs and a regular haunt of celebrities who prove that DUIs, jail time, and rehab are the best ways to quickly and efficiently up one's cool factor, or at least get more face time. Maybe the Republicans vying for more attention should take note.

Republicans Are Bad in Bed

The Myth of the Prude Conservative

But I think once you become a Republican, your nuts shrink and you never score.

—Beavis and Butthead

Picture this: New York City, 2003. A hot summer night on the Upper East Side. After several fish bowls of candied fruit juice and bottom-shelf rum at Brother Jimmy's bar, two young, unattached, lusty twenty-somethings head for a nearby apartment for some hurried foreplay and what will undoubtedly be sloppy and forgettable casual sex. After a glass each of a newly opened bottle of Rosemont Shiraz and thirteen minutes of *Chappelle's Show,* they clumsily begin to fumble at each other's buttons, zippers, clasps, and laces while carefully crab-walking, still conjoined at the face, from the couch to the bed. Once there, in between boozy breaths and heavy petting more reminiscent of *The Three Stooges* than

9 1/2 *Weeks,* the newcomer takes brief glances around the room. And while the owner of the apartment claws at the nightstand for a condom, a poster catches the other's eye, transfixing the visitor, now practically paralyzed with fear and confusion. The slapdash sex dance is begun, nonetheless, but midthrust the guest simply cannot bear another moment. "I can't do this. That thing scares the shit out of me." The owner of the bedroom looks up at the wall behind them, where a prized possession has been hung. The attractive stranger climbs off the bed (and the bed's owner) and begins to dress, leaving a panting, eager (and discreet!) participant alone on the bed, naked, mouth agape, midcoital. "Sorry," the departing stranger says, leaping toward the door. "I can't get off under a poster of George W. Bush."

This *actually* happens. That a poster of our president would disrupt sex is explicable only to a Democrat, of course. All Republicans will meet this story with much the same reaction as the posterowner did: "Are you fucking kidding me?" (Luckily, revenge is a dish best served in print, preserved for all of eternity.) Hurtfully, it is the Republican who has been slapped with the "prude" label, and the image of the uptight, sober conservative who likes to do it with his socks on or only after carefully removing all her Madame Alexander dolls off the bed has been made emblematic by some less-than-sexy conservatives in history. (Who can picture "a steamy night" with Karl Rove? Or Barbara Bush?) And thanks to certain famous Democrats who perhaps went above and beyond their patriotic duty to prove just how suave they were, Republicans like Ken Starr are often berated with schoolyard taunts like, "C'mon, it was just a blow job."

Pop culture, of course, does little to refute this myth. In an episode of *Desperate Housewives,* ABC's megahit dark comedy, the buttoned-up, sweater-set-wearing Bree says to her new boyfriend about giving him oral sex, "I don't do that. I'm a Republican."

While the show's writers were commenting on the stereotypes embedded in existing sexual politics, they were way off the mark. The line should have read "I'm a Republican. Let me first give you a lap dance."

And in addition to the Republicans-As-Prudes stereotype, there's also the idea, bolstered again by popular culture, that politics gets in the way of sex. But, as in the real-life anecdote above, it's seemingly more of an impediment to Democrats, not Republicans. In an episode of *Curb Your Enthusiasm,* with time running out on his "freebie" to engage in sex with another woman as a tenth wedding anniversary gift from his wife, Larry David begins making out with his busty, blonde costar of *The Producers* and stops midkiss, asking, "Is that Bush? You're a Republican?" before deciding that sex with a Republican—though sanctioned—is simply not worth it.

Liberals and pop culture have also worked very hard to convince you that if—against all odds—you were to find yourself alone with a Republican, you wouldn't *want* to have sex with him or her. Katherine Harris, the former Florida secretary of state who certified the 2000 election for George W. Bush, was smeared by a *Boston Globe* columnist who said unless she "was planning to unwind at a drag bar after facing that phalanx of camera . . . the grease paint she wore should be a federal offense."[1] Similarly, *Time* magazine's April 25, 2005, cover featured a grotesque photo of Ann Coulter, which many on both the Left and the Right argued was an attempt to make her look insectlike.

But where does the urge to strip all conservatives of their sexuality and attractiveness come from? And why has it worked? Former MTV VJ Lisa "Kennedy" Montgomery, a self-described libertarian who once aligned more with Republicans (she sports an elephant tattoo and has no plans to officially break from the party) discussed one reason why Republicans might be stuck with the prude label.

* * *

I'm really interested right now in breast-feeding in public, an issue on which I differ from many of my former party-mates. I can't believe that these old farts are outraged that, as mammals, women are feeding their children. No one seems to have an issue with mom giving junior a peanut butter and jelly sandwich, but when she actually uses her functioning body for the purpose of feeding her child people are outraged. I guess Americans hate boobies after the whole Janet Jackson fiasco. And being a breast-feeding mother, I will say, if my child is hungry, and we are in public, I'm not going to take off my top and whip them out for all to admire, although they do look pretty good right now. But I will feed my child in public, if she is hungry, poor thing.[2]

Likewise, former New York Mets pitcher Al Leiter, a known Republican, suggested the stereotype may come from a place of morality. "You know, I would only imagine that's a stereotype because of the whole religious thing . . . because they're worried about Sunday, so they can't swing from the chandeliers on Saturday night." But he also took the stereotype a little personally, as many would. "Speak for yourself. Not true at all. If that's the stereotype I'm definitely not Republican."[3]

The authors of this book, after polling their friends, colleagues, and friendly neighborhood bartenders, can attest that Republicans are not only more fun in bed—they're also more fun on the desk, in the shower, on the Long Island Rail Road, and in the lobby bathroom of the Tribeca Grand Hotel. We have to assume the same is true in the square states (after all, Democrats in Kansas are too busy plotting their escape to have much of a sex life). But don't take our word for it. In 2004, *Primetime Live* and the ABC News Polling Unit surveyed over 1,000 Americans on their sexual attitudes and behavior. The results were surprising (to Democrats), as well as ego-bruising (to Democrats):[4]

* Of those involved in a committed relationship, 56 percent of Republicans reported being satisfied with their sex lives, versus 47 percent of Democrats.
* When asked if they had ever worn something sexy to enhance their sex lives, 72 percent of Republicans said they had, versus 62 percent of Democrats.
* And when asked if they had ever faked an orgasm, 33 percent of Democrats said they had, while only 26 percent of Republicans said they had.

When we tried to come up with some noncircumstantial explanation for what every Republican has always known to be true, well, we couldn't. But an anonymous contributor to *GQ* in a hilarious 2006 article entitled "The Elephant in the Bedroom: Ten (and a half) reasons why Republicans—yes, Republicans—are the best party in bed"[5] gave it her best shot. According to her, Republican men get their sexual prowess from, among other sources, the fact that they have no conscience, a great sense of humor (as was mentioned in another chapter), and better wooing techniques. It makes sense. A conscience can definitely get in the way at times. As she put it, "Democrats are too busy checking if the condoms you keep in the jar by the bed are good for the environment. And by the time they figure that out, we've all lost our erections." Moreover, Republicans have an uncanny sense for when it's "quiet time," a gift Democrats seem to lack. "Republicans, particularly when naked, do not want to sit around and talk about Social Security privatization. Or Iraq, for chrissake. Or why (oh, boo hoo, get over it!) Kerry lost. They don't even want to sit around naked and talk about George W. Bush. They just want you to sit on them."

In an interview with Tucker Carlson on *The Situation, GQ*'s deputy editor Michael Hainey discussed the story:

I think she does a great job of saying what I think a lot of Democrats feel. You and I are the same age, but we grew up believing the Democratic Party is the party of JFK, a very randy and virile party. And just like most domestic issues, the Republicans vaulted over the Democrats, you know, and (took over) . . . the party of free love, you might say. And they've become the more virile party. It's a national disgrace, if you ask me.[6]

Whether the Left truly subscribes to the theory that Republicans are bad in bed is debatable. After all, during the 2004 Republican convention in New York City, the online bulletin board Craigslist became littered with casual encounter ads for liberal women seeking Republican men to deliver "a good Republican spanking."[7] Maybe Republicans are just newly better in bed (it's times like these that the wisdom of a great-grandmother would really prove useful). Either way, this is one misconception that Republicans should be in no real hurry to shake. After all, it's always better to pleasantly surprise than to abruptly horrify.

CHAPTER 11

Republicans Don't Care About You

The Myth of the Heartless Conservative

They had fangs. They were biting people. They had this look in their eyes—totally cold. Animal. I think they were Young Republicans.

—*Buffy the Vampire Slayer*

Perhaps no stereotype about conservatives is more indelible, more recognizable, evoked with more regularity, and uttered with more passion (and less evidence) than the myth of the uncaring Republican, his heart as black as an oil spill in an endangered seal preserve, eyes as steely and piercing as a razor blade in a piece of Halloween candy, and blood cold as a glacier untouched by the ravages of global warming. Republicans are routinely painted as uncaring, unfeeling, stoic, and sober. We joke that Dick Cheney's heart problems stem from his not actually having one. And we hypothesize that Republican policy, domestic and foreign, is born of a severely misanthropic, even homicidal, urge to effect on a national scale the kind of tone set at a funeral for a school bus accident.

There are so many examples of the so-called heartless Republican in popular culture, the media, and political rhetoric itself, it seems needless to cite any specifically. Calling a Republican heartless is as commonplace and unnoticed as calling Paris Hilton annoying.

In March 2005, during the height of the Terri Schiavo tragedy, Fran Shor published a piece on the progressive website Common-Dreams.org called "Brain-Dead Ploys and Heartless Republicans." He writes, "While there are troubling moral issues surrounding matters of when to end a life, some of these Republicans, such as Tom DeLay, and their right-wing evangelical supporters appear to be obsessed with the rights of . . . unborn fetuses and near-dead individuals."[1] Angered that the state tried to keep a dying woman alive, liberal activists like Shor actually tried to brand the conservative position as marked by a *lack* of compassion. What's more touchy-feely than "unborn fetuses" and "near-dead individuals"—in other words, babies and sick people?

The Chief Source, a liberal blog with featured writers like "Kyle," "Chuck," "Robert," and "Terra," posted an excerpt from a *Los Angeles Times* story in February 2007. The excerpt, included in a post entitled "The System Republicans Want," quoted the *Times* story: "A paraplegic man wearing a soiled hospital gown and a broken colostomy bag was found crawling in a gutter in skid row in Los Angeles on Thursday after allegedly being dumped in the street by a Hollywood Presbyterian Medical Center van, police said."

Featured blogger "Chuck" writes, in response to the excerpt, "Fortunately, all three major Democrats (Hillary, Obama, Edwards) see universal care as a goal. On the other hand, the shameful Republicans believe in the status quo . . . which means Republicans are pro-Homeless Dumping, right?"[2] This is how ridiculous the characterization has become. A homeless man is found in an alley, and heartless Republicans—all of them—are to blame.

Compassion is a hard thing to measure. Just as liberals can't prove that the Left approaches policy from a position of compassion, they can't prove that the Right approaches it from a position of heartlessness. David Limbaugh, younger brother of Rush Limbaugh and a noted columnist and author in his own right, explains the heartless Republican myth as one of misappropriation—the result of overextending a basic political assumption. "You know the underlying premise. Since liberals have always promoted the expansion of the welfare state, they care more about the poor and minorities. And since conservatives have generally opposed it, they are compassionless."[3]

Some liberals are even trying to convert heartless conservatives into more compassionate and caring people. Mike Hersh, in a 2000 article in *American Politics Journal* called "Today's Moderate Republicans: Tomorrow's Democrats," wrote in all earnestness:

> Many Republicans are greedy, closed-minded, and hard-hearted. This is true for the top Republican "misleaders." There are times when it seems Republicans are like Patty Hearst in her SLA days, brainwashed by a cult. But the media tells us this cult is legitimate. Even some Democrats more or less accept the Republicans' lies. This makes it hard for moderate Republicans to figure out what's going on. It's up to us to help them understand politics better. That will take a lot of patience on our part. If we brand all Republicans as money hungry, mean and heartless, that won't help them overcome their reluctance. If a Republican is secretly ashamed of what her party is doing, it may be possible to get her to switch. It's certainly worth it to try.[4]

Talk about brainwashing.

*   *   *

If the Republican is like the Tin Man from *The Wizard of Oz*,—that is, heartless—just getting through a day requires that he be constantly checked and maintained, and Democrats have no problem policing his oil can, doling out daily dosages to assure we don't rust and decay into a nation sucked dry of "feelings." The unoiled heartless Republican, after all, explains a whole host of societal ills. Deroy Murdock, syndicated columnist, discusses the heartless Republican stereotype from a race perspective, drawing connections between the portrait of a hardened conservative and that of a racist one.

A lot of this is based on stereotypes and the stereotype of the uncaring, cold-hearted, flinty, greedy Republican trying to hold down the poor person because that's going to benefit him, or maybe just for the sheer joy of holding someone down. I've never quite understood how holding down black or poor people makes your life better, but that kind of attitude prevails. I remember, for example, when Katrina took place, and people were still literally being taken out of their attics by the Coast Guard, and the meme erupted very quickly, as if crashing through the levee walls themselves, that this was all an example of President Bush's racism and Republican bigotry, and this was a combination of Republican neglect for poor people coupled with a very odd conspiracy to blow the levees up so that the lower Ninth Ward would flood and black people would move out so that real estate developers could come in and grab that land . . . because that's where rich, white people want to live—the lower Ninth Ward.

And if that's really what [Republicans] wanted to do, they could just say, We'll give you five hundred thousand dollars per house—but that's too simple. The charge was that all these black people in New Orleans were dying because President Bush, as Kanye West said, doesn't care about black people. And Charlie Rangel said something similar. Charles Barron on the New York City Council here said something very similar. Major Owens said something similar. And the basic charge that they're all making is that the president is guilty of genocide. Not Hitler-level genocide. Not Pol Pot–level genocide. But still, that he's capable of killing twelve hundred or fifteen hundred black people just because they're black. And if they really believe that the president of the United States did that, then they damn well better bring out some evidence that he engaged in genocide. And if it's true, then we should impeach the president, convict him, arrest him, and put him in jail for genocide. But they provided no such evidence, because there was none.[5]

Murdock's example speaks to the regularity and ease with which the Left defames the Right, haphazardly and, even more inexcusably, without retribution. He is quick to point out that Republicans should have—quickly and passionately—defended themselves after this and every other such character attack.

I called the Heritage Foundation. I talked to a guy named Kirk Johnson, who knows the budget inside and out. And I said, Kirk, is it really true that Republicans neglected New Orleans, and that that's what led to this? He called me back about two hours later and said that he looked at the amount of federal spending in Orleans Parish. It turns out that between 2000 and 2003, overall federal anti-poverty spending in Orleans Parish increased per person 24 percent a year. It went up 73 percent between the time Bush showed up and FY 2003. You look at AFDC, you look at food stamps, you look at rent subsidies, you look at all these federal programs. And there are about four or five that went down, and the rest went up, either keeping up with inflation or doubling or tripling. So the Republicans were pouring cash on Orleans Parish, pouring cash on the poor black people, so the idea that they were cutting them off or that they were too starved and suffering from anorexia and could barely

get on the buses to leave, was just, excuse me, fucking crap.
And the White House should have said so.

When pondering the heartless Republican problem, a number of
defenses come to mind. There is the statistical fact that Republicans report being happier than Democrats, and have for some
time. Unless you believe that Republican happiness is born merely
out of schadenfreude, it's somewhat compelling. According to a
Pew Research Center study released in February 2006, 45 percent
of Republicans reported being "very happy," compared with just
30 percent of Democrats and 29 percent of Independents. "Republicans have been happier than Democrats every year since the
General Social Survey began taking its measurements in 1972,"
says Pew, but that statistic is not a reflection of their party's political success. "Since 1972, the GOP happiness edge over Democrats has ebbed and flowed in a pattern that appears unrelated to
which party is in political power." Liberals will be quick to cry
that Republicans are obviously happier because they are wealthier
than Democrats. But, according to Pew, "This explanation only
goes so far. If one controls for household income, Republicans
still hold a significant edge: that is, poor Republicans are happier
than poor Democrats; middle-income Republicans are happier
than middle-income Democrats, and rich Republicans are happier
than rich Democrats."[6] And the study goes even further, declaring
conservative Republicans to be the happiest of them all. "It's true
that conservatives, who are more likely to be Republican, are happier than liberals, who are more likely to be Democrats. But even
controlling for this ideological factor, a significant partisan gap
remains. Conservative Republicans are happier than conservative
Democrats, and moderate/liberal Republicans are happier than
liberal Democrats."

But perhaps the most compelling argument against the myth
of the Uncaring Republican comes from another, closely related
myth—that of the Uncharitable Republican. A Zogby International

poll conducted in 2004 revealed that, according to 43 percent of 2,562 likely voters, "Ebenezer Scrooge" was probably a Republican. Not surprising—a grouchy financier, harassing all of Victorian England with a constant scowl, appalled by the idea of charity, completely unimpressed by the annoying squabbles of the poor, who realizes the importance of giving only when he finds religion in the father, son, and other holy ghosts of Christmas. Dickens was obviously on the DNC payroll.

Likewise, 31 percent of likely voters said "the Grinch" was a Republican, and 27 percent said Santa Claus was a Democrat. (Incidentally, 6 percent believe he is a member of the Green Party—perhaps because of his low-emission sleigh and carbon-free workshop.[7]) The myth of the uncharitable Republican tightwad is an indelible one, thanks in large part to Scrooge, the Grinch, and countless movies like *Trading Places,* in which the money-hungry Republican is written as antagonist to the good-hearted, Democratic hero. And today's creative types keep the myth alive. George Carlin asked, "Have you ever wondered why Republicans are so interested in encouraging people to volunteer in their communities? It's because volunteers work for no pay. Republicans have been trying to get people to work for no pay for a long time."[8] And eternal optimist Noam Chomsky believes George Bush and his colleagues have made an entire career out of such behavior. "The Bush administration do have moral values. Their moral values are very explicit: shine the boots of the rich and the powerful, kick everybody else in the face, and let your grandchildren pay for it. That simple principle predicts almost everything that's happening."[9]

What is surprising, though, is that it's not just the Left that is keeping this myth alive. Some on the right not only seem to believe it, but wear it as some kind of badge of honor. When an ABC News poll revealed that Republicans are more sexually satisfied than Democrats, the Left clamored for an explanation, while the Right trumpeted its virility. Pundits and bloggers from all corners of cyberspace went to work to try to question or justify the results of the survey, and what they came up with was pretty funny. One blogger on conservative site fringeblog.com explained it thus: "Could it be the Left's tendency toward 'charitability' makes them preturnaturally [*sic*] grouchy with the person(s) they're sleeping with, perhaps even turning them off from sex completely? Could the Liberals have 'goodwill fatigue'? The Right has it right on. Republicans are greedy, self-serving, and uncharitable—ideal combinant [*sic*] characteristics for a stunning experience in the sack."[10] So even conservatives think conservatives are stingy?

Of course it's obvious *why* it's beneficial to paint conservatives this way. Where elections are chances to prove one side of the aisle is more giving, more compassionate, and cares more about *you* than the other, it's a useful caricature. But it's completely inaccurate.

Al Leiter, former New York Mets pitcher who also sat on the board of directors of the Twin Towers Fund, is just one example of a philanthropic Republican, and one who was surprised to hear of the miserly conservative stereotype. "They say that? I do not see that at all. I think if anything, people could say that Republicans give more to church-affiliated organizations and do not flaunt or feel compelled to publicize their philanthropic efforts. I see the contributions from the Left, especially when it comes to Hollywood, as a strategic manipulation of charity. 'Give and be seen' kind of money."[11] (Leiter would not discuss his own charitable donations and philanthropy, but his many contributions are not hard to find. He has won nearly every philanthropic award he was eligible for, including the Roberto Clemente Award, the Branch Rickey Award, the Joan W. Payson Award, the Good Guy Award, the Thurmon Award, and countless others. Al and his family have donated hundreds of thousands of dollars to various charities all over the country, and he founded Leiter's Landing, an organization that helps children in need.)

Similarly, another philanthropic ballplayer, Boston Red Sox

pitcher Curt Schilling, who doesn't identify himself with either political party, commented on the hypocritical nature of liberal Hollywood's well-publicized "giving." "The next time I see a movie star screaming some antiwar slogan into an *Inside Edition* camera while two homeless men sleep in a cardboard box in the background I am going to throw up. We have become a country of 'charity by convenience' and 'charity by popularity.' Whatever's hot and whatever gets you 'out there' seems to be where the famous people throw their face and money to, then they move on."[12] Schilling, for the record, along with his wife Shonda, founded Curt's Pitch for ALS, an organization committed to stamping out Lou Gehrig's Disease. Fans can make donations to the ALS Association for every strikeout he throws. He also appears on a weekly WEEI radio show that raises more than one hundred thousand dollars every year for ALS research.

Despite the substantial charitable efforts of these men and conservatives like them, the myth of the uncharitable Republican persists. To get to the bottom of this blatant falsehood, John Stossel, a rogue conservative toiling away in the basement of the vastly liberal media, reported on the charity myths of both parties in a segment for *20/20* in late 2006. In it he interviewed an academic named Arthur Brooks whose book *Who Really Cares?* examined the surprising giving patterns of Republicans and Democrats. The report was eye-opening:

> The idea that liberals give more is a myth. Of the top 25 states where people give an above-average percentage of their income, all but one (Maryland) were red—conservative—states in the last presidential election. "When you look at the data," says Syracuse University professor Arthur Brooks, "it turns out the conservatives give about 30 percent more. And incidentally, conservative-headed families make slightly less money. The people who give one thing tend to be the people who give everything in America. You find that people who believe it's

the government's job to make incomes more equal, are far less likely to give their money away." Conservatives are even 18 percent more likely to donate blood.

In the segment, Stossel and his news team set up Salvation Army buckets in two very different cities—Sioux Falls, South Dakota, and San Francisco, California, to see which city gave more after two days. The experiment was designed to test our basic assumptions about an intellectually elite city on the West Coast and a working-class city in Middle America.

> San Francisco and Sioux Falls are different in some important ways. Sioux Falls is small and rural, and more than half the people go to church every week. San Francisco is a much bigger and richer city, and relatively few people attend church. It is also known as a very liberal place, and since liberals are said to "care more" about the poor, you might assume people in San Francisco would give a lot.

And the results?

> Well, even though people in Sioux Falls make, on average, half as much money as people in San Francisco, and even though the San Francisco location was much busier—three times as many people were within reach of the bucket—by the end of the second day, the Sioux Falls bucket held twice as much money.[13]

While San Francisco and Sioux Falls offer an interesting comparison, perhaps an even juicier comparison is found in two Massachusetts politicians, Democratic senator John Kerry and former Republican governor William Weld. The *Boston Globe*'s story by Jeff Jacoby recalls a Kerry-Weld debate in 1996, during which Kerry was asked the question, "Can you tell us, from your heart, why you think people are poor?" For anyone who remembers the 2004 election, his response was predictable. It's the Republicans' fault:

> As I have gone around this state and been privileged to sit in somebody's kitchen and listen to them talk about their problems, what I learn is that people are poor because the deck is really stacked against them. Because people like the governor fight even raising the minimum wage. . . . Because they don't get the breaks that a lot of wealthy people in this country get. [Because] of the Washington of Newt Gingrich and the Republicans that I am fighting—a Washington that will cut $270 billion of Medicare so they can give a $245 billion tax break, most of which goes to people who are wealthy. And that's what stacks the odds against people, and that's what's wrong.

In that same article, Jacoby discusses the irony of Kerry's compassionate rhetoric by examining the actual spending habits of Kerry and Weld during the 1995 tax year.

> Last year, Weld (and his wife) reported adjusted gross income of $110,418. Of that total, the Welds gave $24,010— almost 22 percent—to charity. They gave to the United Way and the Episcopal Church, to Rosie's Place and Globe Santa, to Harvard College and Mt. Auburn Hospital, to Catholic Charities and the Keene Valley Library, to the Salvation Army and the Special Olympics. All told, they contributed to nearly three dozen charitable institutions great and small. Kerry's income in 1995 was somewhat higher than Weld's—$126,179. But the amount he reported giving to charity was considerably lower. He didn't give anything. Zero dollars, zero cents.[14]

And that year was hardly atypical. "Over the past six years, Weld has reported gross income totaling $1,082,875, of which 15.2 percent has gone to charity. Kerry's six-year total income is $724,042;

according to his federal tax returns, he earmarked just under seven-tenths of 1 percent for charitable contributions."

That John Kerry is somewhat inauthentic is no real surprise. And that many of our liberal friends bemoan so-called fat-cat Republicans but don't engage in any kind of volunteer work themselves is no real surprise either. What is surprising, though, is the *hostility* from the Left toward Republicans who do engage in volunteer work, who are routinely called insincere. The Republican who does not volunteer is selfish, and the one who does is, well, doing it for selfish reasons.

In 2004, a number of Republican delegates and their families, including Republican senator Rick Santorum, traveled to New York City's Bowery Mission, a soup kitchen for the homeless, and were met with, of all things, protesters. Columnist Dennis Roddy of the *Pittsburgh Post-Gazette* explained:

> Because Republicans were doing this, a collection of indignant liberals, some of them from the neighborhood, engaged in the ultimate protest: picketing a soup kitchen because they consider the kitchen volunteers uncharitable. "It's like, 'Oh, let's go feed the homeless. Let's arrive in our air conditioned, magic bus and we'll be here for an hour and then we'll all go back to our five-star hotel,'" said Cole Schneider, 21, a New York University student from Denver.

Another passerby also voiced his disdain for the do-gooders.

> "I think it's a bunch of B.S.," said Darryl Rice, who was putting down both the Pennsylvania Republicans and a plate of pasta one member of the delegation had served him. "They deal with imperialistic dogs. This is all for show, to try to gain votes." Rice might be easily dismissed as another Bowery bum who does not appreciate the charity shown him but for the fact that he is, in fact, a graduate student at Long Island University."[15]

It would seem some liberals would prefer that Republicans keep their time and money to themselves rather than taint the poor, hungry, and homeless with their "all-for-show" charity work, an argument that, needless to say, makes little sense, economic, philosophical, or otherwise. But "sense" has never been the engine that propels politics.

Popular culture will likely always rely on the myth that Republicans hate poor people. An episode of *The West Wing* commented wryly on the pervasive stereotype. When asked why he was a Republican, one character sarcastically replied:

> Because I hate poor people. I hate them, Donna. They're all so poor, and many of 'em talk funny, and don't have proper table manners. My father slaved away at the Fortune 500 company he inherited so that I could go to Choate, Brown and Harvard and see that this country isn't overrun by poor people and lesbians. No . . . I'm Republican because I believe in smaller government. This country was founded on the principle of freedom, and freedom stands opposed to constraints, and the bigger the government, the more the constraints.[16]

The myth that conservatives and Republicans are uncaring, stingy, and uncharitable is actually more than myth—it's pure propaganda, and useful propaganda at that, woven seamlessly into the narrative that the Right lines the pockets of the rich while ignoring the needs of the poor. The invented selfishness of the Right is the go-to reason behind every Republican social and economic program. Keeping this myth alive is *very* important to the success of Democratic candidates and the party itself. And with memorable characters like Scrooge to put a face to the characterization, Republicans may have a hard time rewriting the story.

CHAPTER 12

Republicans Are Religious Extremists

The Myth of the Intolerant Conservative

This experiment, this magnificent experiment in democracy is just being shredded to pieces by these right-wing Christians, the Ashcroft branch of Republicanism. [They're] just shredding the rest of the Bill of Rights which hadn't been shredded already.[1]

—George Carlin

In 2005, Democratic congressman Jim McDermott of Washington State gave a speech to the House of Representatives entitled "Republican Extremists 'Shall Inherit the Wind,'" which detailed the "radical" Republican Senate's plans to target the Supreme Court and judiciary. Following is the part of the speech where he, as some might say, "brings down the house"—no pun intended:

Greed is God to these radicals who are attempting to subvert democracy with religious idolatry. Run for your lives, America, the Republicans are coming. Right wing extremists in the Republican Party control the House, the Senate, and the White House, and they want the new trophy, and it is called the Supreme Court. They want to send their militants into your homes, into your lives, next to your death bed, to force their will upon you. The Republicans in charge today want to replace the Constitution with the Bible. The Republicans in charge today would like nothing better than to enforce a literal interpretation of the Bible in every American home, every American school, and every American mind.[2]

McDermott's sentiments, which range from melodramatic to downright hallucinatory, reflect a common misinterpretation of conservative ideology among many Democrats and liberals, in this country and abroad. In fact, most Americans consider a deep-seated religious conviction to be synonymous with the Republican creed. Terms like right-wing, radical, and compassionate might as well be replaced by Christian.

The fear on the left—and it is fear, in the classical Orwellian sense, propelled by a severe lack of critical understanding of how our country works—that the Right is a group with extremist religious views is no small issue. Throughout his tenure, much has been made of President Bush's use of religious rhetoric in his speeches, his not-infrequent invocations of a higher authority, and his admitted reliance on his faith to help him make decisions of national and international import. And in his second inaugural address, in early 2005, he arguably delivered on what his detractors would consider an abuse of his position by giving a rousing and inspirational speech acknowledging his religious beliefs. *Newsweek*'s Howard Fineman said the speech was "the closest thing to a sermon I can remember."[3] And, not surprisingly, there was even more vitriol from the Far Left, where Bush's faith constitutes an apocalyptic cause célèbre as devastating as a tax cut, and where leaps are routinely made from his belief in God to an abuse of fiscal muscle. In what was perhaps a nostalgic longing for the dignity and nobility of the Clinton era, the *Nation*'s Ari Berman hypothesized in his column *The Daily Outrage,* that "in all, Jesus would've appreciated the absurdity of throwing nine balls, three candlelit dinners, a rock concert and fireworks, followed by an inaugural prayer service."[4]

But even in places where religion is purportedly viewed through a lens of tolerance and inclusion, the president's faith is met with skepticism. Beliefnet, a "multi-faith e-community" that claims to have a "deep respect for a wide variety of faiths and traditions," featured an essay written by David Domke and Kevin Coe criticizing Bush's speeches. "Such rhetoric," they wrote, "positions the president as a prophetic spokesman for God rather than as a petitioning supplicant," questioning his "fusion of politics and religion."[5]

However, when Democratic politicians discuss religion openly, they are somehow perceived as less dangerous. Connecticut senator Joe Lieberman delivered a speech to the Christians United for Israel Conference in July 2007, in which he said:

> This is the long odyssey that has brought us here tonight. By standing with Israel today, each of you has joined that journey and taken up the torch that was lit in God's promise to Abraham 4,000 years ago, and carrying it forward to spread that light. I believe that Israel's rebirth in 1948 was divinely inspired by God, but I know that it was realized by the men and women here on earth who worked so hard to make it happen. Israel will be sustained by the work of men and women like you here on Earth. And I know you know how truly American is your support of Israel.[6]

Here, not only is Lieberman exercising his right to speak openly about his faith and religious beliefs, but he is using those beliefs to make an argument for foreign policy. Where is the undeserved outrage?

The most obvious hypocrisy in this kind of analysis has to do with the very stuff of which American history is made. To assert that our political leaders are somehow above their own personal religious beliefs (or should, at the very least, remain publicly divorced from them) is a dangerous and unfair misunderstanding of history and our sociological makeup. Benjamin Franklin, for example, would have helped to draft an entirely different Declaration of Independence, if he were told that, as statesman, Postmaster, and Founding Father, he was not allowed to simultaneously and publicly explore the realms of philosophy, religion, economics, science, and the arts. The Reverend Martin Luther King, Jr., likewise might have held a very different kind of rally on the Mall to deliver his "I Have a Dream" speech, if he were told that as a minister, his views on U.S. domestic policy and civil rights were best discussed in private, among his close friends and family members.

We have never, to our knowledge, elected an atheist president, nor is it written anywhere in our Constitution that freedom of religion does not apply to those in office. But religion and politics have always been strange and divisive bunkmates, thanks especially to the anxiety over presidents' or other elected officials' abusing their power to close the gap between church and state. But Republican politicians have not been the only targets. In a 1960 speech in Houston, amidst fears that a Catholic president would be beholden to the pope, presidential hopeful John F. Kennedy allayed concerns that his beliefs would inform his decision-making in office by publicly separating himself from his faith. "I am not a Catholic candidate for president. I am the Democratic Party's candidate for president who also happens to be Catholic."[7] And while Kennedy was seen as *too* Catholic, forty-four years later we wondered if another JFK—John F. Kerry, that is—was Catholic *enough*. In what was termed "John Kerry's Catholic Problem," many Catholics, who made up nearly 25 percent of the country's population, feared that his liberal views on abortion meant that he wasn't *authentically* religious. To this, he answered by making very public appearances at church functions, invoking God in speeches, and attending Catholic Mass.

The anxiety over religion has, some would argue, led to a distinctly American obsession with political correctness, something television and radio pundit Glenn Beck knows a good deal about. On his eponymous CNN Headline News show and wildly popular XM Satellite Radio program, Beck frequently discusses the absurdity of political correctness. (He famously changed the lyrics of the Christmas carol "O Holy Night" and renamed it "O Somewhat Important Night.") A self-proclaimed reformed alcoholic and drug abuser, Beck converted to Mormonism after surviving the tragic loss of three family members—his mother and a brother to suicide, and another brother to a heart attack. But luckily, his biting sense of humor remained intact, as did his ability to relate to and understand everyday Americans. He explained the root cause of our political correctness as an ideological one. "We're afraid to talk about religion. We're afraid to offend. Political correctness was made for us. [And] because we are good people by nature, we don't want to offend others."[8]

The pervasive view that conservatives and Republicans are not only religious, but Christian and, in many cases, religious extremists, prompts a number of questions about the makeup of the party: Are conservatives really all that Christian? Are conservatives actually religious extremists? And, most important, what's wrong with religion anyway?

To address this enduring stereotype and all that it conjures—incidentally, neither author of this book is Christian—some basic fact-finding is necessary:

Of the world's more than 6.5 billion people, those representing some belief in God (nonatheists) constitute 98 percent of the population. Of those, Christianity represents the dominant faith, with 33 percent of the population. In this country, of the more than 300 million people in the United States, 90 percent share a belief in God, and 78 percent are Christian.[9] Asserting that most Republicans are "religious," then, is like asserting that most bananas are "yellow." And asserting that most Republicans are "Christian" is like asserting that most dentists recommend Trident. So the (very unscientific) answer to "Are conservatives really all that Christian?" is, yes. But so is the world, and, by a huge majority, so is this country. As Glenn Beck explained, "You have those who seek power, understanding that if a people believe that the ultimate power is with God, the people will not allow the politicians to rise above. Unfortunately, that belief is contrary to our founding understanding . . . God gives rights to man, who loans those rights to the government. A particular religion is not essential to our country, but faith, God, and religions are."[10]

Indeed, there is nothing inherently "Christian" written into conservative ideology, as conservatism, rightly understood and applied, is not a philosophy of rules or strategies. Inherent in conservatism, in fact, is a historical aversion to dogma or treatise. What most conservatives and religious folk (Christian, Jewish, Muslim, etc.) have in common, however, is a commitment to preserving (or "conserving") traditional values, where "traditional" refers to social, cultural, nationalistic, *and* religious mores. The ways in which various religions and a diverse group of conservatives practice this preservation differ widely, of course. Even some of the most conservative Republicans and religious Christians wouldn't suggest that theirs is the only viewpoint. Former Mets pitcher Al Leiter, a Republican and Catholic, put it this way:

> I think it is extremely hypocritical to think as a Catholic or a Christian that our way is the only way to Heaven. There are billions of people who obviously aren't Christian. I'm Catholic because my mother and father were Catholic and their parents

were Catholic, and so I'm Catholic. If I were born into a Muslim family, I would have been raised accordingly. If I were born into a Jewish family, of course I'd believe that as well. And my friends always say, "But you'd still have been given the opportunity to be touched by Jesus Christ, and you could still have been saved." And I say, okay, let's go up that tree. If I were born a little Muslim boy, and I play baseball, and I'm playing ball and hanging out with my teammates, and eventually I come around and decide to become Christian, and I'm born again, I believe that if you're not saved by Jesus Christ, you burn in hell for eternity. Now, I'm thinking as I go back to bed as a little Muslim boy who became Christian, "Remember Grandma, who just passed away? She's burning in hell for all eternity? And remember Uncle Muhammad? He's burning in hell for all eternity?" Come on. Really? It just does not make sense.[11]

But just how Christian are Republicans, compared to Democrats? In a study conducted by the Barna Group in January 2007 called "The God Gap: The Faith of Republicans and Democrats,"[12] the firm, whose self-stated mission is to "partner with Christian ministries and individuals to be a catalyst in moral and spiritual transformation in the United States," uncovered some provocative findings in their polling of over one thousand Americans. According to this study, 61 percent of Republicans considered themselves "absolutely committed to Christianity," or "born-again." And among Democrats 48 percent—nearly half—felt the same way. Likewise, 53 percent of Republicans said they had attended church in the last seven days, compared to 41 percent of Democrats. This means that 47 percent of Republicans don't attend weekly church services, making a tough case for the Republicans-as-Religious-Fanatics argument, especially when 41 percent of Democrats do.

But the real issue here isn't a statistical one. It's a social and political one, of course. The Left's hostility toward religion, which 98 percent of the world embraces in some way, reflects a huge fear for liberals that their own freedoms will be supplanted by the heavy-handed dogma of the Republican regime, a fear that is simply unfounded and frankly somewhat hysterical. And no religion is targeted more often by the American Left than Christianity. Popular author Dinesh D'Souza examined this growing hostility in his 2007 book *What's So Great About Christianity*, which attempts to unpack the leftist and atheist arguments against the Bible, God, and Christ. In it, he discusses the oft-cited "sins" of Christianity—from the Inquisition to the Crusades—proof to the Left and non-Christians that the religion is responsible for most of the world's violence. But, as D'Souza points out, it's the regimes under which atheism is the intended goal from Pol Pot and Mao to Fidel Castro, Ceauşescu and Kim Jong Il, that have historically been the most violent and devastating. For D'Souza, Christianity actually has far less to answer for.

As conservative radio host Laura Ingraham said, "Those who are overtly hostile to religion don't like to concede that there is any force more powerful in their world than the weekend box office. These folks believe *they* are masters of their universe so there isn't much room for God."[13] Pop culture itself often comments on this distaste for and mistrust of religion, and specifically the fear that someone you know and love may in fact be a "God-lover." *Seinfeld* devoted an entire episode to that fear, called "The Burning," in which Elaine suspects her boyfriend David Puddy may be religious after discovering all the presets on his car's radio were Christian rock stations.[14] In a hilarious scene, she takes her concerns to her confidant Jerry:

Elaine: So you think Puddy actually believes in something?
Jerry: It's a used car, he probably never changed the presets.
Elaine: Yes, he *is* lazy!
Jerry: Plus, he probably doesn't know how to program the buttons.
Elaine: Yes, he *is* dumb!

Jerry: So you prefer dumb and lazy to religious?

Elaine: Dumb and lazy, I understand.

What this episode commented on is the liberal aversion to and suspicion of religious folk, and the irony of that point of view in that it fails to acknowledge its own intolerance of other beliefs. "Conservatives are conservative," said Ingraham. "That means that they resist change when it comes to values and tradition. That has worked pretty well for them for twenty-five years, as the Democrats have 'adapted' and 'evolved' to accommodate the views of this or that group that considers itself oppressed by the main-stream culture. Ultimately, the Democrats became a party of fringe coalitions, instead of the party of the 'little guy,' the working folks who are trying to raise their families." As conservative author Ann Coulter adroitly pointed out in her book, *Slander,* the hypocrisy and self-righteousness of the Left are practically tangible. "Liberals deemed voluntary student prayers at high school football games a direct assault on the Constitution. But it was of urgent importance that Islamic terrorists being held in Guantanamo be free to prac-tice their religion."[15] So, where Democrats pose as supporters of minority coalitions, special-interest groups and whatever the new and exciting, have-to-have-it voter contingent (or criminal faction) is, they routinely ignore, lambaste, condemn, or condescend to the actual majority of everyday Americans—Middle America, working families, and the descendants of immigrants.

Former Speaker of the House Newt Gingrich explained this kind of hostility toward religious folk in historical terms. "Much of the modern Left is an outgrowth of the French Revolution of 1789 and then of nineteenth-century socialism. Unlike the American Revolu-tion, the French Revolution was an intensely anticlerical movement. The experience of the two world wars, the Great Depression, and totalitarian systems of antireligious hatred have left an exhausted Europe content to endure life without seeking meaning in it. That is only now beginning to change. Religion is ultimately the deepest opponent of totalitarianism because it asserts that man's relationship to God transcends the state. Those who believe in state power reshaping humans in a plastic way find religion a threatening competitor."[16] Likewise, Glenn Beck described the hostility as a result of the rising influence of science and the false perception that religion and science cannot coexist. "Science has become God for some people on the left. They have fallen into a belief that reason, science, and religion aren't bedfellows, when indeed a proper understanding of a deity is that he works within the framework of the natural laws: he built them."

Boston Red Sox pitcher Curt Schilling, a well-known and outspoken Christian, has taken some flak for being so public with his faith, but makes no apologies for it. "What you have to get past is that other people don't like it. People think that me talking about my faith in God and love of Jesus is somehow a condemnation of who or what they are. That's not for me to decide, that's in God's hands. But that makes for a convenient jumping-off point to slam Christians and it just goes on from there. Fact of the matter is, the more popular you are today, the more people want you to either think and speak like them, or shut up."[17]

And despite the many others in his sport and his field, before him and now—including Sandy Koufax, Andy Pettitte, Kurt Warner, and Evander Holyfield, just to name a few—who have also refused to keep their faith private, Schilling still admits some people still don't understand it. "There is a huge antireligion movement that's becoming more and more public. Much of that has to do with the sheer amount of media and the common person's ability to get information 24/7 from any place in the world. What I think is becoming more prominent is . . . the religion of laziness. Christianity is a religion that you have to work at—hard—and you also have to realize that you never, ever reach the desired goal. The unfortunate part of Christianity for me is that there are Christians, or espoused Christians, who do us more harm than good with their 'We are holier than thou' and everyone else is bad.

I see Christianity as a very personal one-on-one relationship with the Lord and Jesus Christ. If I can help someone else find that same thing then I've done what God put me here for, but the rest of my life is a monumental struggle to do things right that I fail daily at."

This hostility raises the issue of tolerance, one of those feel-good words that everyone agrees is a must-have in today's multiethnic, multigender, multifaith, multieverything world. Tolerance is a myth. It is a utopic, post-Enlightenment fallacy that we have eaten up by the forkliftful for centuries. Religion—an actual belief system not involving Leonardo DiCaprio or the latest trends on the catwalk—*requires* intolerance. Believing in something requires that one does *not* agree with something else. People of faith, and people who understand faith, understand this. There is not a single religion, whether organized or primitive, that agrees that *everything* is good. So to require a group of people who believe inveterately and without wavering in something so vital to their very existence—whether it's that abortion is a sin or that dancing brings the rain—to "accept" beliefs that oppose their own is an unfair, misguided and in fact impossible request. And it misses the whole point of religion and belief.

Conservatives generally agree that in the world there are opposing belief systems, and recognize the insanity (and elitism) of trying to water those belief systems down so that they more closely resemble one another. What matters, and what should matter, is what we do with our natural, instinctual and sociologically binding intolerance. Fortunately, laws exist in this country at least, restricting our actions and behavior when it comes to intolerance—*acts* of violence, *acts* of hate speech, *acts* of discrimination. So relax—you can still be a bad person. Just don't break any laws in the process. It's a far more valuable (and honest) exercise to work toward a better understanding of groups with which we disagree, and *admit* that we are in disagreement, than it is to pretend we can arrive at a place of total tolerance and acceptance.

It seems rather easy to call conservatives "religious extremists." Whatever you think of him, Jerry Falwell once rightly noted that people who are pro-choice and pro–gay marriage are called progressive, while people who are pro-life and pro-family are called extremist. There's nothing more extreme about the latter position, of course, but "extremist" is a very useful label for inciting irrational fear and *decreasing* tolerance and understanding.

The myth of the conservative religious extremist will undoubtedly live on. The Left is far too attached to it to let go now. In the meantime, we'll just have to work on our gag reflex to prepare for that inevitable question posed to every conservative at some point in his or her life: "Can't we all just get along?"

CHAPTER 13

Republicans
Love Them Their Guns

The Myth of the Idiot Cowboy

The hunter gets up early, before daybreak. While shaving, he cuts his face. He tastes the blood and it is good. His desire for the prey has become sexual.

—Richard C. Suquer[1]

Popular culture has done a brilliant job of portraying conservatives as gun toting cowboys who would just as soon shoot at a pigtailed schoolgirl carrying a box full of puppies as they would run a stop sign. The left has maligned hunters and gun owners to the point of absurdity. In 2007, *Time* magazine named the animated Disney film *Bambi* one of the top twenty-five horror movies of all time, because of a scene in which the title deer's mother is shot and killed by hunters. "*Bambi*, directed by David Hand, has a primal shock that still haunts oldsters who saw it 40, 50, 65 years ago."[2] As Chandler said in a memorable episode of *Friends,* when asked if he cried when Bambi's mother died, "Yes, it was so sad when the guy stopped drawing the deer."[3] Michael Moore's documentary *Bowling for Columbine* focused much of its criticism on American gun culture, the so-called ease with which Americans can get guns (the scene in which Moore is offered a rifle as a free-gift-with-purchase for opening a bank account is particularly memorable), and the white man's obsession with firearms, all of which, he claimed, made possible the Columbine killings. (Dylan Klebold and Eric Harris were, apparently, just the messengers.) Charlton Heston contributed to this image when he famously promised, at a 2000 NRA convention, that presidential candidate Al Gore would have to take his Second Amendment rights "from [his] cold, dead hands."

But just how accurate is this characterization? There are of course countless gun advocates on the left, dozens of progun groups backed by Democrats, and a whole contingent of Democrats who won elections by siding with the pro-gun Right. Montana's Democratic governor Brian Schweitzer says of how many guns he owns: "More than I need, but less than I want."[4] In fact, several high-profile Republicans (or at least politicians who call themselves Republicans) are among the most vocal supporters of increased gun control, including the Terminator himself, California governor Arnold Schwarzenegger.

To be fair and honest, Republicans are arguably more comfortable with guns and gun ownership than Democrats. Much of this acceptance can be attributed to the conservative affinity for constitutionality. Although the Second Amendment of the Constitution says that "a well regulated Militia, being necessary to the security of a free State, the right of the people to keep and bear Arms, shall not be infringed," Second Amendment law is largely unsettled. In fact, in March 2007, for the first time ever, a federal court struck down a gun-control law for violating the Second Amendment.

Previously, the Second Amendment was widely assumed to protect only the collective right of the states to maintain militias. Even more surprising, the Supreme Court has never ruled on the constitutional boundaries of the Second Amendment.

Other countries have tried to follow the United States constitutional model and drafted Second Amendment provisions to their constitutions. For example, Cuba's reads " . . . all citizens have the right to struggle through all means, including armed struggle. . . ." Mexico's says that "The inhabitants of the United Mexican States are entitled to have arms of any kind in their possession for their protection and legitimate defense, except such as are expressly forbidden by law, or which the nation may reserve for the exclusive use of the Army, Navy, or National Guard; but they may not carry arms within inhabited places without complying with police regulations."

It may be inaccurate to call the Republican defense of gun ownership, whether from a Second Amendment perspective or not, a myth. But it's not the whole story. While it's true that more Republicans than Democrats own guns, the popular idea that most Republicans own a gun is entirely unfounded. In February 2006, Gallup released a new study revealing that 30 percent of Americans said they personally own a gun, and 12 percent said a member of their household owns a gun. Where 24 percent of Democrats reported owning guns, barely twice that number—41 percent—of Republicans claimed the same. Not even half the population of American Republicans owns a gun.[5]

But as is true with most social causes du jour, the discomfort with guns is not about the numbers. The gun issue is a particularly complicated one. Americans have very visceral feelings on the right to bear arms, self-defense, animal rights and hunting, and gun-related crime, all of which are at the center of gun-control debates. But conservatives who argue for pro-gun legislation are characterized as callous, rash, irresponsible, backward, and even murderous, while liberals who argue for antigun legislation, no matter how invalid or thin their case, are routinely described as humanitarians. And the real disservice to this categorization is that it ignores a huge contingent of Americans who are for the Second Amendment, but advocate common sense restrictions—Americans like Red Sox pitcher Curt Schilling. "I am absolutely for the right to bear arms, but I also think there is absolutely no reason whatsoever for the common citizen to have access to automatic weapons. What is the real problem with having to wait five days to actually take ownership of a weapon? How many deaths might have been prevented with a more thorough set of laws in place to make that happen?"[6]

So what's really at the heart of the beef with guns? We can divide the arguments for and against gun control into two broad categories—crime and hunting, which are inextricably linked to the stereotypes surrounding so-called Republican gun culture. So what do guns really have to do with crime, and what's so bad about the hunter?

Let's look at hunting, for starters. America, like every other country in the world, has enjoyed a long love affair with hunting, and the reason is simple: Humans have always hunted. It is in our DNA to hunt and gather. According to a study conducted by Responsive Management in 2006, 78 percent of Americans approved of hunting. (This statistic does not include those who approve of fishing—nine out of 10.[7]) This means that while more than three quarters of the nation are not gun owners, necessarily, they support the rights of the legal hunter. Thus, categorizing this group as fringe or "backwoods" is inaccurate, and unfairly conjures images of Ned Beatty running naked through Georgia, oinking to dueling banjos. Those who argue that times have changed, that supermarkets and a readily available food supply make hunting unnecessary, should try that out on those Americans who still rely on hunting for some of their food supply—Americans who, inexplicably, do not have regular access to five-dollar lattes and hand-delivered Zone meals. Unlike the leftover pan-seared venison medallions you brought home from Le Cirque, a good-size buck can feed a family for weeks if cleaned and stored properly.

But hunting is more than just a lifestyle or a pastime. The industry contributes in huge numbers to our nation's economy and welfare. In 2001, more than 13 million hunters averaged eighteen days hunting and spent more than $20.5 billion on their sport.[8] In many cases, hunting organizations and interest groups are responsible for huge successes in land preservation efforts. In 2004 the Rocky Mountain Elk Foundation reported that over a twenty-year period it had preserved or improved some 4 million acres of habitat for a variety of wildlife.[9] Hunting is a widely recognized and efficient way of controlling wildlife populations, and in rural areas where man and animal share space, it is often the only means of self-defense. Deer, according to Frank Miniter's *Politically Incorrect Guide to Hunting*, a book rife with unpopular statistics, "kill ten times more people each year than sharks, cougars, bears, and alligators combined, and more people than all commercial airline, train, and bus accidents combined. No alternative methods of reducing the number of deer-vehicle collisions are as effective as hunting."[10] Moreover, hunting has been proven to limit and prevent animal attacks on people and domestic animals, especially in the cases of coyotes, wolves, alligators, and bears, where nonlethal alternatives have proven ineffective. Farmers and vegetarians are also indebted to hunters in ways animal rights activists may not want to admit. According to the book, "if hunting were ended nationally, the costs to taxpayers and consumers would be in the billions because of wildlife damage to crops." In fact, "Every cabbage, carrot, and apple we eat is raised by farmers who kill deer, rabbits, or rodents that would eat them out of business if left unchecked."

Indeed, the modern American hunter performs a service for which he or she should be commended, not vilified. According to Miniter, "Modern hunters in the US have never caused a wildlife species to become extinct, endangered, or even threatened. In fact, every game species that is hunted in the US has increased in number."[11] Moreover, hunters are one of the more philanthropic groups of enthusiasts in the United States, with organizations like Farmers and Hunters Feeding the Hungry processing "1,600 tons (nearly 12,800,000 servings) of venison and other big game for soup kitchens and food pantries" between 1997 and 2004.[12]

Morality and environmentalism aside, hunting is also one of the safest activities adults and children can enjoy, as surprising as it sounds. Hunting, unlike many other athletic activities, requires participants in most states to pass a rigorous safety course and maintain proper hunting etiquette and safety measures while in the field, with severe penalties for disobedience. A hunter's odds of getting killed while in the field are less than five in a million, while the odds of dying while playing organized football is over twice that.[13]

While even hardened liberals should be able to see why hunters should keep their guns, convincing the Left that rabid gun control won't stop crime is another story. No one wants to put dangerous weapons in the hands of children, but those who want to take them away from adult American citizens do the nation, and themselves, a huge disservice. The National Center for Policy Analysis published a number of compelling statistics commenting on the popular myths about gun control that would make any rational personal question the efficacy of such initiatives.[14] Here are just a few:

* After Evanston, Ill., a Chicago suburb of 75,000 residents, became the largest [U.S.] town to ban handgun ownership in September 1982, it experienced no decline in violent crime.
* Among the 15 states with the highest homicide rates, 10 have restrictive or very restrictive gun laws.
* Twenty percent of U.S. homicides occur in four cities with just 6 percent of the population—New York, Chicago, Detroit and Washington, D.C.—and each has a virtual prohibition on private handguns.

* Each year, gun-wielding citizens kill an estimated 2,000 to 3,000 criminals in self-defense, three times the number killed by police. They wound another 9,000 to 17,000 criminals each year.
* The accidental shooting of an innocent person mistaken for an intruder occurs in fewer than 30 fatal firearm incidents a year, about 2 percent of all fatal firearms incidents.
* At a maximum, criminals take a gun away from armed victims only 1 percent of the time (while 10 percent of police who are shot are shot with their own guns).

Additional statistics from other sources are just as provocative:

* As of 2006, the crime rates in the 40 right-to-carry states fell or remained the same after the right-to-carry laws were enacted.
* The serious crime rate in Texas fell 50 percent after it passed a concealed carry law in 1995.
* Robberies occur at a 105 percent higher rate in restrictive states than they do in states with less restrictive gun laws. Murders occur at an 86 percent higher rate, and assaults at an 82 percent higher rate.
* In Florida, which has allowed concealed carry since 1987, you are twice as likely to be attacked by an alligator [as] by a person with a concealed carry permit.[15]

These kinds of findings are not exclusive to the United States. The Fraser Institute released a paper in November 2003 entitled "The Failed Experiment: Gun Control and Public Safety in Canada, Australia, England and Wales." The study found that:

Restrictive firearm legislation has failed to reduce gun violence in Australia, Canada, or Great Britain. The policy of confiscating guns has been an expensive failure. Disarming the public has not reduced criminal violence in any country examined in this study. In all these cases, disarming the public has been ineffective, expensive, and often counterproductive. In all cases, the effort meant setting up expensive bureaucracies that produce no noticeable improvement to public safety or have made the situation worse.[16]

Gary Mauser, author of the paper says, "What makes gun control so compelling for many is the belief that violent crime is driven by the availability of guns, and more importantly, that criminal violence in general may be reduced by limiting access to firearms."

In the wake of the killings at Virginia Tech by student Cho Seung-Hui, Fred Thompson, a former U.S. senator campaigning for the Republican presidential nomination, suggested that, had students been allowed to carry concealed weapons on campus, Cho might have been stopped. "Some people think that power should exist only at the top, and everybody else should rely on 'the authorities' for protection. Despite such attitudes, average Americans have always made up the front line against crime. Through programs like Neighborhood Watch and Amber Alert, we are stopping and catching criminals daily. Normal people tackled 'shoe bomber' Richard Reid as he was trying to blow up an airliner. It was a truck driver who found the D.C. snipers. Statistics from the Centers for Disease Control and Prevention show that civilians use firearms to prevent at least a half million crimes annually."[17]

Time magazine's David Von Drehle wrote a compelling opinion piece on the Virginia Tech massacre and others before it. In it, he argued that killers like Cho Seung-Hui are united by ego—that it's not guns or violent video games or song lyrics that emboldened these murderers, but the fact that they are "raging narcissists."[18]

Following the Virginia Tech tragedy, we heard the familiar outcry over the role of guns in mass murders. But few of our nation's greatest tragedies would have been prevented by more restrictive gun-control laws. Cho, a mentally ill student who killed thirty-two people and himself that day, carried with him two semiautomatic pistols that he bought legally during the months before the shooting. The killers in the Columbine massacre, Dylan Klebold and Eric Harris, also used guns, but they were obtained illegally. They also carried homemade explosive devices. Timothy McVeigh killed 168 people when he bombed the Murrah Building in Oklahoma City. David Koresh killed 79 people when he set fire to his own Branch Davidian compound in Waco, Texas. Killers, and those intent on killing, will use whatever they can to carry out their plans. September 11 is proof of that—not a single gun was fired that day.

"Logic is alive and well in the America that I hang out with," said Ted Nugent in an interview about guns and popular culture. "When the coyotes are attacking, killing and eating the cats in our barn, I personally don't know anyone of intellect or decency that would be so insane as to declaw the cats. Unarmed helplessness is soulless and dangerously irresponsible, and I believe complicit in the next crime committed by the perpetrators we fail to shoot."[19]

Nugent is a bona-fide rock star and legendary guitar player. His television shows "Surviving Nugent" and "Wanted: Ted or Alive" highlight his passion for hunting and survivalism. He is author of *God, Guns and Rock & Roll, Kill It and Grill It: A Guide to Preparing and Cooking Wild Game and Fish,* and *Blood Trails II: The Truth About Bow-Hunting.* His shock-rocking antics in the 1970s earned him a permanent place in the hearts of rock fans, and now his political views continue to shock . . . *and* make a ton of sense.

Touchy-feely bumper stickers like "Bear Hugs, Not Arms" reflect the popular notion that arming our citizens will make them more violent. Nugent, unsurprisingly, does not agree.

It is not a "popular sentiment" that hardware of any kind plays a role in crime or evil conduct. It is, rather, a mental derangement of a lunatic fringe. The liberal cult of denial began with the beatnik and hippie nonculture, which was so dedicated to its cowardly and irresponsible, "comfortably numb" retreat from accountability. The mind-altering religion of substance abuse so thoroughly fogged their brains that they conveniently deny the most discomforting parts of life, and therefore, scramble maniacally to create policies that facilitate recidivism by ignoring evil itself. No thinking human being, for example, could possibly believe that "war is not the answer" when Nazis and their like did and do what they do. The cult of denial has fixated on firearms and refuses to hear a single word of the tsunami of evidence that so completely guts their fantasy. Liberals are a criminal's best friend.

Indeed, in addition to Nugent's unabashed love of hunting, he sees the right to bear arms as a fundamentally human one. "The instinctual urge to protect and procure sustenance is ultimately powerful in all humankind. Though a mother's instinct to do so is unstoppable, I believe the same dynamic surges in men to protect and care for the female so they can deliver and mother our children. For all of us, weapons provide unlimited utility in life."

But he recognizes that, as an entertainer and celebrity, his views are not very popular among his own kind. He attributes that to the superficiality of Hollywood and the liberal media.

I believe that if we could get an honest answer from many of the public figures who espouse a liberal bent in public, that most of them either own a gun or would admit that they and all good people certainly have the right to self-defense. Unfortunately, many celebrities are slaves to their careers and are not only scared to death to make statements against the pulse of the media who they feel control them, but are badgered by management and industry bosses who constantly tell them not to say anything politically incorrect.

Nugent's opinions may sound aggressive and even shocking to the moderate, and downright disturbing to the liberal. But at the heart of his views is a commitment to life and liberty, something no one can really criticize. For the record, the Nuge was pulling for Fred Thompson in '08.

Guns and their many uses, whether self-defense, sport, or survival, are not necessarily integral to the conservative way of life, but the Second Amendment is. While hunting certainly isn't an activity everyone participates in or even agrees with, it is a huge part of antiright mythology, and one that is routinely used by the Left to cast Republicans as irresponsible, murderous, backward, and dangerous. Incidentally, if you're looking to dip your toes into the world of hunting, Nugent has the following advice to get started:

> It is always best to master a simple bolt-action, single-shot, open-sighted .22 rifle that feels good in your hands. With proper ear and eye protection, discover the critical relationship of hand-eye coordination between sight acquisition and trigger-squeeze at short range, say twenty to thirty yards. Once mastered, try longer ranges, then move up to the big game rifle in caliber, action, and design that feels good and is appropriate for the game you wish to hunt.

Advice from a rock star never sounded so good.

CHAPTER 14

Republicans Are Sexist

The Myth of the Misogynist Conservative

A recent event for high-ranking women in the Bush administration was titled "W is for Women." Translation: "W" is for
women who are wealthy and well-connected enough to parlay
their political support into powerful and high-paying jobs.
There's nothing wrong with that, except those women slam
the door behind them as they enjoy the "more." Let's raise our
voices to say that war is not peace, ignorance is not strength,
and "W" is NOT for women.[1]

—Kim Gandy, president of the
National Organization for Women

The left-wing website BeggarsCanBeChoosers.com, which claims
to present "news and opinions with a progressive viewpoint,"
adroitly puts the myth of the woman-hating conservative on full
view. In an essay asserting that Republicans really hate Hillary

Clinton because they "can't stand strong-willed women," writer Marc McDonald contends, "Trying to fathom the various hatreds of the Republicans these days is always a tricky exercise. After all, these are people who despise saintly figures like Jimmy Carter. How, exactly, does one go about hating someone like Carter? It's like hating Mother Teresa." Unless Mother Teresa also visited with terrorist dictators like Fidel Castro, criticized sitting U.S. presidents, and made unfortunate anti-Semitic remarks, it is absolutely possible to hate one and not the other.

The article goes on to explain that an underlying fear of women in positions of power serves as the foundation for the Right's misogynistic modus operandi. "Republicans know damn well that a significant part of their base supports 'traditional family values'—which is simply code for keeping women in their place as docile, cookie-baking homemakers. It's important to remember that for all of the boasting that our nation does about being some sort of 'beacon' of human rights, the fact is, today's America still harbors tens of millions of bigots, whose views on race and gender haven't changed much in the past 100 years. And what party do you think these bigots vote for? It sure as hell ain't the Democrats."[2]

Extreme sites like this aren't the only sources of rhetoric that envisions Republicans (even the women, it would seem) as evil puppet masters to the helpless and mindless papier-mâché voter dolls they control. It's hard to imagine a more insulting viewpoint. Pop culture often caricatures Republicans as members of some stuffy and archaic boys' club where women are either used or laughed at. At the 2007 Emmy Awards, actress Sally Field, well-known for memorable if quixotic acceptance speeches, seemed to confuse her television role on *Brothers and Sisters* with her real life. On that show she plays a mother whose son is about to go to war. In accepting her Emmy she said, "This [award] belongs to all the mothers in the world—may they be seen, may their work be valued and praised—and especially to mothers who stand with an open heart and wait—wait for their children to come home—from danger, from harm's way and from war. I am proud to be one of those women." But it's what she said next that summed up the stereotypical view of conservatives as antiwomen: "If mothers ruled the world there would be no goddamn wars." Field's public challenge to Republicans is an insight into a shared liberal belief that mothers are inherently caring (and therefore liberal) and conservatives are inherently uncaring—and therefore male.

Just after Nancy Pelosi was elected Speaker of the House, a cartoon by Pulitzer Prize–winning artist Ann Telnaes depicted two boulder-shaped, bald, bespectacled, suit-wearing lawmakers at a Washington restaurant (we know they are meant to be Republicans because they are equipped with two *other* stereotypical accoutrements—a martini and a giant steak). One says to the other, "I don't know what upsets me more—that the Democrats control the House or that a woman controls the House." But more than their drawn counterparts, actual flesh-and-blood lawmakers are taking up the Republicans-As-Sexist cause. Democratic New York representative Louise Slaughter unimaginably analogized, thanks to some clever alliteration, the Bush administration's treatment of women to the ravages of actual war. "I want to express my outrage at the Bush administration's way to wage devastating war on women from the first day he took office. The women in America knew from the past 4 years that 'W' is for War on Women."[3] In August 2004, when the Republican National Convention came to New York City, the National Organization for Women (NOW) organized rallies to protest "the Bush Administration's efforts to dismantle and undermine women's rights."[4] NOW-NYC president Rita Haley said, "While distortions and misrepresentations of the Administration's record are told at Madison Square Garden and the public is told that 'W is for Women,' we'll be telling the truth about the Administration's assault on women's rights, including reproductive freedom and the other civil rights we've fought so hard to gain."[5] The National Organization for Women even voted in July 2004 to declare an *immediate state of emergency* through the day of the election in an attempt to unseat George W. Bush.[6] A state of emergency—because, in case you missed it, being a woman these days is apparently akin to living in the Ninth Ward when the levees broke.

Somehow, defending a woman's right to raise a family, reducing the size of government, and opposing abortion are now code for keeping women in the kitchen, or even worse, waging war on them. The genesis of the sexist myth stems from several sources. Carrie Lukas, who is a vice president of policy at the Independent Women's Forum (IWF), a nonprofit organization whose "mission is to rebuild civil society by advancing economic liberty, personal responsibility, and political freedom,"[7] explains the stereotype as the result of sound bites—cute, catchy, and clever bon mots routinely spat out by liberal feminists, activists, academics, and even politicians in mainstream media. She says, "The modern feminist movement isn't about achieving equality for women—a goal that has essentially been achieved and is just about universally supported in the United States. When Hillary Clinton or the National Organization for Women calls for a big government policy, whether it's federally funded daycare or greater regulation of how businesses compensate workers, it's easy for liberals or the mainstream media to paint the opposition as 'antiwoman.' There are serious unintended consequences to big government programs, but those aren't easily explained in the thirty-second sound bite. It leaves conservatives vulnerable to being unfairly caricatured as antiwoman." Lukas also says that "the abortion debate has certainly made it easier for liberals and the media to caricature conservatives, and particularly pro-lifers, as unsympathetic to women."[8]

Much like African Americans who vote Republican, women who vote Republican are often subject to the most scathing criticism of all, cast as pawns and vulnerable dimwits either brainwashed or too dumb to know what they're doing. Feminist activist Gloria Steinem, who once went undercover at the Playboy mansion and revealed the not-so-surprising news that sexism was rampant there, called Republican senator Kay Bailey Hutchinson a "female impersonator," and said, "Having someone who looks like us but thinks like them is worse than having no one at all."[9] Kay Bailey Hutchinson, the first woman Senate majority leader, should serve as a model for women of every political bent—though her historical significance is utterly irrelevant, or at least inconvenient, to someone like Steinem.

K. T. McFarland, a prominent national security advisor and speechwriter in the Reagan administration, addressed the perception that a woman who chooses to get married and raise a family, rather than, say, protest marriage, as Steinem once suggested women should do, is taking an awkward and even dangerous step backward. (Incidentally, Steinem is herself married now.)

> I am one of those women who had to fight against extraordinary odds to get an education and have a career in a field normally reserved for men (national security). I firmly believe that the greatest advance of the sixties and seventies was that women for the first time in world history had the right to choose—choose whether they wanted a career, a family, or both. As the women of the eighties, nineties, and today struggle to find a balance between personal and professional lives, none of us should criticize the choices women make. That was what the women's movement was all about—to give us choices. It is as wrong for people in the twenty-first century to criticize a woman for choosing to be a traditional mother as it was for people in the twentieth century to criticize a woman for having a career.[10]

Ironically (and sadly), when a woman chooses not to have children and goes on to have a brilliant career, she is still attacked by left-wing feminists if her politics are not liberal. During a hearing in Congress in January 2007, Democratic senator from California Barbara Boxer underhandedly sneered at Condoleezza Rice's unmarried status when she asked, about the war in Iraq, "Who pays the price? I'm not going to pay a personal price. My kids are too old and my grandchild is too young. You're not going to pay a particular price, as I understand it, with an immediate family. So who pays the price? The American military and their families."[11] Rice responded afterward by saying, "I thought it was OK to be single. I thought it was OK to not have children and I thought you could still make good decisions on behalf of the country if you were single and didn't have children."[12] Indeed, it would seem that the Republican woman who chooses to not get married or have children is an unsympathetic and hysterectomized she-man, incapable of thinking like a real woman. Likewise, the Republican woman who chooses to settle down, get married, and raise a family is a backward-time-traveling Donna Reed, singlehandedly erasing the women's lib movement from history books. For the Left, apparently, women of value are supposed to be like Hollywood's young starlets—married and unmarried over and over again, pregnant by whichever celebrity or behind-the-scenes man they happened to be bedding at the time, and allowing inexperienced, fame-hungry models/nannies to raise their children while they tipsily make the rounds at Les Deux and Hyde.

Much like the perception that Republicans are racist, the notion that Republicans are sexist is contradicted by historical facts. On August 18, 1920, state legislator Harry Burn cast the deciding vote that made Tennessee the thirty-sixth (and deciding) state to ratify the Nineteenth Amendment, granting women the right to vote. Harry Burn was a Republican (a fact overlooked by the group Tennessee Women for John Kerry, who posed the question on their website, "Why is this Tennessee man so important?").[13] In fact, before 1920, passage of the Nineteenth Amendment had been blocked by southern Democrats. In 1919, Republicans established a majority in the Senate, and it was then that the amendment was passed and sent to the states for ratification.

Another historical source of the sexist-conservative myth is the perception that Republicans opposed passage of the controversial Equal Rights Amendment (ERA), which would have guaranteed equal rights under the law regardless of sex. Although there is no longer much serious discussion about ERA passage, it has been introduced in every Congress since 1982, most recently by Senator Ted Kennedy and Representative Carolyn Maloney. Going back to the early movement to pass the ERA, however, it was two Republicans from Kansas, Senator Charles Curtis and Representative Daniel R. Anthony, Jr., who first introduced the amendment in 1923. Some of the most fervent early opposition to the ERA also came from the Left, with the American Federation of Labor, labor unions generally, and many New Deal Democrats, including Eleanor Roosevelt, opposing the legislation on the grounds that women would be forced to compete with men in the workplace.

Republican support of the ERA was actually part of the official party platform until 1980, when support was qualified. Led by conservative Republican activist Phyllis Schlafly, more Republicans began opposing the ERA on grounds that it would expand the power of the federal government and federal beauracracy and because of the feminist political movement that supported the ERA. It was not sexism that led people like Schlafly, who organized the Stop the ERA movement, to oppose the amendment, but a fear that erasing all distinctions between men and women would lead to a catastrophic loss of identity and rights—resulting in the elimination of laws that actually protected women, and federally mandated unisex bathrooms. Eventually, support for the ERA became associated with left-wing feminist groups like NOW.

Republican women represent many important firsts for women in government. Republican Jennifer Dunn was the first woman majority leader in the House of Representatives. Republican Kay Bailey Hutchinson was the first woman majority leader in the Senate. Republican Jeanette Rankin was the first woman elected to the House of Representatives, and Republican Sandra Day O'Connor was the first woman appointed to the Supreme Court.

Despite many accomplishments and support for women's rights, however, Republicans continue to be caricatured as the party of men. Without a doubt, no single modern-day issue has contributed to this myth more than the abortion debate and the Republican Party's association with the pro-life position. And while it is true that Republicans are more likely to adopt the pro-life position, the significance of that position is more complex than generally portrayed. A January 2003 CBS News/*New York Times* poll of Americans found the following:

* Overall, 39% believe abortion should be "generally available," 38% believe it should be available but with stricter limits and 22% believe it should not be permitted.
* 74% of women believe it should be available, with half of that group feeling it should be "generally available" and half believing that it should be more strictly limited. The remaining 26% felt it should not be permitted.
* 80% of men actually believe abortion should be available, with half of men feeling it should be "generally available" and half supporting stricter limitations. The remaining 20% feel it should not be permitted.
* When it comes to party breakdown, 43% of Democrats support the general availability of abortion, 35% support the right with stricter limitations and 21% feel it should not be available.
* Among Republicans, 29% support general availability, 41% support availability with stricter limits and 28% say it should not be permitted.
* Last, Independents support general availability at a 42% rate, availability with stricter limitations at a 38% rate and non-availability at an 18% rate.[14]

A May 2007 poll of Americans conducted by CNN found 45 percent identified as pro-choice and 50 percent identified as pro-life, and some even accused CNN of trying to cover up the surprising result that more people identify as pro-life than pro-choice.[15] A Gallup Poll conducted around the same time found 49 percent identified as pro-choice and 45 percent as pro-life.[16] These polls reveal some interesting things. First, for a right that is supposedly so "fundamental" it deserves the constitutional protection afforded by *Roe* v. *Wade,* public opinion is certainly divided. Second, the CBS News/*New York Times* poll shows that 70 percent of Republicans actually favor a woman's right to an abortion in some circumstances. This compares with 78 percent of Democrats who favor the woman's right in at least some circumstances, a difference of opinion that is quite narrow.

So, what is one to take away from these numbers? As usual, what many Republicans are saying when it comes to women's rights, and in fact what many Americans are saying on the issue of abortion rights, is being misrepresented. Of course a very large number of people who oppose abortion do so on moral and religious grounds, believing that life begins before birth and that abortion constitutes murder. As IWF vice president Carrie Lukas explains, the issue is not just about women. "It isn't antiwoman to believe that life begins at conception and that life deserves protection."[17] Conservative pundit Glenn Beck says the pro-life position isn't necessarily political. "I see [abortion] simply as a life issue. We either respect life or we don't. Twenty years ago, before technology advanced, we said that life wasn't viable before a certain amount of time has elapsed. Today, that time period has gotten considerably shorter. Life is life, it always has been. This shouldn't be a conservative issue . . . the roles should be flipped. Liberals should be the ones fighting for the weakest among us, and conservatives should be fighting to be able to make their own decisions."[18] In that sense, it could be argued that the pro-life position should be one embraced more enthusiastically by the Left.

Jay D. Homnick, in a 2005 issue of *The American Spectator,* sums up the Republican position on abortion as a compelling combination of intellect and gut: "If you think that abortion is a medical procedure of utmost privacy that is arrived at through a mystical confluence of a woman's agonizing choice and a physician's gentle counsel, you're a Democrat. If you think that it's just a form of retroactive birth control, you're also a Democrat. If you think that it has no moral component, you're a super Democrat. If you think that a human fetus in the womb is a baby who feels pain but is helpless, then you're a scientist. There is no original Republican position on this, other than to respect the science and protect that child."[19]

But for many others, the debate is not about when life begins but is a question of the proper role of government, which has nothing to do with being anti–women's rights. There are many Republicans who support a woman's right to choose but believe that *Roe* v. *Wade* was a poorly decided case (driven by the same legal reasoning that led to the Civil War–era *Dred Scott* decision, which held that blacks constitute property) and that a woman's right to choose should be decided by state governments, not justices on the Supreme Court.

Left-wing feminist organizations also help perpetuate the myth of the women-hating Republican by pointing not just to the abortion issue but to the "gender gap" in America. As Dennis Prager, conservative syndicated radio talk show host, says, "It is inaccurate to speak of a 'gender gap' in Americans' voting. The gap is between married and unmarried women. Single women, especially single women with children, tend to vote Democratic, while married women, especially married women with children, tend to vote Republican."[20] In an analysis that must make NOW members cringe, Prager goes on to say that once a woman marries, "Her need for the state not only diminishes, she now begins to view the state as inimical to her interests. . . . Her urge to be protected, which is now fulfilled by her husband, and her primal urge to protect her nest are now endangered by the government, which as it grows, takes away more and more of her family's money."[21]

So, according to Prager, it is not that the conservative cause conflicts with the interests of women, only that it tends to conflict with the interests of unmarried women (and, in fact, unmarried men as well). The numbers show that Prager, at the very least, is partially correct. Before the 2004 election, a *USA Today* poll revealed that most married women intended to vote for George Bush, whereas unmarried women supported Kerry by a two to one margin. Similarly, married men supported Bush over Kerry 56 percent to 39 percent, whereas unmarried men supported Kerry over Bush 55 percent to 40 percent.[22]

Carrie Lukas also discussed the supposed "gender gap," which Hillary Clinton has attempted to make into an issue this election season. Senator Clinton has reintroduced the Paycheck Fairness Act, which would require employers to prove that they are not discriminating against women if there are disparities in wages. Lukas explained that "women often make very different decisions about careers than men make. Women take off more time to care for children . . . gravitate toward different careers—careers that provide some flexibility so we have more time to spend with families. And even full-time women on average spend about a half-an-hour less per day in the office than men do."[23] Is that a bad thing that perpetuates a patriarchal society? Says Lukas, "Liberals may characterize opposition to workplace regulations as sexist, but conservatives know that this is simply bad policy that can have serious consequences. Imagine if Senator Clinton had her way and the government created a bunch of new regulations and enforcement measures that would micromanage how companies set wages. The very job opportunities that many women crave would become scarcer. If I'm an employer worried about a lawsuit, I'm going to be less willing to negotiate creative arrangements that allow workers to work part-time or from home in exchange for less compensation. That isn't good for women."[24]

So, not only is it unfair to say that conservatives are hostile to women's interests, but conservatives, historically and still today, proactively seek to protect women's interests in ways that are often downplayed. For example, many conservatives are opposed to the proliferation of pornography in society because it objectifies women as sexual objects. Although some feminist groups would agree on this point, many postmodern feminists depart from the critique and consider it part of the liberation and choice of women. Conservatives support harsher penalties for perpetrators of sex crimes. Some Republican women gravitate toward conservatism because they see a commitment to limited government as a real boon to women, and a sign that lawmakers who advocate for less government trust women to make their own decisions about how to spend their money. And others still feel as though the angry cries of modern feminists do not apply to them and force them into uncomfortable boxes that limit their creativity, self-expression, identity as women, and freedoms. The woman who is looked down upon by liberal feminists for getting married or going to church may *become* a Republican if she wasn't already. In admonishing women for making their own decisions, liberal feminists are often sending them right into enemy territory. For good.

Lukas explained that at the IWF, they have a saying that "all issues are women's issues" and that what makes "an administration good for women is advancing the conservative agenda of limiting government and returning power to the people." While Lukas feels as though the Bush administration has not done enough to curb the growth of government and bureaucracy, which would ultimately benefit women, it has "been very outspoken and active in advancing the rights of women overseas, [and that] is where the real attention of any legitimate women's movement needs to focus their attention." Lukas also has high praise for the Reagan administration, which she said is "the only administration that I believe deserves note as advancing women's welfare . . . and that's not because he advanced some pet project specifically to women; it's because Reagan cut taxes and reduced regulations. Women have greatly prospered in the modern economy, which has made it so much easier to find jobs and start businesses. That is part of Ronald Reagan's legacy."

Conversely, Lukas says liberal groups like NOW have very little genuine interest in advancing women's rights. NOW's current brochure admittedly promises, "NOW is one of the few multi-issue progressive organizations in the United States. NOW stands against all oppression, recognizing that racism, sexism and homophobia are interrelated, that other forms of oppression such as classism and ableism work together with these three to keep power and privilege concentrated in the hands of a few."[25] Lukas responds by explaining that, in reality, "[NOW's] mission is to grow government. It is another rent-seeking interest group that exists to obtain government-funded favors for women. They want government-funded health care, child care and preschool; they oppose reforms of the education system or our entitlement programs that would put more power in the hands of individuals. They want more regulation of the workplace." At the end of the day, groups like NOW and liberal feminists "want the government to create rules and regulations to favor women," and "the whole liberal concept that women need help from Uncle Sam to survive is itself sexist. . . . Conservatives simply don't believe that's the government's proper role and also don't believe that tearing men down builds women up."[26]

Gloria Steinem once famously said, "A liberated woman is one who has sex before marriage and a job after," a slam against both the woman with religious or moral convictions and the woman who chooses to work outside the home. Who could blame anyone, liberal or conservative, for rejecting this imagining of a woman's identity as shaped merely by her apathy toward god, men, and family? What would liberal feminists like Steinem prefer that women do with their lives? Chase a paycheck? Fawn over this season's must-have ballerina flat? Seek out the destruction of all mankind to leave women atop the food chain? When one really looks at the so-called women's interest factions, it becomes clear that the "war" being waged here isn't against women. It's against freedom. The feminist today, much like the liberal, is enslaved by a need to fulfill a laundry list of dogmatic criteria that locates her squarely and resolutely in a single camp, whether she actually aligns with all of those criteria or not.

John Fund, in a *Wall Street Journal* article in 2007, made this observation about forcing a viewpoint on unwilling audiences. "Then there's the GreenStone talk radio network started last year by feminists Jane Fonda and Gloria Steinem. It offered cutting-edge liberal thinking pitched to a female audience—and flopped completely."[27] Maybe there's a reason. This faction, led by Fonda, Steinem, and groups like NOW, preserves the image of a white-male conservative boogeyman who is constantly trying to repress women's advances, thus maintaining the relevancy of the feminist message. Given how this boogeyman is cast, perhaps these groups ought to change their official slogan to "Women, stay home until further notice! It's a state of emergency out there!"

CHAPTER 15

Republicans Are Greedy

The Myth of the Money-Hungry Conservative

Apparently, there is no bad economic turn a conservative cannot do unto his buddy in the working class, as long as cultural solidarity has been cemented over a beer.
—Thomas Frank, *What's the Matter With Kansas?*

In 2004, Thomas Frank asked, rather rudely, *What's the Matter With Kansas?* in his book of the same name, which examined the voting tendencies of Middle American Republicans. In it, he claimed that poor and middle class Americans have been hoodwinked into voting for economic policies that actually hurt them, tricked by calculating and money-hungry conservatives who use cheap and transparent ploys (like pulling the God card) that appeal to their family values and American-dream aspirations.

Frank's missive against the thieving and conniving Republican Party is *very* disturbing, and incredibly insulting. It's also very old.

The Marxian trick of false consciousness arguments relies on its ability to claim ignorance somewhere (an accusation that is often impossible to prove). In this case, the ignorance is in Kansas and the rest of the square states. The basic premise is that nonwealthy Republicans vote conservative because they are too dumb to know what they're doing, and if only they could see the light, they would of course vote for the pious and all-knowing Democrats—and fare better economically for doing so. Frank doesn't just come out and say this, however, because though it may be dumb, Middle America don't take too kindly, gosh dangit, to insults. So instead he says things like the following:

> Old-fashioned values may count when conservatives appear on the stump, but once conservatives are in office the only old-fashioned situation they care to revive is an economic regimen of low wages and lax regulations. Over the last three decades they have smashed the welfare state, reduced the tax burden on corporations and the wealthy, and generally facilitated the country's return to a nineteenth-century pattern of wealth distribution. Thus the primary contradiction of the backlash: it is a working-class movement that has done incalculable, historic harm to working class people.[1]

And those poor, working-class folk don't even know it!

Jonah Goldberg, editor-at-large of *National Review,* discussed the problems with Frank's book, which include its inaccuracies ("The guy who reviewed it for *National Review* debunked all of his economic stuff—the factual assertions in the book are simply not true")[2] and the dangers it presents:

> My problem with the argument is not merely that he's calling conservatives rubes or stupid. But it's very similar to the race thing, in that it's this notion that somehow if you disagree with the economic analysis or the worldview of the Left, then

you must have it wrong. This is a really profoundly stupid argument on a lot of different levels. First of all, the idea that somehow politics is only legitimate when people are voting their economic interests is nonsense. That is rank materialism. And it's precisely the line of thought that the Left denounces rich people for having. The idea of the fat-cat Republican who basically only agrees with politics that help his bottom line is supposed to be evil, or at the very least is supposed to be an ignoble way of looking at politics when rich people do it. But according to Thomas Frank, when poor or middle-class people do it, it's friggin' brilliant. And when they don't do it, they're idiots. That's not really a man-of-the-people argument, is it?

Indeed, there are so many problems with Frank's argument that it seems silly to list them all here. The real problem is not *What's the Matter With Kansas?* anyway. It's the myth that props it up: Republicans are all about money. This manifests itself in a great many ways and can be seen in a number of submyths often used to characterize conservatives. There's the argument that corrupt corporate America serves and is served by Republicans and harms small-business owners and "the little guy." Or the argument that tax cuts really only benefit the wealthy. Or that conservative social policies concerning abortion and gay marriage are really just about the bottom line. And that, if only Democrats were running the country, we'd all have slightly larger bank accounts. But all of these submyths ignore some very important Facts of Life that we'd all do well to remember as we trot off to our local bookstore to pick up the next political best-seller, and more important as we head to the polls:

1. Money is a fact of life. It is a fact of America and the world at large. Politics must acknowledge (and deal with) the importance of the economy. Anyone who complains that *either* party is too focused on the economy had best be prepared to relocate to the nearest commune.

2. The Right does not own American wealth. *Both* parties have equally vibrant upper classes. After all, it's not called the "liberal elite" because they're buying their signed copies of the latest Dave Eggers book from Wal-Mart's half-off bin, or their mocha-half-caf-fraps at the local Piggly Wiggly.

3. The Left does not own the right to fix American poverty. *Both* parties speak to issues concerning the poor and the middle class (sometimes effectively, sometimes not) in an effort to make Americans more comfortable. Democrats can't characterize Republicans as both poor rednecks *and* fat-cat executives. Pick one.

4. Calling people stupid is generally a bad idea. And it's just mean.

These caveats, as simple and commonsense as they are, tend to fall by the wayside during election time, or any other time money and conservatism are brought up in tandem. It's bizarre that, for example, we are constantly reminded by liberals, the media, and pop culture at large that George W. Bush comes from a family of money and privilege—as if the Kennedys were coal miners from Pittsburgh. But a closer look at the ecumenical myth that Republicans are all about money and at the submyths concerning corporate America, tax cuts, and Republican economic platforms reveals that there's far less to these stereotypes than one might think.

It's difficult to factually prove that Republicans are *not* "all about money"—how do you prove a negative, especially one that's so ambiguous? Smart folks on the Left routinely cling to stereotypes like this *because* they are virtually impossible to justify or counter with any kind of evidence. But recent studies based on data from the IRS prove that states and districts represented by Democrats are in fact the wealthiest in the country, and that more than half of the wealthiest households are in the eighteen states headed by two Democratic senators.[3] According to Heritage Foundation vice president of government relations Michael Franc, the "pattern shows the likelihood of electing a Democrat to the House is very closely correlated with how many wealthy households are in that district."[4] Likewise, "The vast majority of unabashed conservative House members hail from profoundly middle-class districts."[5]

Voting tendencies also shed some light on the stereotype. America's upper class cannot be characterized as Republican when two of the country's wealthiest cities—New York and San Francisco—vote overwhelmingly Democratic. (Manhattan, as a borough, in fact, has not voted for a Republican in a national presidential election since 1924.)[6] Pundits argue that the Republican economic platform is far more beneficial to poor and middle-class populations than that of the Democrats. Deroy Murdock, a syndicated columnist, for one, defends the Right's fiscal policy as follows:

> If conservative policies are so hurtful, I would wonder, are liberals happy with an unemployment rate now at 4.4 percent or were they happier when Clinton left and it was about 6 percent? Are they happier with an economy that has expanded for something like five and a half straight years? Or are they happier with the previous situation, which was a slowdown while Clinton was in office? Would they prefer having their taxes reduced by something like $800 billion or having that money continue to pour into the Treasury? It seems to me that these policies are actually helpful to people in Kansas and elsewhere.[7]

Taxation is one of those incredibly divisive issues that polarizes the country, and it's often used to gauge just how conservative a conservative is. One of the best Sharptonisms—and there are many—commented on President Bush's tax cuts of 2001: "George Bush giving tax cuts is like Jim Jones giving Kool-Aid. It tastes good but it'll kill you."[8] Indeed, the promise of tax cuts—the horrifyingly misanthropic plan to let you keep more of your own money—elicits the kind of disproportionate outrage and hysteria we see during the defining moments of actual cultural crisis in America, like the "Tickle Me Elmo" panic of 1996. You'd think that tax cuts would sell themselves—after all, it's more money in your pocket. But what's surprising is not *that* we disagree on tax cuts, but *why* we disagree. While the issue is incredibly complicated, the argument for tax cuts is based on a few very simple and compelling points that make the fetishistic raising of taxes by the Left nearly impossible to justify.

"I would say there are three totally different arguments you can use to explain why it's so important to cut taxes,"[9] said Pat Toomey, head of the Club for Growth, a very powerful PAC that works to fund the campaigns of fiscally responsible conservatives—specifically, those who have a proven record of supporting tax cuts and limited government. The group is not shy about denouncing fellow conservatives who do not abide by strict fiscal conservatism, whom they have dubbed RINOs, "Republicans In Name Only." Toomey was a member of the House of Representatives from Pennsylvania from 1999 to 2005, and ran unsuccessfully in the Republican primary race for Senate against big-time RINO Arlen Specter in 2004. Toomey broke down the arguments for cutting taxes as follows:

> One is a fundamental argument for personal freedom. Obviously, the lower your taxes are, the more you're able to keep the fruits of your own labor. That means the freer you are to spend your own money, rather than someone else spending it. So at an ideological level, at a level of principle, if you think it's important for people to be free, then you have to support lower taxes. High taxes are a measure of the lack of freedom.
>
> A second argument for lower taxes is that it's a good way to starve the beast. You don't ever really put serious pressure on government to control spending and to reduce its size until you run some deficits and you put some political pressure on Washington to get spending under control. And we're seeing it now. We're seeing with record deficits that we're just beginning to get some traction on the idea that somewhere, you've got to draw the line on spending.

And the third reason that you ought to support lower taxes is that, especially if you lower them the right way—by that I mean lowering marginal tax rates, lowering or eliminating taxes on savings or investments—you get a very powerful response in terms of economic growth. Taxes impede economic growth. They never help. It's an unfortunate necessity to have a certain level of taxes, but when you're above that level you really impede the ability of our economy to prosper. So for all the things that we all should agree on, like higher wages and better standards of living and better unemployment rates and appreciation of asset values, all of these things happen to a greater degree if you have lower taxes than having higher taxes.

National Review managing editor Jay Nordlinger, a former speechwriter for George W. Bush, put the tax-cutting debate in more philosophical terms to explain the liberal knee-jerk reaction against it. "Milton Friedman says that any tax cut is a step forward. I imagine that some tax cuts are harmful, in theory. But I can't imagine that such a cut would occur in reality. Every itty-bitty cut we manage is like pulling teeth. Here's a test I sometimes pose to liberals: Say you knew—knew for a certainty—that a tax cut would bring in more revenue to the government. Would you support the cut? They have trouble saying yes. Because, at bottom, they don't view taxation as revenue-raising, they view it as punitive. They want it for social reasons, not economic ones."[10]

Bush's tax cuts, specifically, serve as a lightning rod for many who view them as hugely beneficial to the rich and insulting to the poor and middle classes. But the math doesn't really add up in that argument, as liberal online magazine Slate pointed out in a surprising story called "Bush's Tax Cuts Are Unfair . . . To the Rich," by Steven E. Landsburg. The 2004 article examined the breakdown of Bush's tax cuts, and offered up some revealing facts:

If you and your spouse have a taxable income of $60,000 a year, you've had almost a 24 percent income tax cut since President Bush took office. (And ditto if your income was just $20,000.) Meanwhile, the folks who make $350,000 a year got a cut of only about 12.5 percent; those who make $1 million a year got an even smaller cut. Overall, the biggest percentage cuts went to the poorest of the poor (those with incomes in the $10,000 range) and the next biggest to those making about $60,000. After that, with some minor dips up and down, the relative size of your tax cut falls off as your income rises.[11]

Landsburg goes on to point out the incredible irony of the liberal brouhaha over tax cuts, and the Democratic angst over Bush's strategy.

My own opinion is that the rich already pay too much—it seems patently unfair to ask anyone to pay over 30 times as much as his neighbors (unless he receives 30 times as much in government services, which strikes me as implausible). If you share my sense of fairness, you'll join me in condemning the president's tax policy.

But if, on the other hand, you believe that the tax system should soak the rich even more than it already does—or, to put it more genteelly, that the tax system should be more progressive than it already is—if, in other words, you are a mainstream Democrat—then George W. Bush is your guy.

Wise-beyond-his-column-inches pundit George Will, whose Pulitzer Prize–winning work appears in hundreds of publications every week, has not been shy about his criticism of Bush, despite being a conservative himself. However, he considers the Bush tax cuts his greatest legacy. "The greatest achievement has been to further lighten the load of government expenses on the economy by the tax cuts. And the economy has responded in a way that says at the top of its markets that the tax cuts were wise and worked."[12]

Tax-cutting is not the only place where liberals like to sling mud at conservatives, rewriting the issue as bad-for-the-little-guy and good-for-the-fat-cat. Corporate America is routinely politicized as being particularly conservative (read: heartless) and stacked with Republicans (read: money-hungry suits). Business itself—literally, the act of doing business—has come under attack recently, thanks to some highly public scandals involving creative accounting, with the Left deriding big business as a Republican coup d'etat designed to step on and stamp out every small-scale enterprise, including little Jimmy's lemonade stand. The Left's anti–Wal-Mart faction is a surprisingly vocal and vigilant one, with liberals like John Kerry blaming the retail giant and job-multiplier for America's ills. Kerry's billionaire wife Teresa said of Wal-Mart, "They destroy communities." (It was later discovered that she owns $1 million in Wal-Mart stock, making the statement even more mind-boggling.)[13] In a 2006 story called "Dems vs. Wal-Mart," George Will wrote about the irony and hypocrisy of the liberal animus toward Wal-Mart, while offering up some very compelling numbers.

> The median household income of Wal-Mart shoppers is under $40,000. Wal-Mart, the most prodigious job-creator in the history of the private sector in this galaxy has almost as many employees (1.3 million) as the U.S. military has uniformed personnel. A McKinsey company study concluded that Wal-Mart accounted for 13 percent of the nation's productivity gains in the second half of the 1990s, which probably made Wal-Mart about as important as the Federal Reserve in holding down inflation. By lowering consumer prices, Wal-Mart costs about 50 retail jobs among competitors *for every 100 jobs Wal-Mart creates.* Wal-Mart and its effects save shoppers more than $200 billion a year, dwarfing such government programs as food stamps ($28.6 billion) and the earned-income tax credit ($34.6 billion).[14]

According to Will, the rationale behind the attack is a misguided attempt to paint both conservatives and big business as elitist. But the resulting effect is probably not the desired one. "Liberals think their campaign against Wal-Mart is a way of introducing the subject of class into America's political argument, and they are more correct than they understand. Their campaign is liberalism as condescension. It is a *philosophic* repugnance toward markets, because consumer sovereignty results in the masses making messes. Liberals, aghast, see the choices Americans make with their dollars and their ballots and announce—yes, announce—that Americans are sorely in need of more supervision by . . . liberals."[15]

Putting the inexplicable liberal disgust for Wal-Mart aside, is corporate America itself an inherently conservative entity? According to popular culture it is. *National Review* editor-at-large Jonah Goldberg discussed the all-too-familiar depiction of the reviled American businessman in movies and on television.

> Some of these things are so baked into the cake in terms of how narratives work. By definition businessmen are always going to be more sympathetic toward conservatism, and that's just the nature of the universe. And if you look at the popular culture, it's really astounding. How often do you see businessmen portrayed as villains? From *Law & Order* to a thousand private detectives shows and movies and all the rest, there's the idea that somehow good businessmen, when they get in a bind, murder their competition or murder people to help conceal the fact that they're poisoning schoolchildren, or whatever it is. There are all these silly movies predicated on the idea that somehow businessmen are natural villains. I think it's going to be a long time before that is removed from the narrative of Hollywood because it's such an easy cliché.[16]

Perhaps business is inherently conservative. But not because the head honchos of major companies are all evil, or Republican, but rather because doing good business requires the application of conservative principles. "I believe that many large corporations can be viewed as conservative as a result of a reaction to overbearing, expensive, and bureaucratic government interference,"[17] said Chris Milliken, former CEO of OfficeMax. "This common loathing of government creates an accurate picture of corporate America being viewed as conservative. Corporate America today has an inherent dislike of government interference in its businesses. Government mandates, including, but not limited to, Affirmative Action, OSHA regulations, Sarbanes-Oxley conformance requirements, EPA regulations, and of course ever-increasing taxes, are all viewed as expensive, time-consuming, and, although fundamentally sound, are already in place at well-run businesses. As a result, the many pay dearly for the few."

But, as Milliken points out, to view business leaders themselves, small or large, successful or start-up, in a politicized light is incredibly unfair. "I grew up in an environment of extreme conservatism in regard to political ideologies. My father was a card-carrying member of the John Birch Society and was very active in the Heritage Foundation. My own ideology is slightly to the right of center. To characterize the CEO automatically as a Republican is a terrible misconception. Yes, the CEO will revile government interference with its onerous and unnecessary burdens, but the CEO has a huge responsibility to his or her associates and communities where its business is conducted. Constant efforts to support these two vital constituencies are a key role of any CEO and really should not bear any moniker at all—Republican, Independent, or Democrat."

And what of the characterization of CEOs and business leaders as heartless, money-hungry, ruthless, and corrupt (i.e., Republicans)? "Compassion, diversity, and tolerance have absolutely nothing to do with political affiliation—at least in the work place. OfficeMax had 45,000 associates when I was last there. Our associate satisfaction scores were among the highest in the nation. We were 100 percent union-free in the U.S.A. *because* we had compassion, diversity, and tolerance."

Another part of the myth relies on the cliché that big business doesn't care about anything—the earth, its own employees, the community—but lining its owners' and investors' pockets. Ingersoll Rand, a diversified industrial firm more than one hundred years old, manufactures everything from Bobcat farm equipment to Hussman refrigerators, Schlage locks to mobile diesel generators—not, generally, the stuff associated with left-wing business. Nonetheless, Ingersoll Rand is a leader in promoting environmental stewardship, both within the company itself and in the products it manufactures. According to its most recent environmental, safety and health report, "One recent innovation is a Thermo King auxiliary power unit that powers the air conditioning, heating, and electrical appliances in the cab of a truck when it is parked, eliminating the need to continuously run the engine. This new product reduces fuel use and vehicle air emissions, helps customers comply with anti-idling laws, and improves driver comfort."[18] Another is the SmartFAN cooling system—"a hydraulically driven cooling fan that senses machine operating temperatures and then self-regulates to rotate only as fast as needed." Then there's the powder coat paint on Bobcat products, which "results in virtually no hazardous waste at the point of manufacture, as well as nonhazardous propylene glycol in machine cooling systems."

Furthermore, Ingersoll Rand is just one of many big companies committed to community service and philanthropy. In 2006 Bobcat donated $132,000 to the Red Cross and those affected by Hurricane Katrina. In that same year, IR employees donated $52,832 to the United Way and Habitat for Humanity, and the Ingersoll Rand Foundation matched it. IR employees participate in hundreds of community service projects every year, on a local, national, and international level, and while their efforts are admirable, they are not unique. So-called big business donates millions of dollars every year to a variety of worthwhile causes.

Mark Moran, president of Ingersoll Rand's sports-marketing arm, discussed Ingersoll Rand's commitment to the environment, good business ethics, and philanthropy.

> We have a big green push going on, and I think most com-
> panies have changed that way of thinking dramatically. That's a
> major push that's come directly from the chairman, and it's gone
> throughout the entire IR organization and all of what we do.
> It's the right thing to do, it helps the environment. We also have
> a terrific code of conduct. We have training that we have to do
> annually. There's peer pressure within IR to do the right thing.
> And we are very actively involved in the community. We even
> have awards every quarter to employees and employee groups
> who support various causes. During Katrina, for instance, we
> ended up donating around twenty-five thousand locks, and we
> got the President's award for that. Almost every single month,
> people at IR are building homes or they're doing charity. It's
> an individual thing that people do and it's a corporate thing
> that people do. At the end of the day, if people feel good about
> working for a corporation like IR, and I think they do, and our
> customers feel good about working with a company like IR, it's
> the right thing to do and it's right for business.[19]

It would seem morality and making money—something we all have to do—*can* go hand in hand.

Which brings us back to the beginning. Thomas Frank's elitist missive *What's the Matter With Kansas?* raises a very important question: Are liberals just Marxists with better clothes? Marxists and liberals, after all, share a shocking amount of common ground. There's the disgust for the upper-class capitalist; the rank intellectual superiority; the pervasive worldview that dissension is merely a lingering symptom of ignorance; the disdain for religion and other such petty vestiges of pre-Enlightenment Europe; the sycophantic obsession with "the oppressed" (whom they've never actually met, nor would they want to); and the disturbing penchant for creative facial hair. It's all there. Yes, a specter is haunting the Democratic Party—the specter of Marxism. To illustrate this point in even more explicit terms, compare the following excerpts taken from *The Communist Manifesto,* written by Marx and Frederick Engels in 1848, with quotations from well-known contemporary liberals:

Marx: *"The need of a constantly expanding market for its products chases the bourgeoisie over the entire surface of the globe. It must nestle everywhere, settle everywhere, establish connexions* [sic] *everywhere."*

Jane Smiley: "A generation ago, the big capitalists, who have no morals, as we know, decided to make use of the religious right in their class war against the middle class and against the regulations that were protecting those whom they considered to be their rightful prey—workers and consumers. Cheney is the capitalist arm and Bush is the religious arm. They know no boundaries or rules. They are predatory and resentful, amoral, avaricious, and arrogant."[20]

Marx: *"[The capitalist] has pitilessly torn asunder the motley feudal ties that bound man to his 'natural superiors,' and has left remaining no other nexus between man and man than naked self-interest, than callous 'cash payment.'"*

Tim Robbins: "Our resistance to this war should be our resistance to profit at the cost of human life. Because that is what these drums beating over Iraq are really about. This is about business."[21]

Marx: *"[The capitalist] has but established new classes, new conditions of oppression, new forms of struggle in place of the old ones."*

Al Sharpton: "The problem is that Jim Crow has sons. The one we've got to battle is James Crow, Jr., Esquire. He's a little more educated. He's a little slicker. He's a little more polished. But the results are the same. He doesn't put you in the back of the bus. He just puts referendums on the ballot to end affirmative action where you can't go to school. He doesn't call you a racial name, he just marginalizes your existence. He doesn't tell you that he's set against you, he sets up institutional racism, when you have a nation respond looking for weapons in Iraq that are not there, but can't see a hurricane in Louisiana that is there."[22]

Marx: *"[The capitalist] has resolved personal worth into exchange value, and in place of the numberless indefeasible chartered freedoms, has set up that single, unconscionable freedom—Free Trade."*

John Edwards: "I think we've had a failed trade policy in America. The question seems to have been, on past trade agreements like NAFTA: Is this trade agreement good for the profits of big multinational corporations? And the answer to those questions on the trade agreements we've entered into has been yes."[23]

It's hard to say just how much liberals really take from Marx. After all, no one believes liberals would actually want to do away with the upper class in favor of a classless proletariat—where would they shop? But it does reveal something about the Left's discomfort with Republican values, especially where money is concerned. Thomas Frank's Marxist missive is a near-perfect example of the frustration of the Left, and its inability to come to terms with American conservatism and its goals. The idea that Middle American conservatives see Republican economic policy as simply good for their families is inexplicable somehow. So whether it's tax-cutting or corporate America, Republicans will always be left defending their programs as "good ideas," not right-wing terrorist plots to vandalize the American family, and in doing so will undoubtedly come up against condescending leftists who think they know better. Perhaps we'd all do best to remember the wise words of *another* great political theorist, American satirist P. J. O'Rourke: "Anyone who thinks he has a better idea of what's good for people than people do is a swine."[24] Interestingly, an acknowledgment that Republicans are no more tied to big business than Democrats came from an unlikely source in the *Socialist Worker,* which looked to expose "the two faces of the Democrats." In the wake of massive accounting scandals at WorldCom, Enron, Adelphia, Global Crossing, and Tyco, liberals seized on the moment to implicate the Right as corrupt, greedy, and inextricably linked to big business. But where Republicans "pocketed $7.4 million in contributions" from those corporations, "the Democrats, the 'party of the people,' raked in $5.2 million from these same disgraced companies." The *Socialist Worker* concluded, "The Democrats' devotion to carrying out big business's agenda has remained intact despite their recent posturing."[25] Maybe Marx isn't so bad after all.

CHAPTER 16

Republicans Are Undemocratic

The Myth of the Constitution-Shredding Conservative

Democracies have no business running secret prisons. That's what our enemies do.[1]

—Bob Schieffer, *The CBS Evening News*

In late 2007, A. O. Scott reviewed the movie *Rendition* for the *New York Times*. Scott's review of the film, which told the story of the political kidnapping and torture of an Egyptian-born American and the efforts to extract him from a North African prison, read more like a scolding than a critique. He began, "Given the tenor of political discussion these days, it is inevitable that someone with a loud voice and a small mind will label *Rendition* anti-American. (But look! A quick Internet search reveals that some people already have, many of them without even bothering to see the movie.) It is, after all, much easier to rant and rave about treacherous Hollywood liberals than to think through the moral and strategic questions raised by some of the policies of the American government."[2] After agonizing through a few column inches of plot synopsis and briefly complimenting the actors on their performances in what he described as a "well-meaning," but not very good movie, Scott was able to get back to his main agenda—the castigation of those who would dare to defend certain foreign policies that he does not agree with: "But all its clumsy efforts are toward an honest and difficult goal, which is to use the resources of mainstream movie-making to get viewers thinking about a moral crisis that many of us would prefer to ignore. Of course it's disappointing when such efforts don't succeed, but I wouldn't want to live in a country where filmmakers never tried."

Scott's "review" doesn't name conservatives or Republicans implicitly as the driving force behind that "moral crisis" we are accused of ignoring, but one has to assume he's not speaking to liberals. Republicans are often accused of ignoring, if not intentionally undermining, the principles of democracy and the rule of law, and they allegedly do so toward any number of goals. But worse than painting democracy as a pesky nuisance that conservatives constantly try to skirt is the conceit that Republicans wear the disguise of democracy to underhandedly chase other political objectives, like oil, money, land, weapons, and power. The War on Terror is the latest manifestation of a supposedly Republican effort to take what we need from the Middle East under the guise of spreading democracy to the region. To that end, Jon Stewart facetiously wrote in *America (The Book)*, "It is important to remember there still exist many other forms of government in the world today, and that dozens of foreign governments still long for a democracy such as ours to be imposed on them."[3] And yet another variation on the theme suggests that America is not democratic at all, thanks to the Republicans who have worked so doggedly to destroy what might have begun as a noble experiment, but has since gone terribly awry. Jon Stewart compared American democracy, which exists to him only on an alleged basis, to those other great empires that eventually fell under their own massive greed:

The fall of Athens was followed by the emergence, over-night, of Rome. At first glance its people appear to have enjoyed a system of representative government similar to ours. True, behind its façade of allegedly "representative" officials lurked a *de facto* oligarchy ruled by entrenched plutocrats. But the similarities don't end there. In fact, the Founding Fathers bor-rowed many of their ideas from the Roman model, including its bicameral legislature, its emphasis on republicanism and civic virtue, and its Freudian fascination with big white columns. However, there was very little real democracy in Rome. While the Senate theoretically represented the people, in reality its wealthy members covertly pursued pro-business legislation on behalf of such military-industrial giants as JavelinCorp, United Crucifix, and a cartel of resource-exploiting companies known as Big Aqueduct.[4]

The myth of the brash and unrepentant conservative who mani-acally cackles in the face of democracy takes many forms. Republi-cans reportedly enjoy wire-tapping the conversations of law-biding Americans, rounding up political enemies in the middle of the night and shipping them to Guantanamo Bay, ignoring the First Amend-ment's protections, and hijacking elections.

And while some of these accusations are exaggerations, some of them are simply rank hypocrisy. And few are as inaccurate as the accusation that conservatives do not respect the right to speak freely. Given that conservatives are often at odds with the Ameri-can Civil Liberties Union, which is usually an advocate of left-wing policies, it is easy to caricature conservative views as hostile to free-speech rights. However, not only are the protections of the First Amendment among the most sacred to conservatives, but the same cannot always be said for those on the left, as evidenced by the movement by several Democratic congressmen recently to re-introduce the Fairness Doctrine, which conservative columnist and author George Will said is "anything but fair."[5]

The Fairness Doctrine was enacted in 1949 as an FCC rule that required radio broadcasters who covered public issues to do so in a balanced manner under the threat of various punishments. To enforce the rule, the FCC responded to complaints by timing the amount of coverage devoted to each side of a topic in order to assess whether sanctions were warranted. The rule stayed in effect until 1987, when the Reagan administration finally repealed it, rightly believing it blatantly defied constitutional free-speech protections. After repeal of the Fairness Doctrine, conservatives found the great equalizer to an overwhelmingly liberal media in the form of conservative talk radio and, later, the internet. As liberals made strident attempts to create a formidable left-wing talk radio infrastructure with the Air America network and its cast of alarmists like Al Franken and Janeane Garofalo, congressional Democrats decided it was time yet again to regulate "fairness." Democratic senators Richard Durbin, John Kerry, and Dianne Feinstein all called for the return of the Fairness Doctrine. As John Fund wrote in the *Wall Street Journal* in late 2007, "Democrats who have become 'Fairness' mongers insist they simply want to restore civility and balance to the airwaves. Al Gore, in a typically overheated speech last year bemoaned 'the destruction of [the] marketplace of ideas' which he blamed in part on the repeal of the Fairness Doctrine, after which 'Rush Limbaugh and other hate-mongers began to fill the airwaves.'"[6]

Likewise, Senator Durbin self-righteously announced, "I have this old-fashioned attitude that when Americans hear both sides of the story, they're in a better position to make a decision."[7] Senator Feinstein said, "I think there ought to be an opportunity to present the other side. Unfortunately, talk radio is overwhelmingly one-way." Liberal advocacy group Media Matters for America also suggested that in addition to "restoring diversity of fact and opinion to programming," which "has been lost since the 1980's," the number of stations that a company can own should be limited and a quota system ensuring more women- and minority-owned radio stations should be implemented.[8] If there's anything that sounds *less* like democracy and *more* like communism, it would be hard to find. Not surprisingly, Media Matters has yet to call for the same forced intellectual "diversity" in our public educational institutions, on our college campuses, or in print media. Needless to say, the Fairness Doctrine has been opposed with virtual unanimity by those on the right.

Ann Coulter points out that conservatives have a strong grip on the web because "speech is free," unlike space on mainstream media outlets, which is heavily regulated by campaign finance reform and partisan higher-ups. Hillary Clinton, on the other hand, has echoed a liberal concern with free speech on the internet by calling for "a kind of editing function or gatekeeping function for the Internet. . . . It's just beyond imagination what can be disseminated . . . we are all going to have to rethink how we deal with this."[9]

In 2007, the ultraliberal New York City Council passed a symbolic ban (whatever that means) on the use of the "n-word." Later, Democratic Brooklyn councilwoman Darlene Mealy led a campaign to pass a similar measure banning the use of "bitch" and "ho." As Ann Coulter argued, in the Oliver Wendell Holmes tradition of the free marketplace of ideas, "A false argument should be refuted, not named. . . . Arguments by demonization, rather than truth and light, can be presumed to be fraudulent. Real hate speech does not have to be flagged and labeled. It speaks for itself. If a person makes an argument that is, in fact, 'racist' (anti-Semitic, sexist, lookist—whatever), that fact ought to be self evident."[10]

George Will asserts that conservatives in fact tend to be more protective of the right to speak freely as one of the penultimate democratic rights: "Conservatives respect market results—markets are popular sovereignty. That is, the markets allow all appetites and desires to compete and see which one prevails."[11] However, he qualified his statement by reminding us that a Republican (John McCain) sponsored McCain-Feingold campaign finance reform, which he called, "the most severe threat to free speech in our country ever. It is the government asserting a right to regulate the quantity, content, and timing of political speech."[12] Echoing Will's view, thirty-eight of the forty senators who voted against McCain-Feingold were Republicans.

Critics are also quick to point to the erosion of free-speech rights as orchestrated by Republicans in a post–September 11 world. In Saira Rao's *Chambermaid*, a novel about an Indian law-school graduate clerking for a federal judge, the protagonist, Sheila Raj, muses, "everyone knew what became of unpatriotic brown people—Guantanamo."[13] A silly exaggeration indeed, but one mythologized even in fiction. In fact, a similar reference appeared in Jim Nelson's Editor's Note in the September 2007 issue of *GQ*, which was almost entirely devoted to politics: "Are you ready to be 'emotionally compelled' by a politician? Maybe that sounds like something they do in Guantanamo, with a pair of pliers, but no, I'm talking about being moved, wooed, having your brain seduced."[14]

The Bush administration is often accused of subverting democracy through the use of terrorist detention camps like those in Guantanamo. In 2005, Amnesty International said that "the Guantanamo Bay detention camp has become a symbol of the United States administration's refusal to put human rights and the rule of law at the heart of its response to the atrocities of 11 September 2001. It has become synonymous with the United States executive's pursuit of unfettered power, and has become firmly associated with the systematic denial of human dignity and resort to cruel, inhuman or degrading treatment that has marked the USA's detentions and interrogations in the 'war on terror.'"[15] Groups like Amnesty International have a penchant for identifying "symbols" like Guantanamo—symbols that are highly convenient substitutes for substantive analysis.

The War on Terror has fueled other cries of "nondemocracy" from liberals outraged by wiretapping, detentions, and profiling.

Many of these people subscribe to the John Edwards philosophy that the War on Terror is merely a bumper-sticker slogan. They routinely come to the defense of so-called victims like Jose Padilla, who plotted to detonate a "dirty bomb" on U.S. soil and was convicted in federal court of conspiring to commit acts of terrorism and funding terrorist organizations. Glenn Greenwald of Salon.com virtually wept over Padilla's "depressingly familiar" story of detention that "broke Padilla as a human being in every sense that matters." For Greenwald, it was "one of those lines which many people believed would never be crossed in America."[16] Former federal prosecutor Kelly Anne Moore also made the case against trying men like Padilla as enemy combatants. She argued in the *New York Times* that trying terrorists as criminals, as opposed to war criminals, denies them status as warriors or freedom fighters, and shows that "America can protect itself while it respects the rule of law."[17] Never mind that terrorists are not particularly concerned with the status we bestow on them; trying them as ordinary criminals is a costly approach full of evidentiary problems that increases the probability that we will disclose information that should be unavailable to our enemies.

If the Bush administration is guilty of anything, it is viewing the War on Terror as just that . . . a war. Andrew McCarthy, a former federal prosecutor who led the prosecution of Sheik Omar Abdel Rahman, said that of all the wars America has fought, the War on Terror is "uniquely about intelligence." "There is one overriding question: Where are they? Where are they so we can capture or kill them before they mass-murder us?"[18] McCarthy had the following to say in response to accusations that the administration's use of such intelligence techniques flies in the face of democracy:

> For nearly two years since the *New York Times* blew the NSA's warrantless-surveillance program, the Left has transfigured itself into a whirling dervish of indignation over President Bush's imperious trampling of "the rule of law." Why? Because

he failed to comply with the letter of [the Foreign Intelligence Surveillance Act (FISA)], which purports in certain instances to require the chief executive—the only elected official in the United States responsible for protecting our nation from foreign threats—to seek permission from a federal judge before monitoring international enemy communications into or out of the United States. But the president, at least, had an excuse. Actually, not a mere excuse but a trump card. We call it the American Constitution. It empowers the chief executive to conduct warrantless surveillance of foreign threats. . . . When Congress passes a statute, like FISA, that purports to reduce the president's constitutional authority, it is Congress, not the president, that is trampling the rule of law."[19]

Regarding the administration's open decision to treat al Qaeda operatives as unlawful enemy combatants captured in war, and not ordinary criminals, as McCarthy wrote elsewhere:

The laws and customs of war, older than the United States, permit the detention of enemy combatants for the duration of hostilities in order to collect intelligence and deplete the enemy's resources. . . . If these venerable standards are to be tossed aside, and our only alternative in self-defense is to try enemy combatants in the civilian justice system while the war is underway, we will then have to choose between either providing our enemies with discovery that will be extremely useful to them or releasing them to return to the jihad."[20]

Torture, and what that heavily contested term implies, has also been a sensitive subject that has thrown gasoline on the raging antidemocracy fire. When the United States captured the mastermind of 9/11, Khalid Sheik Mohammed, he was apparently impervious to interrogators seeking intelligence until his captors subjected him to a pressure-building technique called waterboarding. Within several minutes of exposure to this technique, which does not cause physical long-term damage when performed properly, he divulged the identities of six high-level terrorists, as well as plans to detonate explosives in U.S. buildings.[21]

Despite these effective techniques, useful in eliciting intelligence from men who are bent on the mass murder of innocent Americans, it was sometime-Republican John McCain who led the political grandstanding to prohibit inhumane treatment of terrorist detainees and limited interrogation techniques to those specified in the Army Field Manual. Andrew McCarthy once again provided a commonsense legal assessment. "Torture is already against the law. It is, moreover, the intentional infliction of *severe* physical or mental pain—which is to say, much of the prisoner abuse that has prompted the current controversy has not been torture at all. Unpleasant? Yes. Sometimes sadistic and inexplicable? Undoubtedly. But not torture. And where it has been either torture or unjustifiable cruelty, it is being investigated, prosecuted, and severely punished."[22]

Given that we are at war, McCarthy explained just how ridiculous the logic of the McCain Amendment is. "If we were to learn where one of those men was, we would attack that target and kill him, and we'd make no apologies for it. By the McCain logic, the killing is fine but the infliction on a terrorist of non-lethal discomfort to obtain the intelligence necessary to do the killing should subject the inflictor to prosecution. That's absurd."[23]

Many Europeans and international rights groups want the United States to go further than constitutional boundaries and prohibit anything that is "cruel, inhumane or degrading," as required by the United Nations Convention Against Torture and Cruel, Inhuman and Degrading Treatment or Punishment (UNCAT). (One would imagine that just being imprisoned is itself a "degrading" experience.) When the Senate ratified UNCAT, it did so with the caveat that the United States would prevent "cruel, inhuman or degrading treatment or punishment," only insofar as the term "cruel, inhuman or degrading treatment or punishment" means the cruel, unusual and inhumane treatment or punishment prohibited by the Fifth, Eighth, and Fourteenth amendments to the Constitution of the United States. Furthermore, the Eighth Amendment barring "cruel and unusual punishment" is inapplicable to enemies captured during war, as the Supreme Court has held. In essence, our leaders continue to be bound by the Constitution of the United States. UNCAT adds nothing of substance, although the McCain Amendment attempts to by prohibiting inhumane treatment of prisoners.

But it's not just the way Republicans supposedly want to treat terrorists that has liberals up in arms. It's also the way they want to treat lawyers. The Bush administration came under fire after former attorney general Alberto Gonzales approved the firing of eight U.S. attorneys, an admittedly uncommon scenario. Outraged Democrats screamed foul, arguing that the administration was subverting the Constitution for political gain. Llewellyn Rockwell, Jr., a libertarian, mused, "Maybe the authors of the *Federalist Papers* were liars. Maybe they were just engaged in political propaganda in order to shove through the Constitution. In secret, perhaps, they were plotting a Leviathan state with a president who can do all that the Bush administration claims he can, which pretty much amounts to whatever Bush wants to do."[24] However, conservative commentator Pat Buchanan defended the Bush administration and Attorney General Gonzales's firing of the U.S. attorneys, arguing that the controversy was contrived. "U.S. attorneys serve at the pleasure of the president. Bush can fire them, retain them, or remove some and retain others. The Supreme Court has upheld that right and denied Congress any role in the presidential hiring and firing of political appointees."[25] The Bush administration's dismissal of these U.S. attorneys is no more illegal than Democrats' systematic failure to approve qualified federal judicial nominees for political purposes.

And of course, the perennial (or perhaps quadrennial) liberal accusation offered as proof that conservatives are corrupt and bastardizing the Constitution is that Republicans steal elections. (Apparently, thanks to Nixon, *all* Republicans now have to pledge that they aren't crooks.) One blog site wrote the following: "Republicans know they can't win (in the aggragate [*sic*]) by playing fair. They have to cheat, lie, and resort to dirty tricks. Those dirty tricks, amounting to everything from clogging get-out-the-vote phone banks to using voter registration operatives to destroy Democratic registrations are blatant attempts by Republicans to sabotage the very system that Republicans claim Bush has instituted in Iraq and Afghanistan. Considering that Republicans claimed the patriotic high road over the past 3 years it begs the question of just how patriotic is it to undermine the very principles our country was founded upon?"[26] Paul Krugman, an editorial writer for the *New York Times,* wrote, "The important point to realize is that these abuses aren't aberrations. They're the inevitable result of a Republican Party culture in which dirty tricks that distort the vote are rewarded, not punished. It's a culture that will persist until voters—whose will still does count, if expressed strongly enough—hold that party accountable."[27]

If you happened to stay up late enough on November 7, 2000, you may have seen every major network call the election for George W. Bush. By the time you woke up the following morning, you might have thought the same man who'd been elected president had instead perpetrated a coup d'état. As the election drama unfolded over the next month and in months after its resolution, Bush was incessantly accused of hijacking the election, and, in fact, it wasn't until the United States unfortunately got a taste of actual hijacking that Bush was downgraded to merely incompetent and inarticulate.

It is worth noting the various ways in which Bush was accused of robbing our electoral process, and the evidence that others presented. The first hysterical charge was that his opponent, Al Gore, was said to have received more votes than he. The only problem is that such a scenario is constitutionally contemplated and, in fact, has occurred previously. Second, Bush's victory in Florida was certified by a supposedly Republican partisan in Katherine Harris. Though she was a pro-Bush Republican, Article II of the Constitution specifies, "Each State shall appoint, in such Manner as the Legislature thereof may direct, a Number of Electors." The Florida legislature passed a law *requiring* the Florida secretary of state to certify election results within seven days, reading, "If the county returns are not received by the Department of State by 5 P.M. of the seventh day following an election, all missing counties shall be ignored and the results shown by the returns on file shall be certified."[28] So, there was nothing unkosher about Harris's certification of Bush. Third, the Florida Supreme Court unfairly ordered a recount, and fourth, a biased U.S. Supreme Court awarded Bush the victory. Had the Florida Supreme Court not decided to relegislate the statute, the U.S. Supreme Court would have faced a much easier decision. Instead, it was forced to consider whether a recount would violate the Equal Protection clause of the Fourteenth Amendment, and seven out of nine justices said it would. Five concluded that the recount would cease, and the state was awarded to Bush and the election was final. In the end, Bush ended up with more votes in Florida when the dust settled.

Since the 2000 election, there have been countless remedial measures to avoid similar scenarios in the future, but as of 2004, only seventeen states require some form of documentation in order to vote. As John Fund discussed in his book *Stealing Elections,* many of the electoral reform proposals have been opposed by Democrats because, as Maria Cardona, spokesperson for the Democratic National Committee, claims, "Ballot security and preventing voter fraud are just code words for voter intimidation and suppression."[29] Fund discussed why most of the examples he cites of electoral fraud are at the hands of Democrats:

> I do not believe Republicans are inherently more virtuous or honest than anyone else in politics, and I myself often vote Libertarian or independent. In their book *Dirty Little Secrets,*

Larry Sabato and co-author Glenn Simpson of the *Wall Street Journal* noted another factor in why Republican election fraud is less common. Republican base voters are middle-class and not easily induced to commit fraud, while "the pool of people who appear to be available and more vulnerable to an invitation to participate in vote fraud tend to lean Democratic." Some liberal activists that Sabato and Simpson interviewed even partly justified fraudulent electoral behavior on the grounds that because the poor and dispossessed have so little political clout, "extraordinary measures (for example, stretching the absentee ballot or registration rules) are required to compensate."[30]

Though it is far too easy to cast one ideological group as sensitive to democratic and constitutional principles and the other as unconcerned, the debate about democracy does reveal certain undeniable trends. For one, ideology rarely leads to a pro-democratic or antidemocratic position, at least explicitly. It does, however, tend to reveal which branch of our constitutional system one is more likely to trust with power. As a general rule, conservatives tend to be far less trusting of the judicial branch than the executive or legislative branches. It is why conservative groups like the Federalist Society, a national group of law students and lawyers, adopt as part of the official platform the advocacy of judicial restraint. It was *Federalist Paper* number 78 in which Alexander Hamilton said, "It can be of no weight to say that the courts, on the pretense of a repugnancy, may substitute their own pleasure to the constitutional intentions of the legislature. . . . The courts must declare the sense of the law; and if they should be disposed to exercise will instead of judgment, the consequence would equally be the substitution of their pleasure to that of the legislative body." Conservatives lack trust in the judiciary because, of all the branches, it can subvert democracy with the most ease. Conservatives are far more comfortable placing trust in the legislative and executive branches because these participants are subject to elections that reflect the democratic will of the people.

Conversely, the American Constitution Society, the counterpoint to the Federalist Society, advocates judicial activism and looks to "bring together scholars and practitioners to formulate and advance a progressive vision of our Constitution and laws that is intellectually sound, practically relevant and faithful to our constitutional values and heritage." It is not enough to interpret the Constitution accurately. Rather, the Constitution must be interpreted progressively. And who should do this interpretation and decide what constitutes progress in our constitutional system? If you ask a liberal, unelected judges—unless, of course, they are deciding an election for a Republican. That would just be undemocratic.

CHAPTER 17

Republicans Are Homophobic

The Myth of the Gay-Basher

Some see the move as an attempt to preserve traditional values, while others see it as a cynical ploy to ensure that Vice President Dick Cheney will never have to pay for his gay daughter's wedding.[1]

—Jon Stewart

Comedian Lewis Black, who routinely skewers both the Right and the Left in hilarious onstage outbursts that seem more like spontaneous mental breakdowns than scripted and rehearsed bits, once attempted to explain the alleged homophobia of the Right. He facetiously wondered if perhaps its fears were founded after all:

Maybe there are a group of gay banditos . . . who, every night climb into a van and go from village to dell, from community to community. They wander, and as the sun is coming down, just setting over a suburban village, the gays drive in. And there in a cul-de-sac, there in the light of a house, you can see a young American family, sitting down for their evening meal. And those gays, those gays put on their masks and their festive colored robes, and sneak slowly into the house . . . and begin to fuck each other in the ass! And another American family is destroyed.[2]

While Black's explanation is probably a little exaggerated (as well as incredibly graphic), he's likely more right than he is wrong, unfortunately. The fear that homosexuality, as a culture and as sexual acts of "perversion," will destroy the American family is a real one for many people who approach homosexuality from either a religious point of view or a point of ignorance and fear (hence, *phobia*). To pretend that this kind of fear has been eradicated over the past few decades thanks to the gay rights movement or television shows like *Will and Grace* would be a lie, and to pretend that everyone who recognizes gays as equal citizens and deserving of equal rights condones or endorses homosexuality would be another. Acknowledging that this fear exists is necessary in understanding homophobia. (And, to be clear, an acknowledgment of this fear is not an apology for homophobia.) One's understanding of homosexuality simply depends on one's perspective, and on what side of the debate one falls.

But it doesn't depend on what side of the aisle one falls. Lewis Black's illustration of the fears Americans have about homosexuality cannot possibly just apply to Republicans. There is nothing inherently Republican or conservative about homophobia. The Constitution never explicitly mentions homosexuality, and neither does the Bill of Rights. Abraham Lincoln's Gettysburg Address never mentions homophobia or the hatred of gays as a Republican requirement (and a number of scholars even claim that Lincoln was himself gay or bisexual). To borrow the platitude of so many middle-class, straight, white folk, the authors of this book "have many gay friends," and are, in varying degrees, supportive of gay rights. They know plenty of Democrats and liberals who oppose gay marriage for myriad reasons, some rational and some blatantly homophobic. And because they went to college, they also know plenty of liberal-minded frat guys who routinely (and without the excuse of alcohol) slammed gays, called their rival fraternity members "faggots" and the like, and denied membership to rushees believed to be gay, all while simultaneously holding fund-raisers to save the rain forests, keep abortion clinics open, and elect Al Gore.

Strangely, though, the gay rights movement has been vocally and possessively coopted by the Left, which has done a tremendous and impressive job of claiming gay rights for themselves and painting the Right as antigay and homophobic. In an episode of *Sex and the City,* the mother of Carrie's new boyfriend recounts her daughter's coming out to her. "When Frannie told me she was a lesbian, I said 'great—just as long as you're not Republican.'"[3] The quotation succinctly captures both the liberal idea that being a Republican is a fate worse than, well, lesbianism, and that Democrats are inherently more tolerant than Republicans are—a point that this character ironically disproves with her blatant intolerance of what is ostensibly half the country's voting population.

And sometimes the Left expresses this embrace of gay rights in bizarre ways. Comedienne, actress, and Air America radio host Janeane Garofalo, for example, described her position thus:

> Our country is founded on a sham: our forefathers were slave-owning rich white guys who wanted it their way. So when I see the American flag, I go, "Oh my God, you're insulting me." That you can have a gay parade on Christopher Street in New York, with naked men and women on a float cheering, "We're here, we're queer!"—that's what makes my heart swell. Not the flag, but a gay naked man or woman burning the flag. I get choked up with pride.[4]

When Illinois senator Barack Obama campaigned for president in 2007, his calculated ambivalence to homosexuality, which was perceived sometimes as patently homophobic and at othertimes as hopelessly out of touch, got him in serious hot water. First, he made the bizarre assertion that he's tried to address the "homophobia among some black voters," suggesting, for one, that homophobia is a problem exclusive to blacks, and two, that he is only concerned with his black constituents. Then, there was Donnie McClurkin. As Dean Barnett wrote in the *Weekly Standard:*

> In an effort to appeal to Democratic values voters (both of them!), Obama has been burning a path through the South in a manner reminiscent of William Tecumseh Sherman. Unlike Sherman, Obama didn't bring tens of thousands of revenge-minded troops with him, but one semi-gay and enormously popular gospel singer, Donnie McClurkin. "Semi-gay?" you ask. Sorry, but that's the best way I can think of to describe McClurkin's lifestyle. McClurkin used to be fully gay, until he was "cured" (his word, not mine) through prayer.[5]

The response was, unsurprisingly, not good.

> To virtually all progressives, as well as many conservatives, the thought of "curing" homosexuality is equal parts offensive and ludicrous. Predictably, Obama's association with McClurkin isn't going over well in progressive circles. The blogosphere took notice of the McClurkin-headlined tour last week, and was universal in its denunciations. Trying to tamp down the rising flames, Obama attempted a characteristically maladroit gambit—he rushed onto the tour an openly gay white preacher to hopefully balance McClurkin's presence.[6]

So maybe most conservatives don't express their support for gay rights by comparing it to a love of flag burning, or by endorsing the idea of "reformed gays." But for every Republican like Jerry Falwell, who considers homosexuality a sin, there is surely his liberal counterpart. There are, after all, Christian Democrats, right? But the myth of the Republican homophobe remains, despite the countless Republican legislators and politicians who are vocally and staunchly pro–gay rights, and despite hard-working advocacy groups like the Log Cabin Republicans.

LCR was founded in 1977 in California as a rallying group against the controversial Briggs Initiative, a measure that sought to keep gay and lesbian teachers out of public schools. In 1978, a future presidential candidate from California sent a letter to a pro-Briggs group opposing the initiative, something that would later be seen as incredibly significant and progressive for the time. "Whatever else it is," the letter stated, "homosexuality is not a contagious disease like the measles. Prevailing scientific opinion is that an individual's sexuality is determined at a very early age and that a child's teachers do not really influence this." Thanks in large part to the opposition by this would-be candidate, the Briggs Initiative was defeated by more than 1 million votes.[7] And in 1981, Ronald Reagan would win the race for president of the United States, and a loud victory for gay rights.

The Log Cabins are named after the birthplace of Abraham Lincoln (again, thought by some to have been gay himself), and have forty-seven chapters and thirty-nine organizing committees in all fifty states, Washington D.C., and Puerto Rico. In their support of Republican ideals and gay rights, they have become an incredibly powerful lobbying agent.

"Being a gay conservative is not an oxymoron," said Patrick Sammon, the newly installed president of Log Cabin Republicans, who also heads the Liberty Education Forum. "The fact of the matter is, there are thousands of gay and lesbian Americans who vote Republican and who support basic conservative principles. I think it's increasingly important for gay and lesbian conservatives to stay in the Republican Party and work to make it more supportive of gay and lesbian issues. The fact that the Left has made some progress on gay issues in no way means that gay and lesbian conservatives should have to somehow put aside their fundamental beliefs about politics or the role of government and become Democrats."[8] Conservative ideology, in fact, is a natural ally in the fight for gay rights, as it acknowledges that one's political beliefs can be just that, political, and that one's personal life should be just that, personal.

"As a gay conservative, I don't believe that government is the answer to every problem," said Sammon. "I believe in less regulation, maximizing individual liberty, a strong national defense, and less government intrusion into people's families and private lives. This desire for less government intrusion is really consistent with the desire to live our own lives, both gay and straight, as we see fit."

Oddly, liberals, who also like to argue that one's sex life should be private (see William J. Clinton), seem selective in their affinity for that dogma. During President George W. Bush's re-election campaign, the topic of Vice President Dick Cheney's lesbian daughter, Mary, which was really immaterial to the campaign itself, was constantly brought up by Democrats who wanted to use her as proof that conservatives are homophobic and hypocritical. And when Dick Cheney, like Bill Clinton before him, refused to enter his daughter into the political fray, liberals were not at all understanding. Bill Maher, like other Democrats around him, criticized Cheney for (gasp!) protecting his daughter's privacy. As Maher put it, "It's an issue in this election. Don't talk about my daughter, who we're trying to discriminate against in a constitutional amendment."[9] Suddenly someone's private sex life is an acceptable item for national debate, and apparently Mary Cheney would have to be elected president—and have an affair while in office—to get her privacy back.

Although groups like Log Cabin Republicans and gay conservatives like Patrick Sammon work hard to marry conservative ideals with the fight for gay rights, Republicans are still lambasted as angry, ignorant, intolerant homophobes who cling to scripture and insist that gay marriage will ruin the institution. But conservatism is an ideology of diversity, and those who align with it are equally diverse. Lisa "Kennedy" Montgomery is one of many conservatives who believe that marriage and adoption should be afforded as freely to gay couples as to heterosexual ones. For her, the lambasting has its roots in a different kind of "redness."

I think most communists assume falsely that Republicans are racist homophobes. I am such a proponent of marriage. I am such a proponent of families. I would fight for anyone, if they were in a loving, committed relationship, to be married. I know there's this argument that gay people are going to screw up marriage if we start allowing same-sex marriages. And I look around, and heterosexuals have done a pretty good job of screwing it up. So they've lost their exclusivity. If two people really love each other, especially people who have been in a committed relationship for ten-plus years, they should be allowed to marry. And if two people who love each other and are committed to each other want to have a family, they should be allowed to adopt or explore their parenting options. There are so many babies in the world who are not being taken care of. And we're trying to create an exclusive club of people.

I can't remember where it was said or who said it, but there was an argument that gay people don't accidentally have kids. Heterosexuals do. And if there are people who really want to adopt kids and provide good homes to them, who cares what their sexual preference is? I think that all boils down to what is supposed to be a cornerstone of Republican and conservative ideology, and that is individual responsibility. If individuals are willing to give their all to their families, then they should be allowed to marry and to adopt. I think that love and commitment are one of those things that doesn't only attach to couples of the opposite sex.[10]

Of course, not all Republicans and conservatives agree with Kennedy. There are Republicans who believe gays should be recognized in civil unions, with all the benefits of marriage, but not the religious or ceremonial significance attached. There are Republicans who disagree with all versions of gay unions, some of whom are gay themselves. Many believe gay marriage is a states' rights issue. It's unfortunate, however, that the Left characterizes all of those who vote against gay marriage as narrow-minded or stupid. "Americans are smart people," says Sammon. "They have a remarkable ability to see through politicians who say one thing, but do another. I think most Americans are concerned with the issues that affect them and their families every day. They're less concerned about wedge issues like marriage and more concerned about how they're going to pay their bills and care for their families."

There is, however, that special kind of Republican who likes to justify his or her homophobia with a perplexing kind of circular argument that makes little, if any, sense. Deroy Murdock, a conservative syndicated columnist for Scripps Howard News Service and a contributing editor for National Review Online, described that kind of conservative viewpoint, which admittedly has some problematic, hypocritical holes.

> I think when conservatives engage in the gay marriage debate, I think some of them do it because they have sincere, moral concerns. I think some of them do it because they believe they'll gain some political advantage out of exploiting this issue. I think it's fascinating that you heard for years that the problem with homosexuality is promiscuity. So then, fine. Why don't we let gay people get married, and then promiscuity will stop. Oh no, no . . . we can't do that! So which is it? A promiscuity problem or a fidelity problem? I always find that to be contradictory.[11]

So it's true. Stupid arguments exist. But stupidity is not the sole property of the Right. The myth that only Republicans are bigots is entirely inaccurate, as Patrick Sammon explained.

That is simply untrue. While the Republican Party clearly has some work to do to get to where it needs to be on gay and lesbian issues, there are countless good, faithful Republicans all across the country who are standing up for gays and lesbians. From Representatives Chris Shays (R-CT), Ileana Ros-Lehtinen (R-FL), Wayne Gilchrest (R-MD), and Deb Price (R-OH) in the U.S. House to Senators Gordon Smith (R-OR), Olympia Snowe (R-ME), and Arlen Specter (R-PA), we're seeing a growing list of Republicans in Congress who consistently support pro-gay legislation.

Also, across the country in statehouses and in local governments, there are countless inclusive Republicans. From Governors Arnold Schwarzenegger in California to Jodi Rell in Connecticut, to New York State assemblywoman Teresa Sayward, who supports marriage equality, to Michigan state representative Lorence Wenke, who consistently takes positions in support of pro-gay legislation; to Wyoming state representative Dan Zwonitzer, who recently gave a very passionate speech in favor of gay and lesbian Americans, we're seeing a tremendous number of Republicans who stand up for basic fairness.

Basic fairness. It's a refreshing lens through which to view gay-rights issues. But homophobia and discrimination will likely persist in this country, and most assuredly throughout the world, where discrimination and antihate laws are less sophisticated and more anemic. But when someone like liberal comedian David Cross says, "I really don't have a problem with gay marriage . . . because I'm tolerant and rational,"[12] let's remember that basic fairness isn't a partisan issue, and that some Republicans do not speak for all. I'm sure Democrats would enjoy the same fairness. Otherwise, they'd *all* have to defend their wacky position on naked-gay-pride-float-flag-burning.

CHAPTER 18

Republicans Hate Foreigners

The Myth of the Nationalist Conservative

> You can take your pick of issues where Republicans are seriously damaging this country: Iraq, global warming, civil liberties. But I resent them most for how they've destroyed the American spirit by using xenophobia and fear to hold on to power.[1]
>
> —Paul Newman

Former Atlanta Braves pitcher John Rocker embodies the oft-cited caricature of the narrow-minded, flag-waving, nationalistic Republican who despises (or just doesn't get) foreigners. He's a loud, obnoxious, shoot-from-the-hip type who used to let baseballs thrown in the bullpen bounce off his chest to pump him up for games. Back in 1999, Rocker sent shock waves through the sports world after he said in a *Sports Illustrated* interview, "The biggest thing I don't like about New York are the foreigners. I'm not a very big fan of foreigners. You can walk an entire block in Times Square and not hear anybody speaking English. Asians and Koreans and Vietnamese and Indians and Russians and Spanish people and everything up there. How the hell did they get in this country?"[2]

Rocker wasn't just taking aim at foreigners, but at that quasi-foreign group known as New York City commuters, when he said, "Imagine having to take the [Number] 7 train to the ballpark, looking like you're [riding through] Beirut next to some kid with purple hair next to some queer with AIDS right next to some dude who just got out of jail for the fourth time right next to some 20-year-old mom with four kids."[3]

Even after the end of his playing days, John Rocker, admittedly a Republican, continues to wax philosophical about nationalism. He and his wife have formed a group called "Speak English," whose goal is "to encourage people to promote and support the sustainment of the American heritage and the American culture," because when "immigrants vote with their feet and come to this country with the intent to live, work, raise a family and enjoy all of the incredible advantages that America has to offer, but make no attempt to learn the language, observe the customs, or celebrate the holidays, these immigrants are showing a tremendous amount of disrespect to their hosts."[4] Although endorsing anything John Rocker has said (including "thank you") feels terribly wrong, he does make one good point: "It's time to stop feeling guilty for living in the greatest nation on earth, and start standing up for America."[5]

Republicans have long been depicted as intolerant and squeamish toward anything that isn't American. And it's not just the John Rockers of the world who are to blame for the stereotype. One can imagine the joy that spread across Democratic political campaigns and comedy news shows when former U.S. Republican senator from Virginia George Allen called an Indian man videotaping his campaign event in 2006 "Macaca." While there are prominent Republicans who have made stupid comments, fueling the Republicans' purported affinity for jingoism, far less is made of Democrats who make equally stupid remarks, like Joe Biden (D-Delaware) who said in 2005 while talking to a group of Indian Americans in Delaware, "You cannot go into a 7-Eleven or Dunkin' Donuts unless you have a slight Indian accent. I'm not joking."[6] Biden found a bit more hot water in 2007 when he said about Illinois senator and Democratic presidential hopeful Barack Obama, "I mean, you got the first mainstream African-American who is articulate and bright and clean and a nice-looking guy."[7]

The myth of the foreigner-hating Republican has been frequently invoked in recent years to disparage the Bush administration, which is cited for its refusal to enter into certain international treaties like the International Criminal Court, for the "go-it-alone" approach to the war in Iraq, for hostility toward institutions like the United Nations, which extend credibility to regimes like Syria by putting it on the Security Council, and for the so-called imposition of our democratic ideals on others. The criticism is even leveled when Bush closes addresses with "God Bless America," both for its religious undertones and for its implication that America is somehow a "chosen" nation.

But these critics then ignore events like the controversy that erupted in February 2006, when the Dubai-based company DP World sought acquisition of a U.K. firm that managed six major U.S. seaports. Members of both parties opposed the deal on the grounds that control of U.S. ports by an Arab country could severely compromise U.S. security. The senator who introduced amendments to block the deal was Chuck Schumer, Democrat from New York, who is no stranger to politically popular maneuvers that earn him camera time. The man who led the charge to approve the deal was President Bush himself, who said, "It would send a terrible signal to friends and allies not to let this deal go through."[8] In the end, DP World foresaw the political obstacles and sold operation of our ports to a U.S. company. It was one of the few times that many Democrats had to give Bush credit for getting it right and resisting the tide of cultural panic. Even Jimmy Carter said, "My belief is that the president, and his secretary of state, the Defense Department and others have adequately cleared the Dubai government or organization to manage their ports."[9]

So, when was the myth of the extreme-nationalist Republican born, and why has it endured? Do conservatives hate foreigners or are we just damn happy to be American?

Perhaps the stereotype is born partially of America's history with colonialism. Republican presidents Teddy Roosevelt and William Taft admittedly made large contributions to colonial advancement in Latin America at the turn of the century, advancements some described as driven by "American exceptionalism," or the belief that the United States is qualitatively better than other nations. Perhaps it is the fact that Republicans tend to shy away from multinational institutions whose motives, policies, and competence they question. Perhaps it is simply based on the hackneyed image of the Republican redneck driving a pickup truck with a bumper sticker declaring "These Colors Don't Run." (Incidentally, such clever displays of American pride are not reserved just for rednecks. White- and blue-collar types alike have been spotted in New York City wearing American flag T-shirts that read "Try Burning This One, Asshole.")

Certainly, the line between patriotism and jingoism is blurry, but those who perpetuate the Republicans-are-nationalist myth are confusing a sense of national superiority with a sense of national pride. Dinesh D'Souza, conservative author and policy advisor during the Reagan administration, explained in his book, *What's So Great About America,* "What is distinctively Western is not ethnocentrism but a profound and highly beneficial effort to transcend ethnocentrism. Only in the West has there been a consistent willingness to question the identification of the good with one's own way. The foreign critique of America would not be so formidable if Americans were united in responding to it" and "[c]onservatism is generally the party of patriotism."[10] He goes on to discuss the possible origins of this American penchant for questioning our own motives. "On the political Left, anti-Americanism has been prevalent and even fashionable at least since the Vietnam War. After 9/11, some of these American critics could not resist the temptation to argue that 'America had it coming,' like columnist Barbara Ehrenreich, who said that the United States is responsible for 'the vast global inequalities in which terrorism is ultimately rooted.'"[11]

Most likely, what really drives the myth of the nationalist Republican is the rise of multiculturalism—and its supreme trendiness in the zeitgeist of the liberal elite, many of whom view America as racist, corrupt, and greedy, or at least like to say they do. Harvard Law School constitutional law professor Richard Parker, a rare proponent of exercising patriotism in Cambridge, agreed. "The rise of multiculturalism in the last twenty-five years has been a powerful force that has accelerated the erosion of patriotism, and multiculturalism, as everybody knows, is most intense in environments like this. What has abided in the culture of the elite Left, not the working-class Left, but the elite Left, is an identification of America with two things: capitalism and racism. And that is, I think, the most powerfully felt and expressed sentiment that they have been purveying for seventy-five years."[12]

After September 11, Parker, who has testified before Congress in favor of a constitutional amendment banning desecration of the flag, authored a paper titled "Homeland: An Essay on Patriotism," setting forth his arguments for patriotism, and why it is good and necessary (and not, as much of Cambridge would insist, racist and narrow-minded). When asked how the essay had been received by his multicultural colleagues, he said, simply, that it hasn't. "They have ignored my views on that." But, he continued, "there is a substantial minority of the students here who, when I bring it up in class . . . basically support what I said and say that they are very patriotic and always have been." And have his students on the left received his message differently than those on the right? "I don't think there is much question there. I think students who self-identify as left-wing or as liberal or as progressive, tend to, without any particular discussion, disdainfully reject my point of view."[13] (To clarify for those who would like to dismiss Parker's account as the perspective of the university's token conservative, Parker is a Democrat.)

In her book *Slander*, conservative commentator Ann Coulter wrote of the Left's bizarre problem with patriotism especially as it arose after September 11. "And they complained about all the damn flag-wavers. The internal flag-waving after 9/11 nearly drove liberals out of their gourds. For the Left, 'flag-waving' is an epithet. Liberals variously called the flag a 'joke,' 'very, very dumb,' and—most cutting—not 'cosmopolitan.' New York University sociology professor Todd Gitlin agonized over the decision to fly the flag outside his apartment (located less than a mile from Ground Zero), explaining: 'It's very complicated.'"[14]

William O'Reilly, a political consultant in New York (who, when we requested an interview, insisted that we must have the wrong guy, since he wasn't the one with the prime-time show on Fox News), explained how patriotism was behind his identification as a Republican. "For someone my age, people were being told that America wasn't good. [Reagan] then came along and it was like he was saying to the whole country, 'Snap out of it. Be proud to be an American.' When Reagan came into office after the seventies, it seemed like everyone in America was ashamed. With the Vietnam War, there was this sense in the country that we had done something wrong. And Reagan came along and said, 'We're America. We're good. We're founded on good principles and this is a great place.'"[15]

Reagan, the father of the modern conservative movement, told a story during his famous "Time for Choosing" speech in 1964 while campaigning for Barry Goldwater. The speech reflected his patriotic view of America. "Not too long ago two friends of mine were talking to a Cuban refugee, a businessman who had escaped from Castro, and in the midst of his story one of my friends turned to the other and said, 'We don't know how lucky we are.' And the Cuban stopped and said, 'How lucky you are! I had someplace to escape to.' In that sentence he told us the entire story. If we lose freedom here, there is no place to escape to. This is the last stand on Earth."[16]

None of this is to imply that Republicans or conservatives have a monopoly on patriotism. Many make the argument that dissent itself is a patriotic performance of our national duty. Of dissent, O'Reilly said, "I'm not suggesting that people on the left are America-haters. But there does seem to be a tendency to look at why Americans are wrong. I remember being a teenager and the kids on the left were talking about boycotting the National Anthem and not standing. And then you had the kids in the Young Republican Club and they would stand straight up when the National Anthem was on."[17]

Professor Parker addressed the nuanced notion that dissent itself is patriotic. "Dissent is part of the ethos of the system about which one is patriotic, but that is just a piece of it."[18] Those who constantly disparage the United States and then claim patriotism are often distorting the meaning of the word. It is like saying you support the troops but oppose their mission, their tactics, and their very presence. As Parker wrote in his essay, part of patriotism is based on "love" and a "personal potent attachment to [the] nation,"[19] and the statistics reveal that the proud-to-be-an-American variety of patriotism is more widespread among Republicans than Democrats.

A June 2005 Fox News poll revealed some glaring differences between Republicans and Democrats, when it comes to love of country:

* 98% of Republicans would not want to live anywhere but the U.S., compared to 89% of Democrats.

* 63% of Republicans were more proud to be an American in 2005 than in the previous year, compared with 44% of Democrats.
* 14% of Democrats were less proud to be an American in 2005, whereas only 2% of Republicans were less proud.
* 64% of Republicans described themselves as more patriotic than the average American, 36% said a lot more patriotic.
* 53% of Democrats described themselves as more patriotic than the average American, 27% a lot more patriotic.[20]

Still another poll reveals that among Bush voters, 83 percent believe American society is generally fair and decent. Seventy-four percent of conservatives believe the world would be better if other nations were more like the United States, and only 15 percent believe it would be worse. However, only 49 percent of liberals think the world would be better if countries were more like the United States and 37 percent believe it would be worse. Even moderate voters believe the world would be better if countries were more like ours at a rate of three to one.[21]

Anti-Americanism, both at home and abroad, seems to be on the rise. "I think [patriotism] has been watered down," Professor Parker reflected. "You talk to anyone my age—I am sixty—and ask them to think back to the fifties and compare it to now and, are we as patriotic? No honest person could say it's anywhere close."[22] Yale University professor and political commentator David Gelernter added another subtlety worth mentioning: "If you declare yourself neutral as between America and her enemies . . . your neutrality in itself is bias."[23]

Polls abroad also show a staggering amount of hostility toward Americans, despite the economic and human sacrifices we have made for these countries throughout history. Recent polls in Europe show that less than 40 percent of both France and Germany have a favorable opinion of the United States; less than 30 percent of Spain has a favorable opinion. Unfavorable views of the United States exceed 90 percent in many Middle Eastern countries.[24]

Conservative commentator Dinesh D'Souza, who was born in Bombay, India, wrote, "America is the greatest, freest, and most decent society in existence. It is an oasis of goodness in a desert of cynicism and barbarism. This country, once an experiment unique in the world, is now the last best hope for the world."[25] After countless celebrities and activists promised they'd leave the country if Bush won re-election in 2004, left-leaning (okay, left-falling-over) *Harper's* magazine published a story entitled "Electing to Leave: A Reader's Guide to Expatriating on November 3," which explained rather humorously and in great detail exactly how one would go about becoming a "renunciant," as one is termed by the State Department. Turns out it's tougher than just burning one's passport (which is illegal) and hopping the next bus to the Canadian border. In light of the bureaucratic difficulty of fleeing to a neighboring country, the story suggests forming one's own nation, which has been successfully and unsuccessfully attempted a number of times over the past century. As the article recounts, "A less fortunate attempt was made in 1972, when Michael Oliver, a Nevada businessman, built an island on a reef 260 miles southwest of Tonga. Hiring a dredger, he piled up sand and mud until he had enough landmass to declare independence for his 'Republic of Minerva.' Unfortunately, the Republic of Minerva was soon invaded by a Tongan force, whose number is said to have included a work detail of prisoners, a brass band, and Tonga's 350-pound king himself. The reef was later officially annexed by the kingdom."[26]

Attempts at secession and sovereignty aren't new. Now, it seems, Vermont is making a serious (well, serious for Vermont) effort to secede from the rest of the country, and has dubbed that effort the Green Mountain Independence Movement. Visit VermontRepublic. org, and you'll learn that the "Second Vermont Republic is a peaceful, democratic, grassroots voluntary association committed to the return of Vermont to its rightful status as an independent republic as was the case from 1777 to 1791, and to support Vermont's future development as a separate, sustainable nation-state."[27] One of our country's poorest states, Vermont's "sustainability" seems the real question mark in that plan. With just under two thousand signatures on their Vermont Independence Resolution petition gathered between November 2006 and July 2007, the movement is small, but gaining publicity.

Nonetheless, as of today, Vermont remains a state. And Alec Baldwin remains an American. So why *didn't* the scores of celebrities and activists who promised to leave actually flee? Baldwin maintains multiple residences in the United States, as do Susan Sarandon and Tim Robbins, Michael Moore, Janeane Garofalo, and others. Is it that they're committed to staying in hopes of changing America for the better? Or did they, as we suspect, have a change of heart after more careful consideration? Living elsewhere, after all, is not always as seductive a reality as it may seem. Below are some frightening facts and statistics about the places Alec Baldwin may one day call home.

According to Aneki.com, a world ranking website that compiles United Nations, CIA World Factbook, and BBC information:

* Russia, Armenia, and Romania are the world's least happy countries.
* Liberia has an unemployment rate of 85%. South Africa's is 31%. (The United States' is around 4%.)
* The highest suicide rates are found in Lithuania, Russia, and Belarus. Hungary and Finland are also highly ranked.
* Norway, Denmark, Switzerland, Germany, and Austria have the highest incidence of testicular cancer.
* Residents of Luxembourg, Norway, and Iceland incur the highest health-care expenses.
* Egypt, Turkey, and Pakistan are ranked worst for gender equality.

* The United Kingdom, Mexico, Austria, Portugal, and Australia have the largest overweight populations.
* Folks in South Korea, Czech Republic, and Poland work the most hours a year.
* Japan, South Korea, Russia, Taiwan, and Norway are the world's most expensive countries to live in.
* Africa's countries, including South Africa, make up the top 19 in the world with the highest AIDS infection rate. Haiti takes the 20 spot.[28]

But it's not just statistics that should give America-bashers like Baldwin pause, it's our way of life. While it's likely that every country in the world has some kind of romantic allure for the traveler, the adventure seeker, the academic, the anthropologist, the honeymooner, and the postcollege backpacker, actually living in another country requires some serious consideration. For example, France, often the subject of unremitting romantic liturgy, is also struggling with an enduring and highly troubling racism epidemic. *Time* put the country's problem under a microscope in a January 2007 article entitled "Racism Unfiltered in France," which made the United States seem like the happy Benetton ads we may one day resemble. The story recalled a recent incident making headlines:

The latest outrage came from second-string TV personality and self-appointed social commentator Pascal Sevran, whose recently published book included the obscenely racist idea that the "black [penis] is responsible for famine in Africa." Elaborating in a newspaper interview, Sevran said, "Africa is dying from all the children born there" to parents supposedly too sexually undisciplined or dumb to realize they could not feed them all. The answer to the problem? "We need to sterilize half the planet," Sevran emphatically replied. Known as a relentless attention-seeker, the defiant Sevran drew only limited fire for his comments, and a public rebuke from his public television employer—though not the cancellation of his Sunday program that many demanded. Appalled at the light punishment, the government of Niger (itself a victim of recent famines) announced it would file libel charges against Sevran in French courts.[29]

In fact, racism abounds in most of Europe. Discrimination, inequality, and blind hatred are rampant for Europe's blacks, Indians, Muslims, Africans, Jews, and every other minority. Staunch Aryan groups have popped up in nearly every country (if they ever left). If you've watched a European soccer game, you know that mocking black players with monkey sounds or by throwing banana peels on the pitch is frighteningly commonplace.

Farther away, in India, a Democratic country since 1947, one segment of the population is suffering an incredibly cruel injustice, as CNN writer Anwa Damon wrote in a July 2007 piece. Widows, ostracized by the rest of the country, are flocking to the holy city of Vrindavan by the thousands—to die. "These Hindu widows, the poorest of the poor, are shunned from society when their husbands die, not for religious reasons, but because of tradition—and because they're seen as a financial drain on their families. They cannot remarry. They must not wear jewelry. They are forced to shave their heads and typically wear white. Even their shadows are considered bad luck."[30] And this isn't just a problem for the few. "There are an estimated 40 million widows in India, the least fortunate of them shunned and stripped of the life they lived when they were married. It's believed that 15,000 widows live on the streets of Vrindavan, a city of about 55,000 in northern India."

While the thought of dying a Hindu widow in India is horrific, the thought of merely visiting Venezuela sounds impossibly worse. In a warning issued by the U.S. State Department for travelers planning a vacation in Hugo Chávez's backyard, Americans are urged to reconsider, and for good reason:

Violent crime in Venezuela is pervasive, both in the capital, Caracas, and in the interior. The country has one of the highest per-capita murder rates in the world. Armed robberies take place in broad daylight throughout the city, including areas generally presumed safe and frequented by tourists. A common technique is to choke the victim into unconsciousness and then rob them of all they are carrying. Well-armed criminal gangs operate with impunity, often setting up fake police checkpoints. Kidnapping is a particularly serious problem, with more than 1,000 reported during the past year alone. There have been several high profile kidnappings that have resulted in murder, including the killings of three minor Canadian brothers, a wealthy Italo-Venezuelan businessman, and the daughter of a senior Venezuelan military commander. Investigation of all crime is haphazard and ineffective. In the case of high-profile killings, the authorities quickly round up suspects, but rarely produce evidence linking these individuals to the crime. Only a very small percentage of criminals are tried and convicted.[31]

In Afghanistan, the turmoil surrounding the release of the movie version of Khaled Hosseini's *The Kite Runner* highlighted a significant culture gap between East and West that positions art as a precarious barometer of ethnic tension and national pride. After filming a hard-to-watch rape scene, the Afghani child actors fled the country to wait out hostile reactions to their performances, and even required the protection of the CIA. Earlier, Hazara peoples in Afghanistan called for the execution of an actor in an Indian film named *Kabul Express* for, as part of a scripted scene in the movie, insulting the Hazara. He fled the country.[32]

Even as close as Mexico, stories of spring-breakers' paying off or outrunning corrupt federal police are as common as parasites and hangovers. While corruption exists in U.S. law enforcement, it's almost unimaginable that a police officer in Daytona Beach would demand "all the money you have" at the business end of a machine gun in exchange for your release after a traffic violation.

There are great places to live all over the world, of course, each with advantages and disadvantages, much like the United States. And anecdotes like these are just that—anecdotes that don't paint the whole picture about the countries in which they occurred, or even come close. But the liberal, knee-jerk, anti-American glorification of places far and exotic (or, in Canada's case, close and ordinary) is the kind of unfortunate pabulum often mistaken for courageous political rebellion—rebellion that is almost always more of a hypothetical promise than an actual ideological prospect. Are Republicans extreme nationalists? Many probably do prefer living in the United States to living in other nations. But who knows? When Alec Baldwin is suddenly a citizen of Trinidad and Tobago, and Michael Moore's passport is issued by the Sudan, and Ben Affleck calls Nicaragua home, the myth of the foreigner-hating conservative just might become truth.

CHAPTER 19

Republicans Are Warmongers

The Myth of the Unilateral Interventionist

The atrocity in New York was predictable and inevitable. It was an act of retaliation against constant and systematic manifestations of state terrorism on the part of the United States over many years, in all parts of the world. I believe that it will do this not only to take control of Iraqi oil, but also because the American administration is now a blood-thirsty wild animal.[1]

—Harold Pinter

A 2004 *New York Times* story about the Republican National Convention in New York City quoted John Price, a veteran of the first Gulf War, as saying of the antiwar protesters, "Anytime in this town when I voice my opinion, I am treated like a warmonger and a hater of mankind."[2]

Republicans in New York City can commiserate in the shared hostility directed at them when they appear at all patriotic or are perceived as generally agreeing with the war in Iraq. Antiwar liberals tend to assume they're in the majority, and are thus extremely comfortable discussing their animosity toward those who support the war, often unprompted. Bumper stickers like "How do you say 'Vietnam' in Arabic?" and "Impeach Bush" are as common in Manhattan as Yankee caps and Whole Foods grocery bags.

Further, they actually believe that anyone who voted for Bush a second time must be, at the very least, a misanthrope of the sociopathic variety, and at the worst, a proxy assassin. War supporters are often asked—in bars, at restaurants, in museums, on the street—"So you're *in favor* of genocide, then?"

Genocide? Warmonger? It's safe to say that most New Yorkers have never committed mass murder, unless you count the roaches that frequent their apartments or the fish they've caught upstate or on Long Island—legally, of course. (Maybe that makes them fishmongers.) But purveyors of war? Shouldn't one have to have voted for more than one wartime president to become an official monger?

In a 2004 speech, Democratic presidential candidate John Kerry said that "George Bush and his armchair hawks" had, with a policy of "unilateral preemption," failed to win the War on Terror. In 2007, California Democratic representative Pete Stark actually said that President Bush sent troops to Iraq to "get their heads blown off" for his own "amusement."[3] He was later forced to apologize, and did so profusely. Everyone from Kofi Annan to Vladimir Putin warned Bush against a "unilateral attack on Iraq."[4] In a cursory search of stories written between September 12, 2001, and September 10, 2006, the words "Bush," "unilateral," and "Iraq" appeared together in the pages of the *New York Times* in 412 separate articles, despite an extensive international coalition in Iraq.

Certainly, the accusation of conservative warmongering is very much driven by the perception of unilateralism. There may in fact be some truth to the idea that conservatives are more inclined to use force in the national interest even if the United Nations is unwilling to throw a society ball endorsing the policy. Nonetheless, there are plenty of examples where conservatives have orchestrated successful policies through multilateral measures. For one, George H. W. Bush commanded the Persian Gulf War in 1991, leading thirty-five nations and authorized by the United Nations to push back the Iraqi invasion of Kuwait, an operation widely regarded as overwhelmingly successful.

George W. Bush, who may well go down at the hands (or pens) of melodramatic academics as the greatest unilateral warmonger of all time, also has many multilateral feathers in his cap. NATO troops were sent to Afghanistan after our invasion in 2001, which most countries—and even Jon Stewart—approved of. Likewise, more than thirty countries have provided some troop support in Iraq. Even more impressive, however, the Bush administration appears to have succeeded in pressuring North Korea to cease uranium enrichment and dismantle its nuclear-weapons program after steadfastly insisting on six-party talks involving China, South Korea, Japan, Russia, North Korea, and the United States. The Bush administration insisted on this multilateral strategy despite North Korea's request for bilateral talks and despite criticism from the Left that Bush wasn't doing enough to deal with the problem.

The administration has also pursued multilateral diplomacy in dealing with Iran, seeking a Middle East solution between Israel and Palestine and pressuring Libya to dismantle its weapons-of-mass-destruction program, including an active nuclear-weapons program that was safely packaged up and shipped to Oak Ridge, Tennessee. Despite successes like these, however, critics refuse to grant credit for skilled brinksmanship in a dangerous, complicated world. Some even dismissed Bush's success in dealing with Libya as nothing noteworthy, given that the military leader of Libya, Muammar al-Qaddafi, previously offered to open its weapons programs to international inspection. This offer was later rebuffed by the Clinton administration (well done!).

That the media are liberally biased and give Bush little or no credit for foreign policy successes is no real surprise, although the "leftness" of the media is still, inexplicably, routinely contested. MSNBC.com investigative reporter Bill Dedman revealed some telling facts in a June 2007 story that surprised many in the field and outside it.

"MSNBC.com identified 144 journalists who made political contributions from 2004 through the start of the 2008 campaign, according to the public records of the Federal Election Commission. Most of the newsroom checkbooks leaned to the left: 125 journalists gave to Democrats and liberal causes. Only 17 gave to Republicans. Two gave to both parties."[5] The question should not be, "Are the media liberal?" But rather, "Does the *San Francisco Chronicle* offer a witness protection program for its two conservative employees?" Indeed, American news organizations make political statements not just by reporting, but by failing to report. As Fox News correspondent Chris Wallace told Steve Malzberg in a radio interview, about a decrease in American soldier deaths in Iraq: "That story is untold. You don't see it in the *New York Times,* and you don't see it in the *Washington Post.* . . . The mainstream media don't like good news from Iraq. The surge is working."[6]

Liberals have long painted Republicans and conservatives as career war-ists, accusing the party of waging "wars" on women, children, the Earth, even science. Saying that they enjoy war is a pet platitude. Indeed, it seems as though the Left and the liberal media are either misinformed or confused about how to characterize Republicans. In the most obvious case, President Bush is routinely portrayed as both a reckless, go-it-alone cowboy who listens to no one *and* a hapless puppet who won't butter his toast without a consensus from his Svengali advisors. It can't be both—is he a bloodthirsty warmonger or a spineless victim of the ruthless company he keeps?

In fact, the history of conservatives-as-interventionists is a short and, ironically, isolated one, as the term came to be associated with Republicans when the staunch isolationist conservatives of the so-called Old Right favored U.S. intervention abroad to fight the communist threat. The New Right that eventually elected Ronald Reagan supported intervention during the Cold War. (Before this, Republicans vehemently opposed intervening in the Korean War.) Kiron K. Skinner, co-editor of *Reagan: A Life in Letters,* wrote in a 2004 *New York Times* editorial that "President Reagan was dubbed a warmonger when, within a span of little more than two weeks in March, he called the Soviet Union an 'evil empire' and then announced that he was authorizing research and development for strategic defense."[7] The term "neoconservative," most often attributed to Irving Kristol, was strictly a commentary on U.S. domestic policy, and over the years has mysteriously come to represent the conservative's supposedly hawkish attitude toward foreign policy. Jeremy Rabkin, a policy analyst who sits on the board of directors of the U.S. Institute of Peace, has examined the misconception:

> I don't think it is true that "conservatives" are inherently "interventionist" while "liberals" are inherently cautious. The positions were largely reversed during the Kosovo conflict. There were some "conservatives" who favored U.S. intervention there but not many. My recollection is that the Congress refused to pass any measure, even retroactively, authorizing or approving Clinton's bombing campaign—because Congress was dominated by Republicans by then and the Republican base was not keen on that war at all. You might recall that back in the late 1930s and early 1940s, "conservatives" tended to be much more cautious about U.S. involvement in the impending (or already fierce) conflicts in Europe. Liberals supported FDR's policies and urged him to be more assertive about helping Britain. To some extent, partisans respond to the political incentives of the moment. Republicans want to support the policies

of a Republican president, when they can, and challenge the policies of a Dem president, when they can—and vice versa for Democrats.[8]

Indeed, one need only look at the anecdotal evidence to see that the myth of the conservative unilateral interventionist is an inaccurate piece of liberal propaganda that has somehow made its way into the popular story of conservative history.

* Democratic president Franklin D. Roosevelt led the United States into war with Germany in 1941, when the United States was attacked by Japan.
* Democratic president Harry S. Truman presided over the end of World War II and in 1950 entered the Korean War, which began as a civil war between North and South Korea.
* In 1962, Democratic president John F. Kennedy started the Vietnam War, which also began as a civil war, between North Vietnam and South Vietnam.
* Democratic president Lyndon B. Johnson continued the Vietnam conflict.
* Republican president Richard M. Nixon ended the Vietnam War in 1975.
* Democratic president Bill Clinton ordered cruise missile strikes on Afghanistan and the Sudan in 1998. Clinton and NATO forces bombed Kosovo and Serbia without declaring war in 1999. Clinton also led U.S. troops into a disastrous military conflict with UN forces in Somalia in the early 1990s, an incident widely credited with emboldening al Qaeda.

Are Republicans really more bloodthirsty than Democrats? Liberal ideologues like to characterize conservatives as aggressive war hawks who *seek out* opportunities to enter conflicts merely for their own sadistic enjoyment. Noam Chomsky said of the United States, for example, just after the terrorist attacks of September

11, "There are hawkish elements who want to use the occasion to strike out at their enemies, with extreme violence, no matter how many innocent people suffer."[9]

A very strong argument against the Republican warmonger myth is the pursuit of defensive technologies, a pursuit that only Republicans have seemed interested in exploring. President Reagan initiated the Strategic Defensive Initiative (SDI, nicknamed "Star Wars" by opponents) and sought to build a comprehensive shield for the United States and its allies against a nuclear attack. Republicans argued that the program was necessary, while those on the left denounced it for a number of reasons, from its supposed infeasibility to its strategic foolishness. While the SDI began under Reagan, the fall of the Soviet Union and lack of funding during the Clinton administration slowed the National Missile Defense (NMD) program. However, funding has greatly increased under President Bush's administration, and the issue has received heightened attention with the president's signing in December 2002 of National Security Presidential Directive 22, which outlined a plan for an operational system.

Despite skepticism from opponents that an NMD program would work, the U.S. government has been increasingly successful in recent tests with improved technology. Nonetheless, there are still those who claim that NMD is a bad, even a hostile policy. The most frequently cited argument is that it would undermine the doctrine of mutually assured destruction with Russia, whereby our respective nuclear arsenals prevent war that an NMD shield might provoke. Despite the fact that the primary motivation behind the NMD program is protection from rogue nuclear states, those on the left would apparently prefer to bear this risk unprotected in order to preserve the ivory tower doctrine of mutually assured destruction and forgo the pursuit of *defensive* technologies. Those damn defensemongers in the White House! Perhaps analogizing a missile defense shield to a condom for the nation that enables us to engage in protected foreign policy, rather than unprotected foreign policy, or worse, abstinence, would change the thinking of the Left on this issue.

President Reagan also was instrumental in achieving passage in 1987 of the International-Range Nuclear Forces Treaty, which eliminated much of the nuclear arsenals of the United States and Soviet Union, and in 1986 Reagan even proposed banning all ballistic missiles, a proposal that the Soviet Union rejected because of U.S. research into the SDI. Reagan used the Reykjavik Summit, which was held in 1986 between Reagan and then Soviet premier Mikhail Gorbachev, as a platform not just to discuss arms control but also to discuss Soviet aggression at home and abroad.

Whether or not one believes that the Far Left—as represented by people like Chomsky and Stark—has helped solidify the idea that the efforts of America's "hawkish elements" to exert power over foreign enemies represent the demise of Western civilization, there is still truth in the classical conservative belief that conflict *will* arise, regardless of attempts at diplomacy. Jeremy Rabkin describes the ideological divide as follows:

> I would say liberalism is strongly inclined to believe that there is some political ground on which everyone can agree—it is, in a way, a philosophy of consensus. So even when liberals do support war, it has to be couched as a war for and even by everyone, humanity, the world. Liberals love the UN (as previously the League of Nations, and before that the war to end all wars—that is, something which, at least potentially, will encompass everyone in a final consensus of the whole world). Conservatives start from the opposite presumption. There will always be evil in the world. There will always be disagreements about how to define or confront evil. Conflict is part of human nature. So we can't hope to settle everything but we need to be prepared to defend ourselves.

As far as unilateralism goes, Rabkin points out that current popular culture seems to have overlooked its past in selectively labeling Bush and Republicans either unilateralists or interventionists:

> I think liberals were drawn to Clinton's Balkan war because it was supposed to be on behalf of humanity. It was not, in fact, authorized by the UN, any more than Bush's war in Iraq. But somehow the Balkan war felt, to liberals, like something multilateral. More nations contributed support to Bush's war but it felt, to liberals, "unilateralist" because there was less talk among war supporters about humanity and more about U.S. interests. And, of course, France was with us on the Clinton war and not on this one. But Bush did round up half the countries in Europe to help in the Iraq War. Most of their contributions were token, but they don't have enough troops to make more than token contributions, anyway. If you look at forces deployed in Afghanistan, which everyone says is a good war, because [it was] approved by the UN, you find that European force contributions there are also very small—and less than promised, in fact. They don't have a lot of force except moral force.
>
> Why liberals are impressed by the moral authority of France or Germany is hard for me to understand, but perhaps they see these countries as standing at the opposite pole from Texas and simply can't resist the impulse to embrace whatever is anti-Bush. But anyway, it is not a serious argument to pretend that a policy is "multilateral" when France approves it but "unilateral" when France rejects it—no matter how many other countries approve it (in this case, Spain, Portugal, Italy, U.K., Denmark, Netherlands, Czech Republic, Poland, Estonia, Latvia, Australia, Japan, etc.).

Indeed, the hypocrisy is evident even now, while mired in an unpopular war in Iraq, as Democrats continue to harangue Republicans for "meddling in other countries' affairs"—and then do just that. In

2007 Democrats came together to support a resolution that would label Turkish attacks on Armenians during World War I, which resulted in as many as 1.5 million deaths, as genocide. Though it may be a worthy cause, President Bush was vocal and adamant against such a declaration, for fear it could jeopardize America's valuable and fragile ties with Turkey. Democrats insisted the resolution was necessary and urgent, despite its relatively symbolic importance and its dangerous implications, prompting the prime minister of Turkey, Recep Tayyip Erdogan, to say, "Democrats are harming the future of the United States and are encouraging anti-American sentiments,"[10] and threatening to cut ties with the U.S.

In 2004, Harvard Law School professor William Stuntz wrote an article for TCS Daily called "Sunrise in the West," in which he compares the geographical East-West divide in the United States to the Democrat-Republican divide. The article sheds further light on why Republicans are often seen as more prone to war. "Easterners like theory and process. Westerners care more about outcomes than procedures, and they like whatever works. Easterners are cautious; Westerners take chances. Easterners like universities, legislatures, and the UN. Westerners like businesses, the executive branch, and the Army. Eastern politicians are more likely to talk down to voters—think of Dewey, Adlai Stevenson, or John Kerry—because they are instinctively less democratic; they come from a world where social and educational class matters and where institutions seem to outlast people."[11]

Indeed, to the Left, according to Stuntz, it's more often about *process* than *progress*. "Legislators, like lawyers (Kerry is both), believe that if you get the process right, if the right people are consulted along the way and the right arguments are made at the right times, good decisions will follow. Executives know better."[12]

Echoing Rabkin's assertion that the Left enjoys the touchy-feely-ness of multilateralism, Stuntz suggests, "Perhaps Kerry's critique of Bush's approach to terrorism didn't sell because it boiled down to two inconsistent claims about process: Don't consult allies in Afghanistan; that's outsourcing. Consult everyone in the world—well, everyone in the United Nations—about Iraq. On the campaign trail, Kerry often said that he 'might' have gone to war in Iraq, but that if he had, 'I'd have done it right.' Meaning, he would have gotten the right process."[13]

The modern manifestation of the warmongering conservative myth may also stem from the need to compensate for a lack of actual foreign policy. Byron York, White House correspondent for *National Review*, says:

> I think it shows that a lot of Democrats have succumbed to Bush hatred—for several reasons. One is that they are still angry about the impeachment of Bill Clinton and the 2000 Florida recount. They just can't let go. Second, they are uncomfortable with the assertion of U.S. military power for anything other than humanitarian purposes—say, for self-defense. They are genuinely appalled by the fact that when Bush speaks of a War on Terror, he actually means a War on Terror. And third, their behavior shows they do not quite know how to be an opposition party. Yes, the job of the opposition is to oppose, but part of that opposition, as Newt Gingrich showed in 1994 and 1995, is to oppose by showing that "we have a better plan." Nobody believed that when Kerry tried to say that in 2004—on Iraq, for example—because he didn't have one, nor did the party.[14]

Likewise, Matt Bai's expertly written "The Framing Wars," which appeared in the *New York Times Sunday Magazine* in 2005, discussed the efforts of John Kerry and his campaign strategists to win voters with words. "Democrats presented a litany of different complaints about Bush, depending on the day and the backdrop; he was a liar, a corporate stooge, a spoiled rich kid, a reckless warmonger. But they never managed to tie them all into a single, unifying image that voters could associate with the president. As a result, none of them stuck. Bush was attacked. Kerry was framed."[15]

Whether the creation is a result of semantic misfires, ideological confusion, or liberal strategizing, it quite clearly seems a historical inaccuracy to categorize Bush, conservatives, or Republicans as unilateral, interventionist, or warmongers. But if liberals insist on calling conservatives mongers of any kind, perhaps "Protect-MyAssMonger" might be the most appropriate.

CHAPTER 20

All Republicans Think Alike

Select First-Person Interview Responses

The Republicans are not very friendly to different kinds of people. I mean, they're a pretty monolithic party. They pretty much, they all behave the same, they all look the same. It's pretty much a white Christian party.[1]

—Howard Dean

Throughout this book we have tried to emphasize that there is no such thing as "all Republicans," a point that should be obvious but is often unmentioned. After all, there are a great many differences—ideological and philosophical—among Republicans, and even more between Republicans, conservatives, libertarians, neocons, moderates, and so forth. Just a quick glance at a list of political interest groups proves the point. With Republicans for Environmental Protection, Republicans for Choice, Republicans for Kerry, Republicans for Obama, Republicans for Black

Empowerment, Log Cabin Republicans, Republicans for Humility, California Conservatives for Truth, and myriad others, it's a gross oversimplification to say that "all Republicans" do anything. Characterizing and stereotyping is, of course, incredibly useful, but often misleading. What follows are the responses to select questions posed to our interviewees for this book, which help to illustrate even further just how nuanced and subtle, in some cases, these differences in opinion can be, as well as the surprising areas where most conservatives seem to agree.

Q. Who is your political hero?

Glenn Beck: I don't think I have one. I guess if I had one it would be Ronald Reagan. My belief in America is reaffirmed when I read Reagan. His belief did not come from the Republican Party. Many people found belief in the Republican Party because of his belief in American principles.

George Will: James Madison, because he understood the role of interest. The fact that government is A) necessary and B) problematic at all times.

Curt Schilling: The one person I've gotten to know better than most is Senator McCain. He is also the person I've come to respect more than anyone I've ever met in that arena because I never ever questioned his morals, ethics, or integrity. Whether I agree with some, none, or all of his policies, stances, or platforms, I know what I am getting and I know what he wants. We all project our beliefs and desires onto our candidates and feel like we think that once they get into office they'll do what we want them to. That's just stupid. There are so many influential events, people, and things that occur on a daily basis with that office that the only thing I know I want, and expect, from my president is total honesty and—where it can be done without risking national security—openness. Senator McCain is just that person to me. I know for a fact that what he has told me, what he has stated as his beliefs, is who and what he is and believes in. I know he won't do a 180 because of special interests and he's never ever going to knowingly be "on the take" for anything, anywhere. He's a decorated war hero, which means more than a little to me, and I think that's something not to be undervalued. His life struggles, both personal and professional, have made him a better man, and a better American than some of the other candidates, in my opinion.

William O'Reilly: Ronald Reagan. He really just opened my eyes up to so many things. For someone my age, I'm forty-two, people were being told that America wasn't good. He came along and it was like he was saying to the whole country "snap out of it." "Be proud to be an American."

Newt Gingrich: Abraham Lincoln, George Washington, Benjamin Franklin, and Theodore Roosevelt were the role models I identified with as a child. I spent the first eleven years of my childhood in Harrisburg, Pennsylvania, within driving distance of Valley Forge, Gettysburg, and Independence Hall. My family made sure I understood their significance.

K. T. McFarland: Reagan. He set his sights on the right goal and then brought the country around to achieve it. He did so out of love for country, not self, and with humility and integrity.

Ted Nugent: [Lt. Gen.] Chesty Puller [the most decorated marine in history].

Al Leiter: Rudy Giuliani asked me to be on the Twin Towers Fund. It was a complete honor, and I felt overwhelmed because of the impressive stature of the people in this group. Contrary to what the press has written about Rudy being the Gestapo, I disagree. I disagree because I saw him in several meetings. Rudy's intelligent. We had $280 million that we were going to disperse to various groups after 9/11. And it was, do we just give it to firemen and police, and there were a lot of little things that we had to consider. Nonuniform FBI agents who ran up . . . were they? There were widows of firemen . . . and they had already gotten a pretty good sum, but there was still a question of what we gave them. And Rudy went around to every single person there with his pad, and asked them what they thought should be done with the money. He listened, he wrote it down, and he went from person to person. And when he was done I watched him go over those notes, and he made a decision, like a true leader should, taking consensus, listening to others. It was really inspiring, and I thought it was the way it should be done.

Q. What are, in your opinion, the core values of conservatism?

David Horowitz: Republicans unite on key issues. I think a core issue is free market, although there's all kinds of policy differences you can have, but Republicans basically believe in the capitalist system and they basically believe in the defense of this country, which you cannot say for the Left.

Newt Gingrich: The core of conservatism is the belief that our rights come from our Creator, that they are inalienable, and that the state should be the servant of the people, not the other way around.

Brian C. Anderson: Conservatives tend to have a less rosy picture of human nature than do liberals and most libertarians, of course. Human beings, most conservatives, whether religious or secular, believe, are capable of good and evil; cultural norms and sometimes laws should try to encourage them to be good.

I think a recognition that the old-fashioned traditional family is worth preserving, that nationhood is valuable and important, that enemies to our security and way of life exist and need to be fought, that government is intrusive and shouldn't be taking your money away so enthusiastically.

Glenn Beck: The shining city on the hill. That our best days are still ahead of us. That any man can create the life that he wishes to create. That while the West is developed, a pioneer spirit still exists in America. It wasn't the land that made us pioneers. But it's also about a real belief . . . conservatives are one of the only groups of people left that don't sneer at those who believe in God. That they don't try to claim that every family, broken or intact, is equal. We should strive for intact families and survive those that break.

Michael Zak: I would say that so many people disagree on it—you've got the Hobbesian view or the Rousseau view—that all these "conservatives" disagree on the meaning of human nature or what they're conserving points to the inadequacy of the term. If there were a simple answer that everyone could agree on, then it would buttress the use of the word. Also the terms "Left" and "Right" came from France. In the National Assembly of France, the opponents of the king sat to the left of the speaker and the supporters sat to the right. So you had left-wing and right-wing. The relevance of that in today's politics is zero. So even more than the term conservative, I'm really slamming the terms "left-wing" and "right-wing." And then what is "hard-right"? Do you have to have a "soft-left"? George Orwell says something like "The first step toward clear thinking is clear terminology." He says it better than that, but you get the idea. I'd go back to respect for the individual by Republicans. If you look at societies that were ruled by an ideology that was the most hopeful for human nature, those are the Nazis, those are the Soviets, Pol Pot, they were all about the wonderful potential of the people—"once enemies were eliminated," "once this and that was done . . ." That's the totalitarian temptation. You could argue that they are the most optimistic about human nature. It's not that [Republicans] say that if we allow people to do what they want they'll make the correct choice, it's that there isn't a correct choice.

Pat Toomey: The conservative view of human nature is that we ought to have enormous respect for the dignity of the individual. It's the dignity of the individual that really inspired the notion of personal freedom throughout Western civilization that arguably reached its pinnacle in the United States, in the way we built our society based on the idea of individual dignity. With that of course goes personal responsibility, and a recognition that it is and it ought to be in the hands of the individual to build his or her life. I would contrast that to the fundamental worldview of American liberals, which is the primacy of the group and society as a whole. They set goals for categories of people, including very broad categories like our entire country. And as I mentioned earlier, they recognize that in order to attempt to achieve those goals, which they often fail at anyway, but in their attempt to get there, they have to use the power of the state, and they advocate a collective responsibility rather than an individual responsibility. So that's the big divide.

I think the conservative view is a more realistic view of human nature—understanding that there is good and there's bad. There is a susceptibility, a vulnerability to evil, as well as the ability to be inspired by good things. There is a fundamental distrust of too much power, so conservatives don't like to see power obsessively concentrated, especially into one entity to which we grant a monopoly on the use of force—and that's government. Whereas liberals have no such qualms about granting great power to government, despite the fact that it costs us the freedom of the individual.

K. T. McFarland: I am a champion of the individual—I believe the greatest thing about the United States is that it allows the individual to strive, and to succeed or fail on the basis of his own efforts. Anything that stands in the way of that is bad government. When in doubt, government should stay out. Specifically, I am a fiscal conservative, social moderate, national security hawk.

Deroy Murdock: I'm a libertarian, not a conservative. We tend to agree on a lot of things. I consider myself a libertarian hawk. I think this country didn't ask for it, but we happen to kind of be the oldest child in a family. I'm the eldest of three kids, and there's something about being the eldest child in a family where responsibilities fall into your lap whether you ask for them or not. I didn't ask my parents to have me first, but they did, and lo and behold, when something happens to my sisters, I'm the one who takes care of them. If I were the baby in the family, I'd scream for stuff and I'd get it, like my baby sister does. We happen to be the eldest child on the planet. We're the sole remaining superpower. So unlike a lot of libertarians, I don't think we should just throw our hands up and say, We'll mind our own business, even though there are a lot of awful people out there who, while you mind your own business, plot to kill you and your neighbors and throw their own constituents into mass graves and gas chambers, what have you.

And in my own life, I want to see my taxes low, my business largely unregulated, have as much choice in the market as possible as a consumer, be able to sleep and drink and ingest substances with anyone over eighteen that I wish, and beyond that it's not really any of the government's concern unless I've got a gun to someone else's head, in which case, it is the government's concern to protect that other person. I'm not an internet gambler, but since Congress just banned it I kind of feel like taking up internet gambling, becoming an online poker player.

And people say, What about the children? I say, What about the parents? Johnny engaged in Internet gambling because he stole Daddy's credit card. Maybe when Daddy gets the bill and wonders where these online gambling debts are coming from, he should put Johnny in a stress position in a corner, or tell him he can't go to the junior prom until he learns how to be responsible and stop stealing. You don't call your congressman and make it so that I, as a forty-two-year-old man, can't engage in online poker if that's what I feel like doing. Nobody's damn business but mine.

Q. Thomas Frank's book _What's the Matter With Kansas?_ implies that middle America is Republican out of ignorance, and that the policies that those working-class Republicans support actually work against them. Is this just another way of calling the Right dumb?

David Horowitz: Bright guy, stupid book. He's a Marxist. He doesn't understand the economy to begin with. I know the thesis, but the fact is that the working class has flocked [to the Republican Party]. There's an element of truth in the thesis. Culturally, working class people, they need strong family values. And they need to keep their kids accountable, because they could slip to the bottom. When your mommy and daddy are paying your way, and they're in the upper middle class, you can afford to be a lot looser. He thinks they were sold a mythological bill of goods, that liberals have stolen their things, when actually it's Republicans who have stolen their things. The core of that book is stupid, but it's the stupidity that's endemic to being on the left. I think the Republican Party has won the working class because it represents its best interests. Marx had a term for [Frank's thesis]. It's called false consciousness. And it's the arrogance of the Left.

Pat Toomey: They might be doing so in a little more nuanced way, but it sounds to me like that's where it's heading. I've heard that before. I've heard liberals make this frustrated, exacerbated claim that if you're not wealthy and you support conservatives, you're supporting policy that harms you. And that is certainly insulting to the intelligence of a lot of conservatives of modest means, who come to the Republican Party and the conservative movement precisely because they're not looking for some liberal to come along and give them a handout. They've got a belief in freedom, in economic freedom and any number of other ideas that are a part of the conservative movement and Republican Party, including some of the ideas of foreign policy and foreign cultural issues.

K. T. McFarland: I won't dignify that with a comment.

Brian C. Anderson: I'm deeply suspicious of false consciousness arguments. They're unfalsifiable and invariably allow a group possessed of the true wisdom to decide things peremptorily for everyone who happens to be blinkered. They're the core of totalitarian thinking.

Laura Ingraham: Frank has a hard time understanding that for a great many Americans, money isn't the most important thing in their lives. This is one of the main reasons Democrats keep losing elections.

Byron York: I think it's more complicated than that. Liberals portray conservative politicians and writers and intellectuals not as stupid but as cynical and dangerous. As far as the everyday Joe is concerned, liberals approach him with a "What's the Matter with Kansas?" point of view: Why does he support policies that run against his best interests? But even then I think the prevailing analysis is that the everyday Joe has been hoodwinked by the Rush Limbaughs of the world. If he just knew the truth, he'd be a Democrat.

William O'Reilly: I started that book and got about thirty pages in and then threw it under a pile of other books out of frustration. I couldn't bear to read another page, actually.

Jay Nordlinger: Of course. This is the condescending attitude: Conservatives aren't so much vicious as they are ignorant. Furthermore, they've been hoodwinked into voting on abortion and all these meaningless things, while impoverishing themselves by so doing. The Left has never understood that some people without money support a free economy because they know that, eventually, they will advance in it. They aspire to be rich, or less poor, and they want an atmosphere in which that is possible. They don't think they're so inept that they have to rely on the government. Plus, they are not so consumed with envy that they want to soak their more successful, or more prosperous, neighbors.

Q. Can you be a "good Republican" and not support cutting taxes?

Pat Toomey: You can't be a good conservative. And if you're not at least reasonably conservative, then I'm not sure what the point of being a Republican is. Given the current pretty high level of taxes we have—when you add up the federal, state, and local taxes, we're really taxed at a very high level—if a person doesn't recognize and acknowledge that, and support lower taxes in this environment, then that person doesn't strike me as a good Republican.

K. T. McFarland: Given the current size and scope and cost of government, no.

Curt Schilling: People somehow drew their own conclusions that I voted for President Bush because of the tax breaks he supposedly offers people in the higher income brackets. I could care less. I pay what the government tells me to pay. Would I like to pay less? Hell yes. But how much I pay in taxes has very little if any impact on who I would vote for."

Laura Ingraham: Not with the rates where they are today. No.

Q. What are the most urgent issues confronting Americans today, in your opinion?

Curt Schilling: The war is absolutely up there, but to me there are a litany of domestic issues that need to be addressed very soon. We aren't going to do squat about the environment alone. That's going to take cooperation on a global, and unprecedented scale. We need to address the dissolving structure of the American family and health care. How is it that as supposedly the most powerful country on the planet, we can have so many of our own citizens without health care? How can we allow cities and states and our legal system to continue to drive the cost to doctors through the roof, forcing them to move their practices and reduce the health-care abilities of some of the more impoverished areas of our country? How can there possibly be that many homeless people in this country? Our homeless rate continues to rise, our children are getting battered and abused, and a million other problems continue to grow, all of them domestic and all of them taking a backseat to foreign relations and other stuff that, while certainly a priority, should take a backseat to taking care of each other here, now.

Jeff Moorad: Well the most immediate issue we're dealing with is of course our presence in Iraq. But in the long term, I think it's more quality-of-life issues, from immigration to social security to taxation.

Shelby Steele: Well probably the Iraq War. I identify myself as an American citizen. That seems to be the preeminent issue. War and peace. Our country is at war at the moment. And it's an issue I take with great seriousness. I happen to support the war, though I've criticized the way we've conducted it and others, like Vietnam and the Gulf War. But we have determined not to win it. We keep saying we're going to fight wars but not win them. We're not going to use the full measure of our power. We never then achieve a victory and administer a defeat. The point of our victory is to end war and save lives. There's something that seems to be missing in the character of our nation today that prevents us from winning wars against extraordinarily weak enemies. And that bothers me more profoundly at this point than anything else. We're sacrificing our military because of some characterological weakness.

I've just finished a book on white guilt, and a good bit of it has to do with the idea that all of whites across the world are stigmatized these days as cruel, evil, avaricious, greedy, racist as a civilization. And we therefore are reluctant, especially against the "brown and weak" enemy, or the "yellow and weak" enemy, to win the wars we reluctantly began. We end up not only in a morass, but it divides our society. And America is a deeply divided society these days because of this characterological lack of will, this faithlessness in ourselves, this belief that we don't have the right to enter a war and win it.

Lisa "Kennedy" Montgomery: I think Social Security is the most important issue right now, for me personally and in general. There is so much said about Social Security by the Left, there are so many scare tactics used, that it's not really a fair debate. It's a hard issue to grasp in nice, little three-second sound bites. And President Bush the younger is doing a nice job. He's got very good intentions. I didn't think there would be a modern politician with the cojones to really take on the issue and to try to attempt to change the system. We'll see how successful he is. Every model for privatizing Social Security, whether it be on the city level or on the international level, has been successful, and it's got a great track record. We are a capitalist democracy. We should be all for making individual decisions and taking responsibility for those individual decisions. Privatized Social Security only makes sense, especially for those people my age and younger, who will not have any Social Security to speak of.

Q. Are rebellion, revolution and counterculture solely the property of the Left?

Byron York: You don't usually rebel against the leaders of your own team. That's what we have now with young conservatives/ Republicans and Bush. If Kerry had been elected, we'd have plenty of rebellious types on the right making noise.

Chris Milliken: Revolution and counterculture are not concepts or even phrases that entered my mind as a CEO. The political overtones that these two concepts convey are not the daily fare of most CEOs. Having said that, I or most other CEOs are not restrained at all from being "creative."

CONCLUSION

By Brett Joshpe

By now you should be thoroughly convinced that the Right is not the crude collection of inadequate and inaccurate stereotypes that the Left, the media, and Al Franken would have you believe. But in case you need one final push, a word on what it means to be a conservative . . .

A friend of mine once asked me what the definition of conservative was. I thought about it and the best I could come up with, in the simplest terms possible, was that we want to preserve what we have more than we want to make what we have better. This sentiment should not be confused with hostility or indifference to progress or to making the world better, but it means that we tend to be more concerned with preserving the rights, freedoms, and securities that we enjoy as Americans than with reshaping society according to some utopian vision.

Like many, I grew up a Republican because my parents were Republicans. They weren't the ideological kind, but the pragmatic kind who wished they paid fewer taxes and that federal bureaucrats wouldn't tell them how to live their lives. But in college I truly began to develop my own political identity. I recall being turned off by the "in your face" public protests and coerced celebrations of the Left, like "wear jeans if you're in favor of gay marriage" day. Although I have always been passionate and intense, many of my political impressions were somewhat tepid before 9/11. Even when a Cornell professor told my class that Jimmy Carter was a good president because relatively few people died during his term, I managed to keep my blood pressure at a somewhat normal level. At that point in my life, I was concerned with one thing: getting an A. So I didn't have the time or energy to let politics get in the way.

September 11 changed my perspective—forever. It became increasingly difficult for me to listen passively to liberal dogma. I recall how disgusted I felt walking through campus in the weeks after 9/11 and our invasion of Afghanistan and seeing radical campus liberals and local hippies marching aimlessly around in a circle protesting . . . something. Luckily, in the days following 9/11, there were plenty of people, on both the left and the right, who looked at the protesters with shame and disdain, and counterprotesters began gathering each morning with clever signs like "Kabul's-eye."

By the time I arrived at Harvard Law School, I was torn between involvement and disengagement, hope and disgust. I often sat quietly in class, irreverently slouched in my chair. Occasionally, I would throw in a smart-ass remark that would generate laughter, particularly from my conservative colleagues, like my proposal for dealing with an adverse possessor who builds on your land: arrive on said land with a bulldozer.

But during that first year of law school, in the months leading up to the Iraq War, I became so disgusted with protests every weekend in the streets and on television that I could no longer remain silent. I formed an organization called Students for Protecting America that began posting flyers around campus and doing interviews with radios and newspapers. The reaction was a combination of relief and gratitude in some circles and angry disbelief in others. We were suddenly stomping on Cambridge's liberal turf and garnering far more attention for our minority position than the Left was for theirs. We even held a rally on the steps of the statehouse on Beacon Hill on a rainy, April Saturday morning. As we walked through Boston Common, a crowd gathered at the top of the steps, anticipating our arrival. Cameras, microphones, and press waited. As we walked up the stairs, a rough-looking guy straight out of *Good Will Hunting* aggressively approached me and asked, "Are you pro-wah, or anti-wah?" "Pro-war," I said. "Good," he responded. "Let me tell you something . . . the anti-wah people are gonna get in your face and push you. You hit 'em right back!"

I laughed to myself and then tried to explain to the press that we did not share our aggressive friend's disposition on the issue as he proceeded to shout obscenities and make graphic hand gestures at spectators on the Boston Duck Tours. And, while I certainly would not teach my children that violence is the first option in dealing with those with whom you disagree, I could not help but think about the common sense behind the notion, particularly in the realm of international politics: If you hit us, we'll hit you back.

After our organization had its say, I remained only tangentially involved in Harvard politics, but I developed a reputation as someone who could be counted on to take a position. When a student organization wanted to hold a debate and needed someone to take a "unilateralist" position, they asked me, and I obliged. It was a somewhat pointless exercise with four law students regurgitating the pundits' positions as if it were *Hannity & Colmes*. But I was reminded at one point during the debate exactly why my passions were stoked enough to participate when one of my opponents remarked, to the nodding agreement of most in attendance, that Abu Ghraib rendered us "no better than Syria." In the Peoples' Republic of Cambridge, such a view of America is mainstream.

Now I am a young, conservative yuppie living in New York City, which can be quite disheartening, because in addition to experiencing firsthand many policies that you loathe every day, most of your friends, acquaintances, colleagues, and service providers are liberal. Every now and then, though, even in a city like New York, you come across someone who just likes you for you, despite your much-maligned and oft-reported lack of compassion, insensitivity to human suffering, warmongering and gun toting, tax cutting, flag-waving, tree-murdering, self-promoting, Republican self. So, when I met S.E. several years ago, I was somewhat taken aback when she told me she didn't often talk politics around people she barely knew, as she tended to offend people. Okay, I thought, I offend people too. I better steer away from this one because if she is as explosive and provocative as I am, this could get ugly. But then it occurred to me: If she usually offends people, and I usually offend people, just maybe we are offending the same people! And so we were. It was a "vilified Republican" match made in heaven. We became friends and eventually decided to indulge in our frustrations by authoring this book about the trials and tribulations of being young, conservative, and misunderstood.

We spent much of the project defending the Right against gross exaggeration, unfair stereotyping, and downright falsehoods. But, in our exploration of what conservatives do *not* personify, we have also affirmed certain common themes defining what conservatives *do* represent, or at the very least, what they tend to represent. Certainly these trends are not absolute. However, it is safe to say that most conservatives and many Republicans adhere to a particular worldview that remains the bedrock of the ideology. Russell Kirk's explanation of the canons of conservatism in *The Conservative Mind* remain largely true today.

"Belief in transcendent order, or body of natural law." Although not all conservatives are religious, believe in God, or constitute the Christian Right, most conservatives tend to identify right and wrong, moral and immoral, good and evil. Conservatives are often not shy, for example, about asserting that the United States is, emphatically, *not* the moral equivalent of Iran or Syria. Because not all conservatives believe in natural law, the genesis of moral judgment might be questioned, but moral judgment is possessed and practiced, nonetheless. Justice Potter Stewart famously

explained how he recognized hardcore pornography by saying "I know it when I see it." Morality, like porn, is sometimes easier recognized than explained. I cannot always articulate the principle that makes one thing right and another wrong and I cannot always explain the source of my moral judgment, but I am capable of moral judgment nonetheless.

"Affection for the proliferating variety and mystery of human existence, as opposed to the narrowing uniformity, egalitarianism, and utilitarian aims of most radical systems." The modern manifestation of this is advocacy of states' rights and judicial restraint. It is another version of the belief that we are not all the same. The law of Alabama should not necessarily be the law of New York, even if five justices on the Supreme Court think it is fundamental, in their humble opinions.

"Conviction that a civilized society requires orders and classes, as against the notion of a 'classless society' . . . equality in condition . . . means equality in servitude and boredom." Certainly this principle rings clear and true for conservatives today. It is not that we are the party of the elites. We are the party of economic freedom, of allowing and encouraging people to achieve their own places in society. Naturally, when the government retreats from intervention and regulation, differences will arise and not all will prosper equally. That is a good thing. Not only does it encourage innovation and growth, but society would not function if it were made up only of wealthy investment bankers.

"Persuasion that freedom and property are closely linked. . . . Economic leveling, they maintain, is not economic progress." Freedom requires the ability to possess for oneself, to purchase rights and to sell rights. Societies that are free respect and protect private ownership rights. Conservatives generally favor less government regulation, intervention, and taxation, as these things not only erode wealth, they erode freedom.

"Faith in prescription and distrust of 'sophisters, calculators, and economists' who would reconstruct society upon abstract

designs." This principle can be seen through the conservative's distrust of academics, the media, and, often, the judiciary. We often find the notion of "fundamental rights" offensive, not because we do not believe in the right or we do not believe certain rights are fundamental (we know certain rights are because the Constitution says they are) but because the phrase "fundamental rights" should really be prefaced by "in my opinion." The people who hand down these edicts dictating what is fundamental are almost always judges who see themselves as the caretakers and arbiters of Truth (with a capital T), similar to the philosopher-kings Plato described in the *Republic.* The principle also speaks to the professors in their ivory towers who think terrorism should be defeated by theory and talk. Conservatives tend to believe that real-world problems require real-world solutions, and when those problems arise, we do not turn to the professors who wax philosophical about those problems, or the reporters who write about those problems, or the judges who issue rulings about those problems.

"Recognition that change may not be salutary reform: hasty innovation may be a devouring conflagration, rather than a torch of progress." This last idea can be summarized simply as "prudence." Pragmatism is one of the most salient reasons why we are conservatives. It is why one of the experts we interviewed for this book, William O'Reilly, said he is a Republican "because I detest committees."

Going back to my original simplistic formulation, the conservative inclination to defend, protect, and preserve, rather than progress, illuminates what tends to be the conservative view on many of the core issues. We tend to favor a strong military so that we can *defend* our country. We favor free markets and *protecting* property rights. We believe that morality is something that society should *preserve.* We believe in defending the Constitution, not dismissing it as an antiquated document in need of a facelift.

In fact, when public officials take an oath of office and pledge to "defend and protect the Constitution of the United States from enemies both foreign and domestic," they are saying something inherently conservative. Fundamentally, they must *conserve* it, as the first and highest duty. Of course, this assumes that what we are conserving is good and worth protecting, which we tend to believe, and statistics indicate that those who are conservative are more inclined to believe in the decency of the American cause than those on the left (although we certainly do not possess a monopoly on such views).

We tend to hold a view of human nature that begins with a belief that certain people, like murderers, rapists, terrorists, and demagogues, are evil, and we are less concerned with psychoanalyzing them to determine how they became that way or with determining what our role may have been. We also believe that humanity is capable of great things when left to its own devices. George Bush repeatedly has invoked freedom as a goal that people around the world are capable of attaining for themselves and their families. He has dispensed with the paternalistic notion that people in the Middle East want to be ruled by dictators and has declared this goal within reach of historically oppressed societies. We believe that minorities are more than capable of meeting the standards of society, just like the majority, and should not be propped up or excused with social programs or affirmative action that only prolongs their inequality.

Conservatives also believe in the vast differences between individuals, which accounts for the sense of individualism championed in conservative communities versus the sense of community praised in liberal ones. After all, why champion the individual if we are really all the same in character, equally good, equally right, and merely the victims or beneficiaries of our surroundings?

Because of these tendencies, we are sometimes accused of stifling change, of being unable to see through the plumes of cigar smoke emanating from fat, white men in boardrooms to the sort of "progress" that could lead us to utopia. As conservatives, we certainly cling to tradition at times, and I think many of us maintain an appreciation for history and our ancestry. We like to think that this does not result in an impediment to progress but is a facilitator of it. As has often been said, "One cannot know where one is going unless one knows where one comes from." As Republicans, we try to maintain a keen sense of our origins, and as a result, we maintain a cohesiveness in our party that Democrats arguably lack.

Our sense of preservation, rather than progression, is in some ways illustrated deftly by our last two presidents. Bill Clinton was a southerner who spent most of his life in the South before reaching Washington. Yet, most people would probably identify him as far more of a northeasterner or Washingtonian now. He barely speaks with a southern accent and he infrequently evokes his southern roots. After serving his terms in Washington, no one knew for sure where he would go next, but everyone knew that it would not be Arkansas. He would go where the next opportunity presented itself, which, not surprisingly, was New York City. From here, perhaps he will one day find Washington again.

Consider, in contrast, George W. Bush. Although Bush grew up in the Northeast, he eventually found a home in Texas. Like Clinton, he served as governor of his home state. Unlike Clinton, he brought that identity with him to the White House. Nobody ever accused Bill Clinton of bringing his "Arkansas attitude" with him to Washington. Bush, to the contrary, has been criticized for the way he walks, even, because of how it reeks of "Texas arrogance." As Bush said during his 2004 campaign, "In Texas, we call it walking." He is a man who knows the origins of his disposition and he embraces and celebrates it. For George Bush and many Republicans, discarding the memories of our past—even the scars left by them—is not always progress.

When George Bush spoke to the nation after John Kerry conceded the election in 2004, he emotionally addressed his home state of Texas:

Let me close with a word to the people of the state of Texas. We have known each other the longest, and you started me on this journey. On the open plains of Texas, I first learned the character of our country: sturdy and honest, and as hopeful as the break of day. I will always be grateful to the good people of my state. And whatever the road that lies ahead, that road will take me home.

"Home." It is a conservative, backward-looking concept. The notion of a home base even helps explain why George Will says that baseball is America's most conservative sport. None of this is to deny that change and looking forward are good, if not imperative, sometimes. There is a thing called progress, and blind adhesion to tradition can impede the betterment of society and mankind. However, as Republicans and conservatives, we tend to believe in certain principles that formed the foundation of our party at its inception and will continue to guide us into the future. We believe that the power of individuals to possess the freedom to make their own decisions and chart their own path through life is the highest form of achievement. We believe that there is good and evil in this world and that evil must be dealt with accordingly, at times through force. We believe that government is here to protect and defend, not to provide. We believe that human beings are capable of making decisions and ought to bear responsibility for those decisions.

During the 2004 election season, *The Daily Show with Jon Stewart* mocked the divisiveness and lack of cohesion among Democrats. One of the *Daily Show* reporters went into a room with a collection of diverse Democrats at their convention. As soon as they began talking, they immediately began fighting with each other because each considered his pet issue paramount to his support for the party. The lesson is humorous but not surprising, because progress is hard to define. Change is hard to prioritize. Not that we should never pursue progress or change, but I think that maybe as Republicans and conservatives, we start with what we know is good. We start with where we came from and what we can learn from that. And before we try to figure out what to change, we try to preserve the great things we, as the United States of America, have already built.

Some Useful Conservative Lingo

1854 (ā-tēn' fif'-tē fôr) *n.* Point in American history after which civilization began.

Army brat (är'-mē brat) *n.* Hybrid breed of parent-activist who blames the U.S. government for conspiring to kill his or her child in battle. Activism may include press tours, television appearances, marches, and well-timed pledges to no longer pay taxes. (e.g., Cindy Sheeham, Mary Tillman.)

Berglerize (ber'-gl[ə]-rīz) *v.* The act of removing classified documents from the National Archives, stuffing them in one's clothes, and shrugging when questioned about it.

Bigfoot (big fŭt) *n.* A celebrity whose carbon footprint size is in direct proportion to the size of his or her mouth.

Bloggle (bläg[ə]l) *v.* To use a pet liberal medium, the blog, to coo sycophantically over whichever demagogue of the Left is most popular at the moment.

Call (kôl) *v.* Demand by Democratic official or activist that Republican leader apologize, form a committee, or resign after doing something said Democratic official or activist didn't like. Example: "Won't you join me in calling for the president to apologize, form a committee to investigate this matter, and then resign?"

Carbonista (kär'-b[ə]-nēs'-tə) *n.* A person noted for his self-righteous indignation and superiority complex over his own low carbon emissions and yours, which are genocidally high. Native tongue: hyperbole. Some struggle with massive carbon credit debt.

Cash Bar (kash bär) *n.* Social event where guests are asked to pay for their own alcoholic beverages. Event will, as such, feature a significantly high Republican-to-Democrat ratio, as Democrats generally believe that charity balls and fund-raisers should provide food and beverages, as well as hospitality suites, gift bags, and spa certificates.

C.C.S. (Catty Cheerleader Syndrome) (sē-sē-es) *n.* Democratic tendency to gossip uncontrollably about a public figure's physical appearance simply for the purpose of ostracizing him or her from the clique. (e.g., Democrats and Ann Coulter; Democrats and Katherine Harris; Democrats and Barbara Bush.)

Charity (chār'-i-tē) *n.* The act of helping those in need by donating time, money, or resources to a worthy cause. For liberals, charity is specifically limited to well-publicized Third World adoption and organizing or attending a televised live concert, which may or may not produce an album or DVD.

Chick-anery (shi-kā'-n[ə]-rē) *n.* Deception by trickery or sophistry—and involving a sexual abuse of power. (e.g., Bill Clinton.)

China (chī'-n[ə]) *n.* World's fourth-largest country, where, under a thriving communist regime, 130 million people live below the international poverty line, childbirth is regulated, execution is routine, food safety is an urban legend, and human rights laws are viewed as annoyingly meddlesome. Nonetheless, liberals often warn conservatives that this country will become "the next superpower."

Christianity (kris'-chē-an'-i-tē) *n.* The boogeyman.

Closet conservative (klȯz'-it k[ə]n-ser'-v[ə]-tiv) *n.* Pussy.

Committee (k[ə]-mit'-ē) *n.* A body formed to investigate and then write a report on any major incident or problem. Antonym: Action. (Note: the term "Action Committee" in no way changes the above definition of "Committee.")

Fool's gold (fūlz gōld) *n.* Political contributions by or to George Soros.

Gored (gord) *adj.* Term describing Al Gore's cult followers. Example: "Leo DiCaprio is totally Gored. I wonder if they're doing it."

Green (grēn) *adj.* Ecotastic bromide describing any environmentally sound entity, real or fictitious, and requiring no proof or verification, which will eventually cost the consumer more money to use. Example: "On the plus side, the Good Earth Coffee Café went green when it replaced paper towels in the bathrooms with Frette Triplo Bourdon bath towels. But now a muffin costs $8.75."

Hill-Billy (hil bil'-ē) *n.* Any American of voting age who somehow thinks that a Hillary Clinton administration would resemble Bill Clinton's in any discernible way.

Marxmen, Expert (märks'-m[ə]n ek'-spert') *n.* Liberals who routinely employ the credos of the *Communist Manifesto,* i.e., blaming the wealthy for societal ills, insulting the middle class, denouncing globalization, free trade, capitalism, and other economic phenomena as "evil," disavowing religion, embracing violent overthrow, and generally believing that they're smarter than everyone else that lived before them.

Moore-on (mōr´än´) *n.* Particular breed of liberal who is vulnerable to the caustic and sensationalistic, self-promoting, entertainment-masquerading-as-journalism type of propaganda shoveled out by figures who may or may not be rotund, hirsute, and disheveled.

PETA rally: (pē'-t[ə] ral'-ē) *n.* Excuse to take off one's clothes.

Petty-Cure (pet'[ə] kyur) *n.* A symbolic call to end petty bickering among the parties by liberals, often enacted with feigned exasperation and disingenuous altruism, and immediately ignored upon vocalization.

Plati-nudes (plat'-i-nūd's) *pl. n.* Ditz-arific, scantily clad celebutards who, when attempting social commentary, speak only in empty cliché, but believe they are making genuine political statements. (For example, Paris Hilton and the "Vote or Die" campaign, which did not even bring Paris herself to the voting booth on election day.)

Republican't (rē-p[ə]b´-li-kant) *n.* A Democrat who espouses entirely conservative ideals but can't call him or herself a Republican.

Resolution (rez'[ə]-lū'-shən) *n.* Nonbinding symbolic gesture, passed at the behest of liberals, expressing an opinion that no one cares about, and having no real consequences.

Small-plate tasting menu (smȯl plāt tāst'-ing men'-yū) *n.* Indulgent and expensive option at highbrow restaurants in liberal U.S. cities, whereby one is served a variety of small dishes, often from whatever ingredients the chef has in the kitchen. The middle class calls this "getting by."

Introduction

1. UrbanDictionary.com.
2. Ann Coulter, *Slander,* Crown, 2002.

CHAPTER 1. Republicans Are Racist

1. A. Alexander, "Racist Republicans: If They Can't Stand the Heat, They Shouldn't Stand So Close to the Burning Cross," *Progressive Daily Beacon,* October 28, 2006.
2. First-person interview.
3. Digitalhistory.uh.edu.
4. "Hollings Remark Stirs Anger and an Apology," Associated Press, October 13, 1983.
5. First-person interview.
6. First-person interview.
7. Bill Maxwell, "Black Republicans Are Strange Indeed," *St. Petersburg Times,* December 8, 1999.
8. First-person interview.
9. First-person interview.
10. First-person interview.
11. Alvin S. Felzenberg, "Race and Republicans, From Williams Lloyd Garrison to Trent Lott," *Weekly Standard,* June 7, 1999.

12. First-person interview.

13. First-person interview.

14. First-person interview.

15. Bill Cosby speech to NAACP on fiftieth anniversary of *Brown v. Board of Education*, May 17, 2004.

16. First-person interview.

17. Julian Bond speech at 2003 NCAAP convention, Miami Beach, Florida.

18. As heard by Milton Coleman and reported by Rick Atkinson, *Washington Post*, February 13, 1984.

19. Meghan Clyne, "President Bush is 'Our Bull Connor,' Harlem's Rep. Charles Rangel Claims," *New York Sun*, September 23, 2005.

20. CNN, "Biden 'Stumbles' Over Education Question," October 25, 2007.

21. Jack White, "Lott, Reagan and Republican Racism," *Time*, December 14, 2002.

CHAPTER 2. Republicans Are Elitist WASPs

1. First-person interview.

2. Gawker.com, August 30, 2004.

3. Andrew Hacker, "Liberal Democracy and Social Control," *American Political Science Review*, 1957.

4. CNN.com

5. Maps and cartograms of the 2004 U.S. Presidential Election Results, Michael Gastner, Cosma Shalizi, and Mark Newman, University of Michigan, 2005.

6. Adherents.com.

7. Richard Baehr, "The Exit Polls and the Jewish Vote," *American Thinker*, November 15, 2006.

8. Melissa Radler, "US Republicans Support Israel: Poll" *Jerusalem Post*, April 18, 2002.

9. Rjchq.org.

10. Aaron Klein, "Jimmy Carter: Too Many Jews on the Holocaust Council," Worldnetdaily.com, January 25, 2007.

11. Abraham A. Foxman, "Judging a Book by Its Cover and Its Content," ADL.org, November 13, 2006.

12. Daniel Pipes, "The Clout of Christian Zionism," *Jewish Magazine,* August 2003.

13. Rjchq.org.

14. Irving Kristol, *Reflections of a Neoconservative: Looking Back, Looking Ahead,* Basic Books, 1983.

15. Stephanie Ebbert, "Asian-Americans step up to the Ballot Box," *Boston Globe,* April 26, 2005.

16. Journeyswithgeorge.com.

17. Daniel Henninger, "Bush is Back. Will it Matter?" *Wall Street Journal,* March 24, 2006.

CHAPTER 3. Republicans Are Humorless

1. Hunter S. Thompson, *Pageant,* July 1968.

2. First-person interview.

3. George Will, *Newsweek,* December 11, 1978.

4. First-person interview.

5. *Washington Post,* June 20, 2001

6. First-person interview.

7. Nicholas Wade, "Is 'Do Unto Others' Written Into Our Genes?" *New York Times,* September 18, 2007.

8. Ibid.

9. First-person interview.

10. Tmz.com.

11. First-person interview.

12. First-person interview.

13. David Rising, Associated Press, May 22, 2007.

14. Anonymous, "The Elephant in the Bedroom," *GQ* April 2006.

CHAPTER 4. Republicans Don't Care About Education

1. *Majority Report,* April 21, 2005 broadcast.

2. Bill Clinton, *Between Hope and History,* Random House: 1996.

3. Noam Chomsky, *Class Warfare,* 1995.

4. Noam Chomsky, *Chomsky on Miseducation,* 1999.

5. Gareth Davies, "The Great Society After Johnson: The Case of Bilingual Education," *Journal of American History,* March 2002.

6. First-person interview.

7. David Horowitz, "Republicans Lost in Space," Salon.com, November 29, 1999.

8. "No Child Left Behind Is Working," Ed.gov, December 2006.

9. Ibid.

10. Sourcewatch.org.

11. TedKennedy.com.

12. Bill Steigerwald, "Conservatives Take Wrong Turn on Education," HumanEvents.com, October 03, 2006.

13. Nea.org.

14. Clubforgrowth.org.

15. Peter Brimelow, *The Worm in the Apple: How the Teacher's Unions are Destroying American Education,* Harper Collins, 2003.

16. David Gelernter, "A World Without Public Schols," *Weekly Standard,* June 4, 2007.

17. Associated Press, "Uproar Over Kerry Remarks," November 1, 2006.

CHAPTER 5. Republicans Are NASCAR-Loving Rednecks

1. Jeff Foxworthy, *Totally Committed,* 1998.

2. First-person interview.

3. First-person interview.

4. Juliet Macur, "Nascar At Crossroads After Years of Growth," *New York Times,* April 15, 2007.

5. First-person interview.

6. All NASCAR info provided by Andrew Giangola, head of NASCAR business communications

7. First-person interview.

8. First-person interview.

9. Jefffoxworthy.com.

CHAPTER 6. Republicans Hate the Planet

1. P. J. O'Rourke, *All the Trouble in the World: The Lighter Side of Overpopulation, Famine, Ecological Disaster, Ethnic Hatred, Plague and Poverty,* Grove/Atlantic. Inc., 1994.

2. Ellen Goodman, "No Change in Political Climate," *Boston Globe,* February 9, 2007.

3. Julia Seymour, "Kennedy Calls Skeptical Politicans 'Traitors,' and 'Corporate Toadies,'" NewsBusters.org, July 9, 2007.

4. Jeffrey P. Schaffer, *Yosemite National Park: A Complete Hiker's Guide,* 4th ed., Wilderness Press, 1999.

5. EPA.gov.

6. President.gov.

7. "G8 Leaders Agree to 'Substantial' Greenhouse Gas Cuts," ReutersAlertNet.com, June 7, 2007.

8. Jeff Mason, "Gore: Bush Should Follow Reagan's Lead on Climate," Reuters, September 26, 2007.

9. Crea-online.org.

10. As told to Robert Siegel, "All Things Considered," NPR, October 29, 2007.

11. Walter Sullivan, "Scientists Ponder Why World's Climate Is Changing; A Major Cooling Widely Considered to Be Inevitable," *New York Times,* May 21, 1975.

12. James Taylor, "Alarmist Global Warming Claims Melt Under Scientific Scrutiny," *Chicago Sun-Times,* June 30, 2007.

13. Rob Marciano, "American Morning," CNN, October 5, 2007, broadcast.

14. Steve Lyttle, "Gore Gets a Cold Shoulder," *Sydney Morning Herald,* October 14, 2007.

15. First-person interview.

16. Richard Lindzen, "On Global Warming Heresy," March 16, 2007, MIT.

17. IPCC Fourth Assessment Report, Climate Change 2007.

18. Richard Lindzen, "On Global Warming Heresy," March 16, 2007, MIT.

19. Ibid.

20. First-person interview.

21. UNFCCC.int.

22. U.S. Senate Roll Call Votes, 105th Congress (s. res. 98).

23. James Inhofe in speech on Senate floor on September 28, 2006.

24. First-person interview.

25. First-person interview.

26. Richard Linzden editorial, "Is Global Warming a Cause for Alarm?" written for the Ford Hall Forum, April 22, 2007.

27. Charles R. Smith, "Enron and Clinton," NewsMax.com, May 14, 2003.

28. Kyle Smith, *New York Post,* "Inconvenient Truths," October 7, 2007

29. Bjorn Lomborg, "Our Priorities for Saving the World," speech given at TED Conference, February 2005.

30. John Tierney, "'Feel Good' vs. 'Do Good' on Climate," *New York Times,* September 11, 2007.

31. "Mayer: Not Especially Green, Kinda Bitchy," Blog.Vh1.com, July 9, 2007.

32. Sherylcrow.com.

33. Linda Laban, "These Rockers Are a Little Green," *Boston Globe,* May 26, 2006.

34. People.com, September 24, 2007.

35. Amy Gunderson, "Making Your Second Home Green," *New York Times,* February 28, 2007.

36. Jennifer Loven, "Bush Moving on California Wild Fires," Associated Press, October 23, 2007.

37. "Global Warming to Blame for Fires, Says Harry Reid," WorldNet-Daily.com, October 23, 2007.

38. Newt Gingrich, *A Contract With the Earth*, 2007.

39. Russell Kirk, *The Conservative Mind: From Burke to Eliot*, Regnery Publishing Inc., 1986.

CHAPTER 7. Republicans Are Stupid

1. TV.com.

2. Ellis Weiner, "Why Conservatives Aren't Funny," *Huffington Post*, September 25, 2007.

3. "Obama Calls Republican Policies 'Tough and Dumb,'" Associated Press, September 30, 2006.

4. Jeff Jacoby, "Democratic Demagoguery Poisons the Tax-Cut Debate," *Jewish World Review*, July 30, 1999.

5. Ann Coulter, *Slander*, Crown, 2002.

6. Lionel Trilling, *Liberal Imagination*, Viking Press, 1950.

7. Grand jury testimony (August 17, 1998).

8. Melinda Henneberger, "Gore Campaign, Trailing Among Women, Sharpens Its Pitch to Them," *New York Times*, July 6, 1999.

9. David Maraniss and Ellen Nakashima, "Gore's Grades Belie Image of Studiousness," *Washington Post*, March 19, 2000.

10. Ann Coulter, *Slander*, Crown, 2002.

11. Alan Fram, "Book Chief: Conservatives Want Slogans," Associated Press, August 21, 2007.

12. Ibid.

13. William Saletan, "Liberal Interpretation," Slate.com, September 14, 2007.

14. Ibid.

15. Ibid.

16. Ibid.

17. Alan Wolfe, "Defending the PhD's," *New York Times*, September 10, 2006.

18. Vice presidential debate, Omaha, Nebraska, October 1988.

19. Robert David Johnson, "Re-Visioning America," *New York Sun,* September 17, 2004.

20. Stanley Fish, "George W. Bush and Melville's Ahab: Discuss!" *New York Times* blog, October 21, 2007.

21. First-person interview.

22. First-person interview.

CHAPTER 8. Republicans Are Intolerant

1. WhiteRoseSociety.org.

2. RepublicansHateAmerica.com.

3. WhiteRoseSociety.org.

4. First-person interview.

5. Joe Conason, "A Gay Old Time for the GOP," *New York Observer,* September 5, 2004.

6. Dennis Prager, "Ann Coulter Wants Jews to Become Christian—So What?" Townhall.com, October 16, 2007.

7. First-person interview.

8. Bill Maher, *New Rules: Polite Musings from a Timid Observer,* Rodale, 2005.

9. Bad-mother.blogspot.com.

10. Fuckthesouth.com.

11. Rightwingnews.com.

12. First-person interview.

13. First-person interview.

14. Bridget Johnson, "Rebels with a Cause," *Wall Street Journal,* July 21, 2004.

15. Richard Johnson, "Rebel Group," *New York Post,* October 23, 2007.

16. Bridget Johnson, "Rebels with a Cause," *Wall Street Journal,* July 21, 2004.

17. First-person interview.

18. Toby Harnden, "Bush Like Hitler, Says First Muslim in Congress," *Telegraph*, July 17, 2007.

19. Cindy Sheehan, "Pulling No Punches," LewRockwell.com, April 15, 2005.

20. Morrisseymusic.com, October 28, 2004.

21. Dave Lindorff, "Bush and Hitler: The Strategy of Fear," Counterpunch.org, February 1, 2003.

22. Jonah Goldberg, "The New N-Word," *Jewish World Review*, June 30, 2004.

23. MuslimAmericans.com.

24. Ethan Cole, "Bush Tells Muslims That US Defends Islam," Christiantoday.com, June 29, 2007.

25. "Bush Creates Muslim Ambassador Post," www.aljazeera.net, June 28, 2007.

26. First-person interview.

27. Interview with Tom Brokaw, NBC News, April 24, 2003.

CHAPTER 9. Republicans Aren't Cool

1. NewYorkCool.com.

2. Jack Anthony Matel, "Punishing the Frat Boy," Watchblog.com, November 4, 2004.

3. First-person interview.

4. First-person interview.

5. Broadcastingcable.com.

6. First-person interview,

7. First-person interview.

8. First-person interview.

9. First-person interview.

10. John Solomon, "Why Are All Jock Politicians Republicans?" Slate, June 13, 2001.

11. First-person interview.

12. First-person interview.

13. First-person interview.

14. Warren St John, "A Bush Surprise: Fright-Wing Support," *New York Times*, March 21, 2004.

15. First-person interview.

CHAPTER 10. Republicans Are Bad in Bed

1. Ann Coulter, *Slander*, Crown, 2002.

2. First-person interview.

3. First-person interview.

4. *Primetime Live*, ABCNews: "American Sex Lives 2004 Survey."

5. Anonymous, "The Elephant in the Bedroom," *GQ*, April 2006.

6. MSNBC.com.

7. "Even Republicans Can Get Laid With Craigslist," Gawker.com.

CHAPTER 11. Republicans Don't Care About You

1. Fran Shor, "Brain-Dead Ploys and Heartless Republicans," CommonDreams.org, March 20, 2005.

2. "The System Republicans Want," TheChiefSource.com, February 16, 2007.

3. David Limbaugh, "Conservative Racism Myth," *Jewish World Review*, January 10, 2003.

4. Mike Hersh, "Today's Moderate Republicans: Tomorrow's Democrats," AmericanPolitics.com, January 25, 2001.

5. First-person interview.

6. PewResearch.org.

7. Zogby.com.

8. George Carlin, *Brain Droppings*, Hyperion, 1997.

9. Interview by Steve Scher on KUOW, Seattle, Washington, April 22, 2005.

10. Fringeblog.com.

11. First-person interview.

12. First-person interview.

13. John Stossel, "Who Gives to Charity," Townhall.com, December 6, 2006.

14. Jeff Jacoby, "Kerry's Charity Gap," *Boston Globe*, May 16, 1996.

15. Dennis Roddy, "Liberals Take Umbrage At Soup Kitchen 'Photo Op,'" *Pittsburgh Post-Gazette*, September 1, 2004.

16. *The West Wing*, Season 3, "Ways and Means."

CHAPTER 12. Republicans Are Religious Extremists

1. George Carlin interview with Michael Deeds, *Idaho Statesman*, January 24, 2004.

2. Jim McDermott speech to House of Representatives, May 18, 2005.

3. Howard Fineman, "The Inaugural Blog," *Newsweek*, January 20, 2005.

4. Ari Berman, "Outrageous Outtakes," TheNation.com, January 21, 2005.

5. David Domke and Kevin Coe, "How Bush's God-Talk is Different," BeliefNet.com.

6. Joe Lieberman speech to Christians United for Israel Conference, July 16, 2007.

7. Address to Southern Baptist leaders, September 13, 1960.

8. First-person interview.

9. CIA World Fact Book, CIA.gov.

10. First-person interview.

11. First-person interview

12. Barna.org.

13. First-person interview.

14. *Seinfeld*, "The Burning," Season 9, Episode 16, 1998.

15. Ann Coulter, *Slander*, Crown, 2002.

16. First-person interview.

17. First-person interview.

CHAPTER 13. Republicans Love Them Their Guns

1. Richard C. Suquer, "Ban All Guns Now!" Adequacy.org, November 7, 2001.
2. Time.com.
3. *Friends,* "The One Where Chandler Can't Cry," 2000.
4. Paul Nussbaum, "Red, Blue—and Purple: A Closer Look at America's Political and Cultural Divide." *Philadelphia Inquirer,* June 20, 2006.
5. Gallup.com.
6. First-person interview.
7. ResponsiveManagement.com.
8. TheOutdoorWorld.com.
9. RMEF.org.
10. Frank Miniter, *The Politically Incorrect Guide to Hunting,* Regnery, 2007.
11. Ibid.
12. Ibid.
13. Ibid.
14. NCPA.org.
15. GunFacts.info.
16. FraserInstitute.org.
17. Fred Thompson, "Signs of Intelligence?" *National Review,* April 20, 2007.
18. David Von Drehle, "It's All About Him," *Time,* April 19, 2007.
19. First-person interview.

CHAPTER 14. Republicans Are Sexist

1. NOW.org.
2. Marc McDonald, "The Real Reason Republicans Hate Hillary Clinton," BeggarsCanBeChoosers.com, December 29, 2006.
3. NCRW.org.

4. NOW.org.

5. NOW.org.

6. CommonDreams.org.

7. IWF.org.

8. First-person interview.

9. IWF.org.

10. First-person interview.

11. "Boxer's Low Blow," *New York Post,* January 12, 2007.

12. Helene Cooper and Thom Shanker, "Passing Exchange Becomes Political Flashpoint on Feminism," *New York Times,* January 12, 2007.

13. Kay R. Daly, "Women's Suffrage, Republicans Suffer," GOPUSA. com, October 18, 2004.

14. CBSNews/*NYTimes Poll,* 2003.

15. Gudrun Schultz, "CNN Caught Falsifying Results of Abortion Poll," LifeSiteNews.com, May 15, 2007.

16. Gallup.com.

17. First-person interview.

18. First-person interview.

19. Jay D. Homnick, "Turning On a Dime," *American Spectator,* November 15, 2005.

20. Dennis Prager, "When Women Marry, Democrats Lose," Townhall. com, September 23, 2003.

21. Ibid.

22. Susan Page, "Married? Single? Status Affects How Women Vote," *USA Today,* August 25, 2004.

23. IWF.org.

24. First-person interview.

25. NOW.org.

26. First-person interview.

27. John Fund, "'Fairness' Is Foul," *Wall Street Journal,* October 29, 2007.

CHAPTER 15. Republicans Are Greedy

1. Thomas Frank, *What's the Matter with Kansas?* Henry Holt, 2004.
2. First-person interview.
3. Donald, Lambro, "Study: Democrats the Party of the Rich," *Washington Times,* November 23, 2007.
4. Ibid.
5. Ibid.
6. OurCampaigns.com.
7. First-person interview.
8. Al Sharpton in Democratic debate, Columbia, South Carolina, May 3, 2003.
9. First-person interview.
10. First-person interview.
11. Steven E. Landsburg, "Bush's Tax Cuts Are Unfair . . . To the Rich," Slate.com, October 21, 2004.
12. First-person interview.
13. FrontPageMag.com.
14. George Will, "Dems vs. Wal-Mart," *Jewish World Review,* September 14, 2006.
15. Ibid.
16. First-person interview.
17. First-person interview.
18. IngersollRand.com.
19. First-person interview.
20. Jane Smiley, "Why Americans Hate Democrats—A Dialogue," Slate.com, November 4, 2004.
21. Tim Robbins, "Against Fundamentalism," TheNation.com, October 18, 2002.
22. Al Sharpton at Rosa Parks Funeral Speech, November 2, 2005.
23. John Edwards, Democratic primary debate on *This Week,* August, 19, 2007.
24. P. J. O'Rourke, *All the Trouble in the World: The Lighter Side of Famine, Pestilence, Destruction and Death,* Picador, 1994.

25. Lance Selfa, "The Other Party of Big Business," SocialistWorker.org, August 2, 2002.

CHAPTER 16. Republicans Are Undemocratic

1. Bob Schieffer, CBS Evening News, September 13, 2006 broadcast.
2. A. O. Scott, "When a Single Story Has a Thousand Sides," *New York Times,* October 19, 2007.
3. Jon Stewart, *The Daily Show with Jon Stewart Presents America (The Book): A Citizen's Guide to Democracy Inaction,* Time Warner Books, 2004.
4. Ibid.
5. First-person interview.
6. John Fund, "'Fairness' Is Foul," *Wall Street Journal,* October 29, 2007.
7. Byron York, "An Unfair Doctrine," *National Review,* July 30, 2007.
8. Ibid.
9. Ann Coulter, *Slander,* Crown, 2002.
10. Ibid.
11. First-person interview.
12. First-person interview.
13. Saira Rao, *Chambermaid,* Grove Press, 2007.
14. Jim Nelson, Editor's Note, *GQ,* September 2007.
15. AM.org.
16. Glenn Greenwald, "The Padilla Verdict," Salon.com, August 16, 2007.
17. Kelly Anne Moore, "Take Al Qaeda to Court," *New York Times,* August 21, 2007.
18. Andrew McCarthy, "Enact the President's Code for Military Commissions," *National Review,* September 13, 2006.
19. Andrew McCarthy, "FISA: Don't Mend it, End it," *National Review,* August 7, 2007.
20. Andrew McCarthy, "Lawfare Strikes Again," *National Review,* June 12, 2007.

21. Deroy Murdock, "Terrorist Rogues' Gallery," *National Review,* September 27, 2006.

22. Andrew McCarthy, "Say 'No' to the McCain Amendment," *National Review,* November 15, 2005.

23. Ibid.

24. Llewellyn H. Rockwell, Jr., "Sic Semper Tyrannis," *American Conservative,* April 23, 2007.

25. Patrick J. Buchanan, "Don't Give Up Rove," *American Conservative,* April 23, 2007.

26. Paul Krugman, "Block the Vote," *New York Times,* October 15, 2004.

27. Ibid.

28. Florida State Legislature, Section 102.111.

29. John Fund, "Democracy Imperiled," *National Review,* September 13, 2004.

30. Ibid.

CHAPTER 17. Republicans Are Homophobic

1. Jon Stewart, *The Daily Show With Jon Stewart,* March 2004.

2. Lewis Black, "The Carnegie Hall Performance," September 24, 2005.

3. *Sex and the City,* Season 2, "Shortcomings."

4. Trish Deitch Roher, "Don't Tread On Janeane," *Buzz,* 1993.

5. Dean Barnett, "Obama Stumbles . . . Again," *Weekly Standard,* October 29, 2007.

6. Ibid.

7. Lou Cannon, "Reagan Country, Then and Now—California Has Become Clinton Country" *National Review,* April 17, 1999.

8. First-person interview.

9. Bill Maher, *Real Time with Bill Maher,* October 15, 2004.

10. First-person interview.

11. First-person interview.

12. David Cross, *The Last Laugh,* 2005.

CHAPTER 18. Republicans Hate Foreigners

1. Paul Newman in an email solicitation for Democratic fund-raising effort.
2. Jeff Pearlman, "At Full Blast," *Sports Illustrated,* December 23, 1999.
3. Ibid.
4. JohnRocker.net.
5. Ibid.
6. Sher Zieve, "Sen. Biden Shows Contempt for Indian Americans," The Conservative Voice, July 7, 2006.
7. Jason Horowitz, "Biden Unbound," *New York Observer,* February 4, 2007.
8. Speech given by President Bush, White House South Lawn, February 21, 2006.
9. "Jimmy Carter Backs Dubai Ports Deal," Newsmax.com, February 21, 2006.
10. Dinesh D'Souza, *What's So Great About America?* Penguin, 2003.
11. Ibid.
12. First-person interview.
13. Ibid.
14. Ann Coulter, *Slander,* Crown, 2002.
15. First-person interview.
16. Ronald Reagan speech "A Time for Choosing," October 27, 1964.
17. First-person interview.
18. First-person interview.
19. Richard Parker, "Homeland: An Essay on Patriotism,"
20. Dana Blanton, "Fox Poll: Feeling Patriotic," Fox News, June 30, 2005.
21. Rasmussen Reports, "62% Say World Better if More Like USA," April 27, 2004.
22. First-person interview.
23. David Gelernter, "A World Without Public Schools," *Weekly Standard,* June 04, 2007.

24. Pew Global Attitudes Project, "America's Image Slips," PewGlobal. org, June 13, 2006.

25. Dinesh D'Souza, *What's So Great About America?* Penguin, 2003.

26. Bryant Urstadt, "Electing to Leave: A Reader's Guide to Expatriating On November 3," *Harper's,* October 2004.

27. VermontRepublic.org.

28. Aneki.com.

29. Bruce Crumley, "Racism Unfiltered in France," *Time,* January 6, 2007.

30. Arwa Damon, "Shunned From Society, Widows Flock to City to Die," CNN.com, July 5, 2007.

31. Travel.State.gov.

32. David M Halbfinger, "The Kite Runner Is Delayed to Protect Child Stars," *New York Times,* October 4, 2007.

CHAPTER 19. Republicans Are Warmongers

1. Harold Pinter, address given at the University of Turin, 2002.

2. Dean E. Murphy, "About 300 Antiwar Protesters March in Downtown San Francisco, and Disruptions Are Few," *New York Times,* March 20, 2004.

3. Jonathan Weisman, "Stark Language Angers Republicans," *Washington Post,* October 19, 2007.

4. Patrick Healy, "Kerry Speech Blasts Bush's 'Unilateral Preemption,'" *Boston Globe,* February 28, 2004.

5. Bill Dedman, "Journalists Dole Out Cash to Politicians (Quietly)," MSNBC.com, June 25, 2007.

6. Richard Johnson, "Untold Truth," *New York Post,* November 2, 2007.

7. Kiron K. Skinner, "The Odd Couple," *New York Times,* January 19, 2004.

8. First-person interview.

9. Noam Chomsky, *9-11,* Open Media, 2001.

10. "Angry Turks Ready to Cut US Ties," CNN.com, October 12, 2007.

11. William Stuntz, "Sunrise in the West," TCSDaily.com, November 9, 2004.

12. Ibid.

13. Ibid.

14. First-person interview.

15. Matt Bai, "The Framing Wars," *New York Times Sunday Magazine*, July 17, 2005.

CHAPTER 20. All Republicans Think Alike

1. Carla Marinucci, "In S.F., Dean Calls GOP 'A White Christian Party,'" *San Francisco Chronicle*, June 7, 2005.

This book is the product of more than two long years of blood, sweat, and tears—if blood, sweat, and tears are actually espresso, Red Bull, and hard liquor. We didn't know what we were getting ourselves into when we began this twenty-chapter exercise in self-defense, but it brought us to the White House, Lowe's Motor Speedway, a New York City Council campaign, and half a dozen or so not entirely hygienic rest stops along I-95. A few months into this project, we promised each other that if we ever finished the thing, we'd use the so-called "Acknowledgments" to call out all the haters who've tried to keep us down. So that's just what we're going to do. We call this section "Comeuppance Happens."

To the lunatic literary agents who told us, with varying degrees of vitriol, that we conservatives were horrible people who didn't deserve to live, much less to publish a book—good luck with your upcoming series on the migration patterns of the Black-tailed Godwit. Sounds like a page-turner.

To the colleagues and business associates who smirked as we toiled away and smugly called our project "cute," or "misguided," or "the devil's work"—have fun at the company retreat in Passaic. Pass the ambrosia salad!

To so-called friends who said, "I can't believe you actually support that"—better get your believers fixed.

To everyone we ever met socially who refused to talk to us once they learned of our politics—you're boring. Get out more.

To any ex-girlfriends who might have shed tears at the thought of one author leaving his job to pursue such a "bad idea"—it turns out motivation often comes from the doubters as much as the believers. SO weird!

To the people who make political bumper stickers like "Impeach Bush" and "Can't Wait Till 2008!"—thanks for making all the Hummers and BMWs in New York City so much prettier!

To every teacher or professor who underestimates his students' intelligence by pushing his personal political agendas on them—you don't deserve to mold young minds. Try Play-Doh instead.

And to the New York Mets—we love you, but can you please add some pitching?

Revenge is fun. Now, for the people who supported us—you win! In all sincerity, this book is the result of the hard work, support, and graciousness of many people. First, we'd like to thank our contributors, who gave us their time and insight without the promise of anything in return (except maybe this acknowledgment). Especially to the contributors who went out of their way to assure they were giving us an opportunity to write the best possible book we could—Andrew Giangola, Al Leiter, Tucker Carlson, Tony Stewart, Deroy Murdock, and Chris Milliken—thank you. Thanks to our agent, John Talbot, whose support, expertise, and enthusiasm have been a refreshing change of pace. And thank you to our publisher, Threshold—we are humbled to be in the company of your incredibly talented authors.

S.E. would also like to thank Patty and Ken Cupp, the hardest-working people she has ever known, as well as the most devoted. Many have called them role models, and she is lucky enough to also call them Mom and Dad. Thanks to the *New York Times* Index Department, which has always treated its resident conservative, well, as if she were a liberal. Thanks to the friends, family, colleagues, and mentors who have acted as part-time researchers, assistants, editors, brainstormers, advisors, ego boosters, and confidants, regardless of their own political beliefs: Grandma Blanche and the DePaolo Family, Harvey Holmes, John Sexton, Lyle Chastaine, James Pincow, Matt Laflin, Farhad Manjoo, Michael Sharp, Jason Weinstein, and Keith Payne. You will see yourselves in this book. And last, thanks to Brett, the best partner in crime a girl could ask for.

Brett would like to thank his friends and family, a list that always begins with his parents, Glen and Vicki. Thanks also to his grandparents, Pedge, Betty, and Stuart, all of whom exemplify America's "Greatest Generation," and who have helped shape many of his political views. Thanks to his grandfather Ralph, who is gone but not forgotten. Thanks to his brother Chad and his friends at Wrobel & Schatz, who have provided him a place to hang his hat in times of uncertainty. A special thanks to Aaron Stupple, whose thoughts and contributions, although from a different part of the political spectrum, are always honest, thoughtful, and appreciated. Last, and most important, thanks to S.E, from whom he has learned a great deal about character through her persistence and belief in this book. Although at times he doubted how far they could take the project, he never doubted S.E., and his faith was certainly well placed.

LIST OF CONTRIBUTORS

Glenn Beck

Tucker Carlson

George Will

Laura Ingraham

Bubba the Love Sponge

Newt Gingrich

K. T. McFarland

Pat Toomey

Al Leiter

Tony Stewart

Andrew Giangola

Curt Schilling

Patrick Hickey

Jeff Moorad

Byron York

Jonah Goldberg

Jay Nordlinger

Deroy Murdock

Lisa Kennedy Montgomery

Ted Nugent

Randy Douthit

Jeremy Rabkin

Richard Parker

Naomi Orsekes

Herb London

Jon Zimmerman

Richard Lindzen

David Horowitz

Ted Hayes

William O'Reilly

Chris Milliken

Patrick Sammon

Brian C. Anderson

Carrie Lukas

Shelby Steele

Michael Zak

Mindy Kramer

Mark Moran